Just-in-Time
Manufacturing
in Perspective

W9-AEO-887

The Manufacturing Practitioner Series

Just-in-Time Manufacturing in Perspective

Alan Harrison

Prentice Hall

London   New York   Toronto   Sydney   Tokyo   Singapore

First published 1992 by
Prentice Hall International (UK) Ltd
Campus 400, Maylands Avenue
Hemel Hempstead
Hertfordshire, HP2 7EZ
A division of
Simon & Schuster International Group

© Prentice Hall International (UK) Ltd, 1992

Typeset in 10/12 pt Times
by Mathematical Composition Setters, Salisbury.

Printed and bound in Great Britain by
Hartnolls, Bodmin

Designed by Lesley Stewart

Library of Congress Cataloging-in-Publication Data

Harrison, Alan,
    Just-in-time manufacturing in perspective/Alan Harrison.
        p. cm. — (Manufacturing practitioner series)
    Includes bibliographical references and index.
    ISBN 0-13-514175-3
    1. Production management. 2. Just-in-time systems. I. Title.
II. Series.
TS155.H2955 1992
658.5'6–dc20   92-6611
                                                             CIP

British Library Cataloguing in Publication Data

A catalogue record for this book is available from
the British Library

ISBN 0-13-514175-3

---

1   2   3   4   5   96   95   94   93   92

Contents

Foreword

This book shows how manufacturing methods developed and perfected by the Japanese can and do work in a Western setting. It also explains many of the pitfalls on the way. It blends theory and practice. It explains the basic importance of the vision of an excellent company, and of the determination by the top team to achieve this elusive goal.

UK experience has much to teach. More Japanese companies have established their base here than anywhere else in Europe. Some have turned round existing companies, while there is a burgeoning wave of new companies setting up on greenfield sites. Many UK companies have set out to emulate Japanese ideas – with mixed success. Unfortunately others have little to show in the race towards world class manufacturing.

Alan draws lessons from a wide variety of sources. The theory is liberally illustrated by example of both good and not so good practice from companies in the UK and elsewhere. His material comes from research, from study tours to Japan and the USA, from consultancy work and from the many just-in-time training programmes which we ran together at Warwick. It is also derived from some of the best texts on the subject. The aim has been to put just-in-time into perspective, to show that it is not a passing fad, and that it is and always will be on the critical path to World Class manufacturing.

This book does not set out to idealize just-in-time, nor to promote how easy it is to implement, as so many previous books have done. And yet the attractiveness of the simple yet strict philosophy shines through. While the application may start in manufacturing, we are inevitably lead on to other areas of the business. Design, purchasing and administration are three areas which receive particular attention. In each such area, sufficient detail has been given to show how just-in-time philosophy can be applied. The rest is up to the company concerned!

This is not just a valuable reference for managers in a wide range of industries but also a good textbook for students. Its wide-ranging view of just-in-time takes us across many functional barriers, both within and outside manufacturing. Such barriers must be broken down. So issues such as management of change and new measures of performance are discussed. It is the first book on just-in-time to go into detail on crucial issues such as design for manufacture and maintenance, and to show how such issues relate to the overall just-in-time philosophy.

As part of the Manufacturing Practitioner Series, my hope is that this text becomes influential in improving manufacturing performance in Western business.

Professor Chris Voss
BT Professor of Total Quality Management
London Business School

Preface

The task of manufacturing management has changed irrevocably as a result of changes developed in Japan and used with devastating effect in Japanese products and services around the world. Our view of manufacturing has broadened and deepened to encompass other business functions like design and logistics. It is no longer an isolated function whose only impact on business performance is a negative one! Many companies have responded to the changes and are developing cultures where the elimination of waste, total quality and people preparation are key elements. Many are not, especially in the United Kingdom where surveys and personal experience show that manufacturing companies are relatively slow in the adoption of the new methods of modern manufacturing, a factor which seems to contribute to the relative continuing decline of manufacturing industry. Today, it is not enough to show improvement in key areas like cost, quality and delivery performance: it is necessary to improve faster than the competition.

This book is primarily a text for students and managers who need to understand better the modern era of manufacturing. It aims to explain many tools and techniques and how they can be applied in design, manufacturing, purchasing and other business areas towards making a business leaner and fitter. So many tools and techniques have been 'marketed' in recent years, each vying for attention, that it is often difficult to 'see the wood for the trees'! Within the confines of a single work, I have set out to describe and review a wide range of such aids to modern manufacturing. These have been constantly related to the following:

- The vision of an excellent company (or 'world class manufacturing' as it is usually referred to).
- Strategy and priorities for implementation.
- Examples of good and bad practice from around the world.

The aim has been to describe techniques in sufficient detail to show how they can be applied in developing the excellent company, but also to avoid unnecessary technical detail. Numerous references have been added for further reading.

There is an increasing amount of practical Western experience to draw on to show examples of problems and wrong turnings on the road to excellence. Many so-called 'Japanese techniques' had Western origins, none more so than the United Kingdom, where cellular manufacture was developed from Russian ideas, where John Burbidge developed production flow analysis, and where Taguchi optimization owes much to the work of Sir R. A. Fisher. But it is not only a matter of applying tools and techniques: much careful thought must be given to the timing and scope of what is done, and how the new methods can advance progress towards the vision of excellence. Many mistakes have been made by companies who have tried to cherry-pick the new ideas and have ended up by going back to the bad habits of crisis management. We can learn from those mistakes as well as from the sound principles of Japanese manufacturing techniques on which they are based. The real challenge, however, is to develop new tactics which use Western strengths in combination with Japanese methods rather than to copy what another company has done. Otherwise, it will be like trying to play tennis with the racquet in the wrong hand! Today, there is a greatly enriched choice of techniques to use, and a much better understanding of how they can be applied with discretion to improve business performance. The real breakthrough is to embrace the new philosophy. The real challenge is to make an appropriate selection of techniques which take a particular business closer towards excellence.

So an objective has been to present the richness and variety of just-in-time (JIT) techniques arranged in a logical sequence for consideration. I make no apology for bringing in more techniques like design for manufacture and electronic data interchange. It is necessary to show how such techniques fit in with the overall JIT philosophy. Simplicity is not the only theme. It is also necessary to accelerate the pace of learning and to encompass wider ideas into the overall pattern. Some of these techniques – such as electronic data interchange – are more advanced in the UK than elsewhere in Europe and are strengths which need to be built on.

My thanks are due to Professor Chris Voss of London Business School who first introduced me to just-in-time, and to the many companies and people whose experiences have helped to form my views. Richard Schonberger, Dr W. Edwards Deming and Shigeo Shingo have been major influences, both via the written and the spoken word. I am very grateful to Kazuo Murata for helping me to understand better the strong determination necessary to pursue excellence, and for the many things I learned while we worked on our jointly authored book on his experiences in setting up Yuasa Battery in the UK. A special mention is also due to Les Gill and Colin Tivey of Jaguar Cars, Steve Long and Brendan McCarthy of Ford, Dr Malcolm Evans and Les Graham of SP Tyres, Iain Halliday of Rover Group and to Brian Francis and Stewart

Fletcher of Albion Pressed Metal. While many improvements could still be made and my book is far from ideal, that is down to me. I am deeply grateful for the knowledge and assistance they have shared with me.

Alan Harrison
Warwick Business School

Introduction

Developing excellence in manufacturing has been the focus of many Western writers in recent years. Of increasing concern has been the widening gap in manufacturing performance, particularly with respect to Japanese equivalents. It is unfortunate that many such comparisons have come up with simplistic solutions like quality circles. To listen to consultants and trainers in the early 1980s, one could be misled into thinking that such employee involvement activities were the reason for Japanese industrial success! While quality circles undoubtedly have a role to play in the excellent company, that role has been progressively put back to later stages in the development of such a company as our understanding has improved [1,2].

Today, we can look back on such early attempts to rationalize manufacturing excellence as only one of the many techniques which must be competitively managed. They are facets of the same diamond. Individual 'programmes' or 'installations' will not achieve their full potential unless they act as a catalyst to force the company to re-examine everything it does, and to aim ever higher. After leading the turnaround in Toyo Kogyo's perilous business position following the first oil shock in the 1970s, company president Yoshiki Yamasaki stated in a New Year's address to employees:

> I would ask you never to be self-satisfied, but always to aim for a higher objective. No matter how hard you try, there is no victory if your competitors work harder. I would ask you to continue striving, not only to best the competition but also to keep on improving yourself [3].

Manufacturing personnel who perfected the Toyota Production System (which became the inspiration for many Western improvement programmes) went on to help streamline other business areas like sales and distribution.

Use of the term 'just-in-time' is one example of our programme-oriented approach in the West. Originally used to encapsulate manufacturing techniques developed and perfected by the Japanese, it has become a less than adequate term to describe what we know about the new management philosophy and methods. It appears to focus on the delivery of parts to the production process only as needed, which is a very limited view of what JIT is about. Many companies use their own alternatives. However, it is still the most widely used term to describe development of excellence in manufacturing, and will be used in that context in this book. The reader is asked to appreciate the limited nature of the term 'JIT' and the comprehensive intent! In fact, it is impossible to encompass all of the ramifications in a single book, and so it has been necessary to focus on key aspects and techniques. The company which understands the basics will know how to develop from there.

However, it would be a fatal mistake to dismiss JIT as a passing fashion. Companies which have embarked on the JIT journey are becoming 'leaner, stronger and fitter' [4]. Those which have not are doomed to be shaken out in the race to world-class performance.

■ What is different about JIT?

Although the JIT philosophy and supporting techniques were developed mostly in Japan, many of the concepts are not specifically Japanese. Although applied mostly to manufacturing, the concepts are not limited to this area of the business. Indeed JIT concepts are always applied to non-manufacturing areas in the same way as in manufacturing areas in the excellent company. There is also an increasing array of papers and case studies which describe JIT applications in service businesses [5]. Many techniques are based on good Western operations practices, whose origins can date back as far as the early days of the Industrial Revolution.

What is it, then, which has made JIT different from other approaches to improved business performance? There are three key reasons:

1. **Techniques:** A number of core techniques are used to attack waste across a broad front. It is the combined effect of applying these techniques which makes JIT such a formidable competitive weapon. The whole is greater than the parts.

2. **Everyone participates:** JIT is a 'total' system, which means that all company members work towards improvement goals. If only some of the members are involved, then only some of the problems will be solved. It is on this aspect of JIT that another Western embodiment of Japanese ideas – total quality – most closely impacts. Total quality is used here to describe the organization development (OD), or culture changes, needed to support development into the excellent company. The 'war on waste'

[6] must be extended from operations to all other company activities. It is not a war fought by operations personnel on their own!

3. **Continuous improvement:** The JIT task is never completed because the goal of perfection can never be reached. But we can get closer to this goal this year than we were last year. So JIT has been described as a 'journey with no end'. Each improvement generates the opportunity for further progress to be made.

In the early stages, it is usually necessary to experiment with selected techniques in pilot areas. But once the necessary lessons have been learned, a full-scale attack must be launched.

■ Scope of JIT

JIT is about doing the simple things well, and gradually doing them better. It is about developing competence and simplification in the way we do things. It is about squeezing out waste every step of the way.

But there are no short cuts to excellence. We can learn from, and so avoid the pitfalls of, companies which have already embarked on the JIT journey. It is not necessary to make the same mistakes. The order of development towards an excellent company is fundamental. It is not like going around a supermarket, where you can pick up the goodies in the order you feel like; it is more like going along a motorway, where progress is measured by the sequence of the exits which you pass. This is a very difficult lesson for Western management to learn. There is always the temptation to believe the prophet who claims he has 'been to the other side of the mountain', and who can guide you to the promised land more quickly than your competitors by means of a secret tunnel which only the elite know about!

The most important thing to understand is that it is necessary first to believe in an excellent company, and that yours can become one. This is real breakthrough strategy! In an excellent company, it is possible to:

meet demand instantaneously, with perfect quality and no waste.

While this may seem beyond the realms of possibility at present, we can embark on a journey which will get us ever closer to this goal. Stages in the development towards this JIT ideal are shown in Figure I.1. which also shows how progress in the development of JIT is dependent on progress in total quality (TQ) development. While the Japanese developed TQ first under the auspices of Drs Deming and Juran [7,8] there seems to be no reason why multi-stage progress on TQ must precede JIT development. Therefore, it should not be necessary to complete all five stages with a TQ emphasis before starting the stages with JIT emphasis. Indeed, early application of JIT

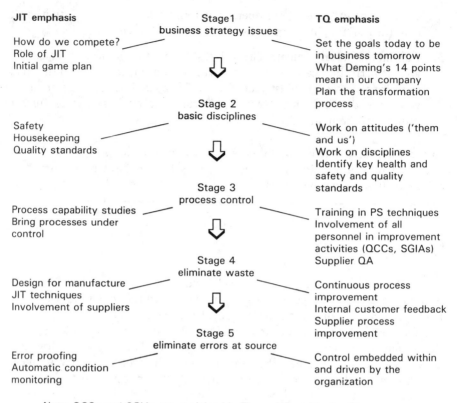

JIT emphasis

How do we compete?
Role of JIT
Initial game plan

Safety
Housekeeping
Quality standards

Process capability studies
Bring processes under
control

Design for manufacture
JIT techniques
Involvement of suppliers

Error proofing
Automatic condition
monitoring

Stage 1
business strategy issues
⇩

Stage 2
basic disciplines
⇩

Stage 3
process control
⇩

Stage 4
eliminate waste
⇩

Stage 5
eliminate errors at source

TQ emphasis

Set the goals today to be
in business tomorrow
What Deming's 14 points
mean in our company
Plan the transformation
process

Work on attitudes ('them
and us')
Work on disciplines
Identify key health and
safety and quality
standards

Training in PS techniques
Involvement of all
personnel in improvement
activities (QCCs, SGIAs)
Supplier QA

Continuous process
improvement
Internal customer feedback
Supplier process
improvement

Control embedded within
and driven by the
organization

Note: QCCs and SGIAs are explained in Figure 4.5 and in the Glossary

Figure I.1   Developing JIT/TQ

techniques to attack waste provide company members with the opportunity to apply the new thinking and training. However, it is important that JIT development does not exceed the equivalent TQ development. Some UK companies have made disastrous mistakes in this area, by, for example, aiming for a sophisticated, management-led TQ 'implementation' while ignoring the pressing need for stage 1 and stage 2 reforms. Such programmes overlook the current problems, and forgo the essential discipline and learning which must precede further progress. The Japanese refer to this as *nemawashi*, or watering the roots. Unless its roots have been established in fertile soil, the tree will not bear fruit in the long term. In one of the traditional UK engineering companies, total quality management (TQM) was referred to by shop-floor cynics as 'the quiet man' when after 2 years, cascading of TQ training was still lodged in management layers of the organization. The case study in Appendix C describes such a company. Senior managers had received many days of training, and debated the new issues at length. But shop-floor personnel understood little of what was going on other than that which they had read in the company newsletter and heard about in briefing meetings. It was only planned to give them 2 days of 'TQ training'. Yet these were the very people who would be expected to contribute most to the war on waste!

JIT and TQ are so complementary that they are often combined into 'JIT/TQ', a term which will often be used in this book to emphasize the joint waste elimination/cultural route to excellence. Where a company starts with JIT/TQ depends on a careful and honest pre-assessment of the current situation. If the manufacturing part of the organization is performing badly against yardsticks (benchmarks) of competitive performance, then it is essential to go back to stage 1 and completely overhaul attitudes and disciplines. (The term 'world class' is often used to refer to best global performance, and the term 'excellent company' has been used in this book in the same way.) Figure I.2 shows a striking example of the use of benchmarking by a Western firm, the Reprographics Business Group (RBG) of Rank Xerox at Venray in Holland, with a Japanese equivalent (Fuji Xerox). Because Fuji Xerox is 50% owned by Rank Xerox, it was possible to make specific comparisons using compatible company information. Here, the comparison is based on cost of production (COP), and tracks the immense strides made by the European plant over the period shown. But Figure I.2 also shows how disheartening such comparisons can be:

■ The Japanese company has been working on improvements for 20 years, so the opening gap in performance is very large.
■ The Japanese company continues to improve while the Western one is trying to catch up.

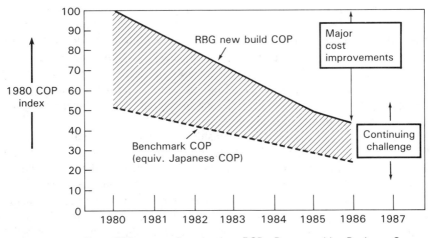

Note: COP = cost of production, RGB = Reprographics Business Group

Figure I.2 Costs v. competitive benchmark at Rank Xerox, Venray, Holland (Source: Rank Xerox)

However, Western companies also have some advantages to play with:

- They are not starting from scratch.
- There are reference companies to look at.
- Japanese companies did not improve continuously for 20 years. They made some mistakes on the way. Western companies can learn from these mistakes and save time and resources.

Whatever happens, a clear and pervading understanding of how the company competes, what course of action is needed to become an excellent company, and a long-term understanding of and belief in the transformation process are fundamental to success.

The foundation for the development of JIT/TQ is a set of beliefs. While these will vary from one organization to another, some key examples are as follows:

- The headings of the five stages which are shown in Figure I.1 (business strategy, basic disciplines, process control, eliminate waste, eliminate errors at source).
- The consuming need to satisfy customers, and so become a 'market-in' rather than 'product-out' organization. This need can be embedded within the organization by applying Ishikawa's famous belief that 'the customer is the next process' [9].
- The aim to become process oriented rather than output oriented. Improve the process and you improve the product of that process. Every business activity constitutes a process which can be improved to give lower cost and better service.

The tools and techniques of JIT/TQ are secondary to such beliefs. Techniques are simply means to an end. JIT and TQ 'implementations' have often foundered in the West basically because company management never really believed in what they were doing, or left it up to consultants to do the believing for them. A rush to install techniques such as cellular manufacture gradually fizzled out when the gains achieved meant nothing to the philosophy by which the company was managed. Dr Deming's famous '14 points for management' [10] constitute one extremely learned person's version of the beliefs necessary to compete with Japanese companies.

Finally, JIT/TQ is not about slavishly following best Japanese practice. That is a route which dooms the Western company to at best second-rate performance, because it will never catch up. I have come to believe less and less in Schonberger's fourth lesson [11] that 'culture is no obstacle'. The fact is that JIT/TQ Japanese style plays to Japanese cultural strengths. The beliefs are transportable from East to West. Japanese manufacturing techniques undoubtedly work in Western settings. But the capability to apply such beliefs and techniques to compete successfully with Japanese companies based in Japan requires recognition of British cultural strengths and weaknesses. This recognition is fundamental to making Japanese management methods work in the West. Murata and Harrison [12] propose how winning behaviour from company members can be developed by grafting Western cultural specialties on to the essential points which have made Japanese companies successful. Our 'transformation list' is shown in Table I.1. Eight features of the successful Japanese way have first been listed. Japanese cultural specialities like tradition and habit are then discarded to leave eight 'essential points' which are key characteristics shared by members of excellent companies. In order to make these essential points work to best effect in the UK setting, they must be brought to life by applying British cultural specialities like individualism and enjoyment of sport. For example, teamwork activity can be enhanced by encouraging a sporting spirit in work. Rules such as safety and quality standards mean much more when linked to the cultural values of rules in sport. If only company members showed the same commitment to work as they show in supporting their team on the football terraces... The motivation is surely there, but few leaders have succeeded in allowing it to be brought undamaged through the factory gates. The transformation list proposes key areas where this could be rectified over time in a Western setting.

Table I.1 Transformation of the management approach

Successful Japanese way	Discard Japanese speciality	Essential points	Add Western speciality	Successful Western way
1 Traditional conservation of teamwork	Tradition from feudal past	Teamwork activity	Sport, games	Encourage a sporting spirit in work
2 Loyalty to work	To the company	Loyalty	Individualism	Work for himself/herself
3 QC circle motivation	Group behaviour	Interest	Sport, games	Promote individual interest
4 Working is respectable	Society view	Value of working life	Time consciousness and excitement in life	Being excited about and being conscious of the importance of life at work
5 Work together (management and workforce)	Working from scratch after World War II	Integrated teamwork	Sport, family activities	Supervisors and managers set good example in working together; eliminate 'them and us'
6 Flexibility in work	Working from scratch after World War II	Curiosity	'Do-it-yourself' car maintenance	Promote interest of individual and provide opportunities; no demarcation
7 Seniority system	Traditional conservativeness	On-the-job training and evaluation of experience	Community activity	On-the-job training and domestic promotion
8 Lifetime employment	Traditional conservativeness	Job change and promotion	Moving jobs and community activities	Domestic job moves and promotion

■ National issues

In his *Competitive Advantage of Nations*, Michael Porter [13,14] lists many factors which have contributed to Britain's relative industrial decline. Some of the major factors are listed in Figure I.3. 'The pattern of gains and losses [in world ratings of UK industrial sectors since before World War II] is most worrying' [15]. While we have some world class industrial clusters (like chemicals, confectionary, insurance and pharmaceuticals), 'there are scarcely any with the high shares that characterise leading Japanese, American and German companies.'

National direction of industrial efforts through the Department of Trade an Industry (DTI) has been subject to numerous structural, ministerial, and policy changes, pointing to a historic low standing [16]. While well meaning and with some successes, many DTI projects, such as the Computer Aided Production Management (CAPM) project, have produced few tangible benefits to UK industry. There is a stark comparison with the Japanese Ministry of International Trade and Industry (MITI), described as central to the economic and political history of modern Japan [17].

While Porter proposes many remedies for Britain's declining position, cultural strengths should not be overlooked. Individualism, creative flair, and an ability to fight when cornered are all natural specialities which can be

Weak educational system in schools
- made worse by low company investment in training

Lack of management professionalism
- far fewer graduates in industry than in other developed nations (24% of UK top managers have degrees v. 85% in USA, 65% in France)

Lack of commitment to companies by institutional investors
- short-term pressures passed on to company management

British cultural weaknesses
- downplay competitiveness in personal terms
- unwillingness to complain publicly
- penchant for tradition
- narrow definition of responsibility
- high level of concern for form and order
- failure is unforgivable
- low motivation of management and workforce

R&D spending relatively low in industrial other than defence;

British consumer more price conscious
- less sophisticated demand base in many markets

Economic drift
- downward spiral of wealth-driven (decline) of economic development. Difficult to reverse.

Poor government support for industry
- preoccupation with macro-economic policy
- flawed model of competition (subsidy, consolidation, protection)
- sharp policy reversals

Figure I.3 Summary of factors affecting Britain's industrial decline (Source: after Porter [13], with permission of Macmillan Ltd, © Michael E. Porter, 1990)

harnessed in developing the competitive spirit which is so fundamental to becoming an excellent company. Harnessing such strengths is the theme which drives our transformation list described above.

The central importance of JIT/TQ in preparing a company for world-class manufacturing has been repeatedly emphasized by Schonberger [18]. Virtually, however a company decides to compete, the philosophy and techniques of JIT/TQ lie on the critical path to success. It is therefore of further concern that a conclusion of our recent comparison study of JIT implementations in the United States and the United Kingdom [19] was that:

> these findings, and our experiences both sides of the Atlantic, indicate a greater current awareness in the USA of JIT and its benefits, giving rise to our assessment that the UK requires an increased and sustained emphasis on promotion and education regarding the role and mechanisms of JIT.

Many old-established UK institutions have been slow to promote the new manufacturing era in a sustained way. As part of the Manufacturing Practitioner Series, this book is an opportunity to press on and encourage more UK firms along the lengthy road to manufacturing excellence.

■ JIT in perspective

If one reviews the history of presentation of Japanese methods in the United Kingdom, it is apparent that a piecemeal series of offerings has been made. When Western companies began to wake up to the seriousness of the Japanese challenge in the late 1970s, and to send their executives on study tours, the reaction was often to 'package' what had been seen into specific programmes. For example, Ford Motor Company came up with 'AJ' (After Japan), and 'EI' (Employee Involvement). As previously observed, quality circles became a fashionable elixir of business success in the early 1980s. Just-in-time followed in the mid 1980s (a couple of years behind the USA), then total quality management, and most recently design for manufacture.

It is unfortunate that, in the West, we have regarded these approaches as separate programmes and failed to understand their integrative nature. Given the basic beliefs of just-in-time, it should be possible to re-invent the whole philosophy of the Japanese approach to operations management in the same way as Taiichi Ohno and Shigeo Shingo did at Toyota in the 1950s and 1960s. My friend Kazuo Murata started off at Yuasa Battery in the United Kingdom not with Yuasa management standards or even a set of programmes, but with a set of beliefs. He concluded that a new situation existed in setting up the UK subsidiary, so he exhorted his managers as follows:

> let's create the best management system to fit this company and sort out problems by seeking the best way, as in a business school. [20]

Tools and techniques have only a subordinate role to play in the journey to becoming an excellent company. It is quite feasible to visit a Japanese factory and to marvel at the many detailed methods which are in operation without understanding how this progress has been achieved. It is easy to go and not to see. The vision of the excellent company must be to orchestrate the many initiatives which must be taken, and to coordinate them into a winning sequence.

The purpose of this book is to explain to students, academics, and industrialists how just-in-time ideals have been developed over time as a logical progression, and how they integrate with other approaches to improved business performance. A summary of the history and development of JIT and of the challenge posed to Western companies is given in Chapter 1. The organization of the book is illustrated in Figure I.4.

■ Chapter 2 provides a JIT overview, and explains both the development of JIT methods and early Western reactions to them and the core JIT/TQ philosophy and supporting techniques.

■ Chapter 3 explains the fundamental importance of design to the achievement of world-class manufacturing. Modern design methods are reviewed, and related to design for manufacture ideals.

■ Chapter 4 begins the process of explaining the development of an excellent company through cultural and teamwork aspects of its key resources – its people.

■ Chapter 5 shows that a sound start is made by doing the simple things right, like safety, housekeeping, and process control. This provides the essential foundation on which more difficult methods can be built.

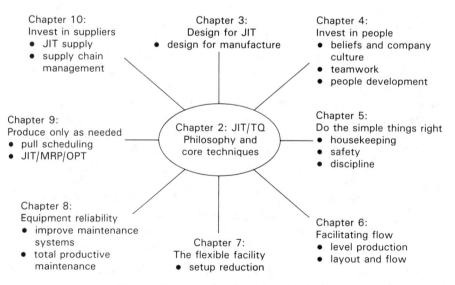

Figure I.4 How this book is organized

- Chapter 6 develops the theme of flow in manufacture. The ideal is that parts should never stand still and should enter and leave the manufacturing process by the shortest possible route.
- Chapter 7 shows how the flexible facility can be achieved by cutting setup times, and hence batch sizes.
- Chapter 8 describes the crucial role of maintenance in assuring a reliable facility. Maintenance has been so undermanaged in the past that the chapter begins by reviewing maintenance systems before going on to describe total productive maintenance.
- Chapter 9 explains the introduction of pull scheduling once other supporting techniques are in place. The role of computerized systems (material requirements planning and optimized production technology) is also analysed.
- Chapter 10 extends the JIT philosophy to suppliers and to supply chain management.

The concluding chapter draws together ends and means, and shows how these need to be coordinated into an implementation strategy. Numerous examples have been used to illustrate particular implementation issues, and a selection of three case studies has been included in the Appendices to illustrate particular issues. A Glossary is available for the reader to check basic definitions and abbreviations of terms used in the text. Now that JIT is no longer a new management fad, the aim is to show that JIT has not passed into history but is and always will be on the critical path to the excellent company: that is, to put JIT into perspective.

■ References

1. *Just-in-Time: A Global Status Report*, C. Voss and D. Clutterbuck, IFS, Bedford, 1989.
2. *Japanese Manufacturing Techniques: Nine Hidden Lessons in Simplicity*, R. Schonberger, Free Press, New York, 1982.
3. 'Tokyo Kogyo B', Harvard Business School Case no. 682–093, 1982.
4. *World Class Manufacturing*, R. Schonberger, Free Press, New York, 1986.
5. 'JIT implementation within a service industry: A case study', S. Mehra and R. Inman, *International Journal of Service Industry Management*, **1**, no. 3, 1990.
6. The term 'War on Waste' was first coined by Lucas Engineering & Systems
7. *Out of the Crisis*, W. Edwards Deming, MIT Center for Advanced Engineering Study: Cambridge, MA, 1986.
8. *Juran on Planning for Quality*, J. M. Juran, Free Press, New York, 1988.
9. *What is Total Quality control? The Japanese Way*, K. Ishikawa, Prentice Hall, Englewood Cliffs, NJ, 1985.
10. W. E. Deming, *ibid*.
11. R. Schonberger, *Japanese Manufacturing Techniques*, *ibid*.
12. *How to Make Japanese Management Methods Work in the West*, K. Murata and A. Harrison, Gower, Aldershot, 1991.

13. *The Competitive Advantage of Nations*, M. Porter, Macmillan, London and Basingstoke, 1990.
14. 'The competitive advantage of nations', M. Porter, *Harvard Business Review*, March–April, 1990.
15. *Director Magazine*, April, 1990.
16. 'The Department that lost its way', *Management Today*, February 1990.
17. *MITI and the Japanese Miracle*, C. Johnson, Standford University Press, 1982.
18. R. Schonberger, *World Class Manufacturing*, *ibid.*
19. 'Just-in-time; A US–UK comparison', T. Billesbach, A. Harrison and S. Croom-Morgan, *International Journal of Operations & Production Management*, **11**, no. 10, 1991, pp 44–57.
20. K. Murata and A. Harrison, *ibid.*, p 2.

1 | The Just-in-Time Challenge

When one looks back on the size of the task facing Japanese manufacturing companies after World War II, it seems incredible that so much has been achieved in such a short time. Economic and political reasons for this have been analysed in many excellent publications [1]. But the underlying operational factors which helped to arm the Japanese with some of the best factories in the world were much longer in the making.

The origins of just-in-time are somewhat clouded. But it is clear that JIT principles were largely developed in Japan, that the adoption of what we now call total quality laid the necessary foundations, and that techniques such as use of pre-prepared dyes and JIT steel deliveries began in the shipyards in the 1950s. Much of the credit for the development of JIT, however, goes to Taiichi Ohno of Toyota. Toyota's ability to ride the first oil shock in 1972–3, and to continue to grow, was a testament to how much had already been achieved. This had a big impact on other Japanese automotive companies, and Toyota's ideas spread rapidly throughout that industry and subsequently to other manufacturing and service industries in Japan. For example, Toyo Kogyo (maker of Mazda cars) was nearly bankrupted by the sudden loss of its market for the heavily petrol-consuming, rotary-engined cars it produced at the time. One of the major factors in the company's turnaround was the introduction of the Toyota Production System (as JIT is more widely known in Japan) in its factory at Hiroshima [2]. Dr Nakayama of Sumitomo Tyres describes the introduction of the Toyota Production System at the Nagoya factory under the supervision of Toyota engineers in 1976 [3]. The factory was told that it must introduce the Toyota Production System or face loss of Toyota as a customer.

While it is apparent that Japanese companies were vigorously applying Toyota's ideas throughout the 1970s, adoption in the West was very slow to get going. Partly this was due to lack of understanding, and partly to ignorance of the competitive threat which was posed. Ohno wrote a book entitled *Toyota Production System* in 1978 [4], and an article appeared in the West under the interesting title 'Toyota Production System and Kanban Production System: Materialisation of Just-in-Time and Respect-for-Human System' [5] which emphasizes an aspect of JIT which it is all too easy to lose sight of. But because of the fact that books and articles were often in Japanese, and that it was (and often still is!) very difficult to extract meaningful data from Japanese companies, the development of understanding in the West continued to be slow.

By the end of the 1970s, the economy of the free world was hit by another oil shock. Again, it was Japanese companies who seemed to escape most easily, and to take rapid advantage of the new opportunities which arose for lighter, longer-life products. But by this time, Western companies with manufacturing bases in Japan were taking a much closer interest in what they were doing. Xerox began to establish its famous benchmarking measurements of its Western plants against its Japanese subsidiary, Fuji Xerox (see Figure I.2). Capital liberalization programmes in Japan led to joint ventures between Mitsubishi and Chrysler, Isuzu and General Motors, and between Toyo Kogyo and Ford [6]. Of these, the Ford–Toyo Kogyo partnership seems to have been the most productive in terms of Western understanding [7]. Some of the horror stories which began to emerge by the close of the decade were as follows:

- A landed cost advantage in North America of $1,500 per car in favour of the Japanese for an Escort/Lynx-type vehicle [8].
- The time to change the press tool for a front fender at Ford/GM in North America was 6 hours, of Volvo in Europe 4 hours, and at Toyota in Japan 12 minutes! [9].

Comparison studies between Ford plants in North America and Toyo Kogyo plants in Japan showed that the major reasons for Japanese success were as shown in Figure 1.1. While political issues like Japanese government protection of their automotive industry and a wide-open US trade policy (the so-called 'tilted table' referred to by Lee Iacocca [10]) were important, the reasons for the Japanese productivity advantage were key learning points for a Western manufacturer. These were to eliminate waste, optimize the

Japanese success
- Japanese governmental protection of their automotive industry
- Wide-open US automotive trade policy
- Labour cost differentials

Yes, but do not overlook the need to

- eliminate waste
- optimize the manufacturing process
- minimize investment levels

Figure 1.1 Japanese success (Source: Bill Harahan, Ford Motor Company)

manufacturing process using the talents of their people, and minimize investment levels (in plant space requirements, inventories, and equipment) [11].

Western automotive manufacturers became extremely concerned about the threat posed by the Japanese. Responses varied from one company to another, but three examples serve to illustrate the actions which were taken in the early 1980s:

1. GM decided in 1978–9 to use its vast financial resources to outspend its rivals and stall the import invasion. A $40 billion investment programme was conceived, with the objective of redesigning all of its cars and re-equipping all of its factories. It was a strategy which only GM could afford. By 1986, when the US market share had fallen from 48% to 41% and GM's break-even point was moving inexorably upwards, signs of disappointment and self-doubt began to set in [12]. Newly automated plants like Buick City and Hamtramck had disastrously slow start-ups. Meanwhile, GM's joint venture plant with Toyota at Fremont, California [13] – New United Motor Manufacturing Inc. – was outperforming other GM plants on a platform of simplicity and worker teams. Worse was to come. By 1990, GM's market share had slumped to 36%. A 1989 GM comparison between Ford and GM factories producing comparable models concluded that 'automation was not a factor' in the large productivity gap which was found in Ford's favour. Although the GM plant was the more heavily automated, key issues in the gap were design for manufacture (41%) and factory practice (48%) [14]. While other problems have contributed to GM's decline in market share, the company has been very open about the shortcomings of its automation strategy. In particular, GM concluded that shop-floor improvements are needed as a necessary precursor to automation.

2. Based on its increasing knowledge of Mazda, Ford in the United Kingdom launched its famous 'After Japan' (AJ) campaign in 1980. The stated aims were to improve product quality, reduce scrap, and encourage worker involvement. This was interpreted by many trade union officials as 'an attack on manning levels, demarcation and all practices which interfere with flexible working' [15]. In spite of some early successes, union support was withdrawn in April 1981 and workers and shop stewards were instructed not to take part. It proved impossible to continue implementation of quality circles without this support. So, far from encouraging company members to become more efficient, the campaign had the reverse effect, and stalled progress on joint improvement plans for years. The failure of quality circles at Ford has been ascribed to the attempt to use an involvement technique which was a feature of 'a very different management approach from that practised by Ford' [16].

3. The ailing Dunlop Tyres found itself in an increasingly desperate trading position in the recession of the early 1980s [17]. Losses for the UK

operation alone were running at over £20 million per year. Dunlop fell into the vicious cycle of:

results bad − do not invest − results worse − invest less

The marketing manager stated that: 'we were making tyres then finding out where to sell them, rather than making them with customers in mind.' Bureaucracy was rife. 'We were told one Thursday that we should apply Quality Circles the next Monday', stated a company director. Sumitomo Rubber Industries, formed from Dunlop's former Japanese subsidiary in 1960, bought Dunlop's tyre operations in January 1984. By 1986, the UK tyre operation made its first profit for 14 years. The new masters focused on quality, and embarked on major re-investment in new plant and machinery. JIT techniques like housekeeping, maintenance, and development of flow were early priorities [18]. Open communications replaced one of the key weaknesses which had been a feature of UK management: only bad news was communicated, and this was done through the unions.

These three illustrations from actions taken by Western companies show how careful we must be in pursuing strategies which impact on the operations function of a business. Mistakes, once made, can take years to rectify, and greatly damage prospects for the business as a whole.

■ Improving business performance

Increasingly, one is forced to the conclusion that operational changes need to take place in stages. Incremental changes are easier to manage, and allow the organization to learn at each stage. The risks of failure of one stage then mean that you only fall back by one small step [19]. 'Breakthrough' strategies are far more risky to manage. If the change fails, then far greater potential progress is lost. And yet Western management is so often tempted by the prospects of early gains from a new programme. Consider the company which pursues continuous, incremental improvement over a long time (Figure 1.2). After a couple of years, it will have opened up a considerable gap in performance against a company which is only acting as a steward over its existing processes, and dealing with day-to-day problems. Once management of the latter company see that they are now in an unfavourable position relative to the improving company, the temptation is often to try to bridge the gap rapidly. So quickfix solutions are put in place, such as quality circles, JIT, and TQ programmes. These often do not work out because the necessary preparation and learning is not applied to each stage, and payback is expected too early [20]. On the other hand, many small improvements which involve all company members achieve far more over time than a few big improvements made by experts or consultants from outside the company.

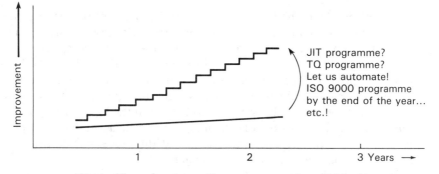

After a few years, the performance gap can be considerable.
How do we close it?

Figure 1.2 The effect of incremental improvement

A proposed relationship between four approaches to improved business performance was made by Ingersoll Engineers, and is shown in Figure 1.3 [21]:

■ Following the creation of a vision for the business (mission, values, guiding principles), the achievement of that vision needs to be planned from first principles. All aspects of the business must be examined: its objectives, products, markets and its people. Resources must be reconstituted to support achievement of its long-term aims. A key part of the strategy-setting process is that of determining the manufacturing strategy, and of linking it to the business strategy [22]. Implementation of the manufacturing strategy demands simplicity, practicality and attention to detail

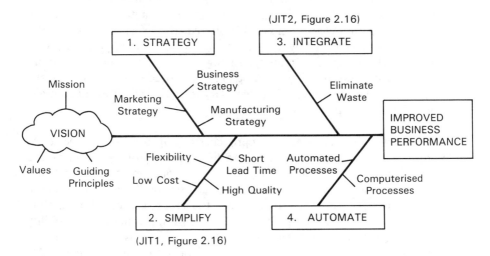

Figure 1.3 Four Approaches to Improved Business Performance

[21]. This is where just-in-time takes over: JIT becomes the manufacturing strategy for the business. It is *the* route to world class manufacturing.

■ Developing competence and simplification in the way things are done is a low-risk approach to improved business performance. It is also a high return approach. The combined effect of many small simplification projects typically results in substantial savings in work-in-progress and in operating expenses. This is where JIT techniques have their greatest impact in the early stages of becoming an excellent company. Capital investment is typically comparatively low at this stage: low cost/no cost solutions to business problems are sought.

■ Once considerable progress has been made on simplification, integration is made much easier and less risky. Integrated manufacture breaks down traditional departmental barriers and replaces them with communications pathways that are simple for people to understand and want to use. Integrated manufacture is the business philosophy that forces out unnecessary waste by reducing complexity and cost whilst improving quality in order to be much more competitive [21]. Voss [23] defines the dimensions of integration as those of strategy (above) plus material flow, technical choices, information and organisation. Computer Integrated Manufacture (CIM) is one of many enabling tools towards the goal of integration, directed primarily at the information dimension.

■ Automation (the introduction of automated and/or computerised processes) leads to a substantial escalation of risks. While past gurus like James A. Baker of General Electric may exhort us to 'automate, emigrate [to low wage economies] or evaporate', and former Department of Trade and Industry initiatives exhort us to take similar actions, many companies are extremely wary about making breakthrough changes by means of heavy investment programmes − witness the GM experience outlined above. Although there are many attractions in the automation approach to reduce operating costs, the field is littered with expensive failures. But the risks can be reduced by progress in the previous two approaches. Such progress also helps to generate the savings necessary to fund automation. Although the level of payoff can be high, the speed of payoff is typically longer-term because of the time necessary to select, procure and commission the new equipment.

It is proposed that the above four approaches to improve business performance form a logical sequence: first, set a new strategy for the business and develop a plan to implement it. Start off by developing competence and simplification in the way things are done. Once that essential foundation has been laid, the business is in a fit state to proceed to the next stage, that of integrating processes and communication pathways. This helps to preclude the possibility of developing the notorious 'islands of automation', or 'islands of JIT' for that matter. One of Schonberger's 'principles of operations management' [24] is to automate incrementally when process variability cannot otherwise be improved – in other words, to go as far as possible on the simplification/ integration route until little further progress can be made. This way, learning can be applied at each stage, and the highest level of risks associated with breakthrough automation strategies can be mitigated.

■ The challenge to manufacturing companies

After the first oil crisis, markets for many goods were changed irreparably. Figure 1.4 illustrates what happened. Prior to 1974, there was sufficient demand in the market place for attractive products to create demand for themselves. Most markets were growing strongly enough for the products to sell largely on the initiative of the producer. But after the first oil crisis, markets increasingly began to exhibit the effect of saturation, and a period of low growth followed. The consequence to manufacturing companies was that they were forced to compete more strongly for the limited number of customers. The successful ones typically reacted by offering more versions and so expanding possible demand. For example, television sets with more features (teletext, stereo sound, high definition, etc.) make the consumer want to trade up long before the useful life of his or her set is at an end. Portable versions which can be used in other rooms expand the number of sets in each house. There has been growing demand for products which match individual needs. The period before the first oil shock has therefore been called the 'product-out' period; the subsequent one is referred to as the 'market-in' period.

The greatly increased competition which the saturated market brings means that firms that do best are the ones which most closely meet those individual needs. For example, a customer wants to place his or her order as late

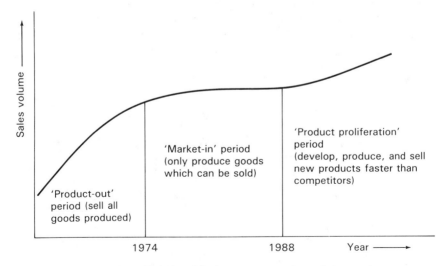

Figure 1.4 Relationship between supply and demand

as possible, yet once having decided to buy, the customer wants to take delivery immediately or by a fixed date. If the manufacturer makes the potential customer wait too long, then that customer may lose his or her desire to buy, or go elsewhere. So delivery dates become a key competitive factor.

Domestic sales of passenger cars in Japan have grown from about 3 million (1985) to about 4 million (1990). People are replacing their cars more quickly than in any other country, cars are increasingly viewed as fashion items, and new, fast-growing segments are emerging for sports cars and recreational vehicles having off-the-road capability. In virtually every market which is saturated, there is evidence that increased product variety is the key to improved market share. The rewards for the market leader are price leadership and hence profit leadership. Matsushita leads the Japanese domestic market for colour television sets, and offers far more models than its rivals. Providing that Matsushita continues to spend more than its rivals on the development and launch of improved new models, its rivals will find it virtually impossible to catch up because they are incapable of matching Matsushita's resources. We can confidently predict that Japanese auto makers will use development of superior products and product diversity to expand their assault on the US market. The famous 'motor cycle war' between Honda and Yamaha was won by the superior ability of Honda to overwhelm its rival by new product launches into a strongly fashion-conscious market [25]. Many companies like Sanyo in electrical goods and Mazda in cars have been forced to target most of their sales away from the domestic market and into exports. The result of intense rivalry in the domestic market has been to create companies which are very competitive on an international basis. Porter [26] sees such intense local rivalry as a key driver in the creation of world-class companies.

A further consequence of such rivalry is the reduction of product life cycles. Manufacturers also follow built-in obsolescence policies, often encouraged by advances in technological innovation. Figure 1.5 shows product life cycles as they notionally appeared in the 1970s and 1980s, and how they are expected to appear in the 1990s. Greater proliferation of products with

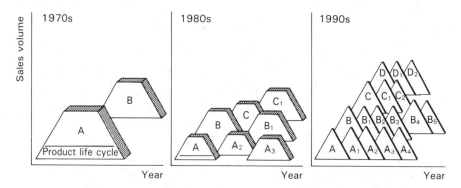

Figure 1.5 Product life cycles during the 1970s, 1980s, and 1990s
(Source: after Professor H. Yamashina)

shorter life cycles can be expected. Such pressures lead to what Yamashina [27] calls the 'three most unfavourable conditions to manufacturing':

■ Increasing diversity of demand.
■ Increasing difficulty in being able accurately to forecast demand.
■ Reducing product life cycles.

Competitive manufacture is about using the manufacturing function of a business to improve a firm's capability for meeting these conditions.

■ Implications to manufacture

The main implication of the above conditions to manufacturing is to interface manufacturing more and more closely with the market. This means that manufacturing lead times must be sufficiently short for customers to be able to select increasingly specific products delivered within increasingly competitive lead times. Manufacturers with the lowest lead times can be rewarded by premium prices, yet lower costs and inventories. Boston Consulting Group describe this favourable state of affairs as 'Time-Based Competition' [28]. Two possibilities for satisfying customer needs are shown in Figure 1.6:

1. **Mass production system:** Manufacture is decoupled from the market by a buffer of finished goods inventory. This maintains a stable manufacturing situation with large batch sizes. Unfortunately, finished goods stocks are high, but often the very item which the customer wants is unavailable. So capital employed is relatively high, and there is high risk of stock obsolescence.

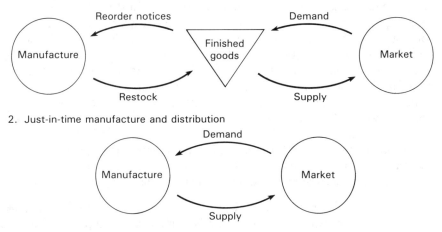

Figure 1.6 Two solutions to competitive delivery dates

2. **'Just-in-time' manufacture and distribution:** Market demands are quickly satisfied by very short manufacturing lead times. Goods are only made to order, an ideal solution for offering diverse products to a market where it becomes increasingly difficult accurately to forecast demand for individual products.

Because of the key role of delivery speed in fashion-conscious markets, manufacturers with JIT manufacture and delivery capability will continue to win orders from those who are weak in this area. The weak companies have two extra sources of waste caused by mismatches between sales and production:

1. Excess production of goods for which there is no demand.
2. Loss of sales potential of needed goods for which there is no stock available.

Japanese car manufacturers deliver home market orders to exact customer specification 4 days after confirmation of the order. Car production is still largely based on dealers' estimates in the West. Up to now, Japanese manufacturers have competed in the European market in terms of value for money – very high accuracy and extras as standard. The situation is likely to change with the advent of European transplants, which offer the opportunity to repeat Japanese delivery speed in the European market. This will of course take time, and Nissan UK's current target is to reduce the order lead time to 30 days with help from its DIANA (Distribution Information and Network Architecture) system. At present, this is somewhat behind Ford.

JIT manufacturing requires that a new element – flexibility – becomes a key factor in a manufacturing system. To achieve flexibility, manufacture needs to be in small batches with short setups (flexible machines) and with rapid delivery from one activity to the next. This is further facilitated by a flexible workforce where individuals can be moved from areas of low demand to areas of high demand. Finally, equipment capacity must be sufficient to meet peak requirements, a concept referred to as 'undercapacity scheduling'. This concept is anathema to many Western managers who have been trained to think in terms of high equipment utilization. But being market oriented today means that equipment utilization is often less important from a competitive point of view than ability to respond quickly to changing market needs. A combination of low lead times, zero inventories, and high equipment utilization is impossible! So JIT companies are prepared to trade equipment utilization for the other two.

Another central issue for competitive manufacture is to produce only as needed to meet actual demand. So JIT manufacture starts with understanding that demand as accurately as possible. There are basically two possibilities:

1. Where actual demand can be identified, we can build to specific customer orders. Not only does this mean that specific orders can be met, but also production planning becomes a much simplified task in the long run.

While many Japanese auto companies set out to achieve this goal, it is not so easy in export markets. So Toyo Kogyo (Mazda) buffers exports with 20 days of stock, and Komatsu buffers demand for excavators (also mainly export) with 1·5 to 2 weeks of stock. No doubt, over time, these inventories will be reduced.

2. Where demand cannot be accurately known in advance (for example, supplying goods to retail stores and to after-market operations) actual demand must be captured immediately, and replacement action triggered. One of the best companies in Japan in this area is Kao Corporation, the largest domestic manufacturer of soaps and detergents, hair care, and cosmetic products. Kao's integrated manufacturing and delivery system is shown in Figure 1.7. Kao short-cut Japan's multi-stage wholesaling system by appointing a network of wholesalers who distribute Kao's products exclusively. Daily orders and deliveries operate between retailers and the distribution centres. It is claimed that a customer can get any product within 12 hours. Retailers store mostly standard items, using the 80/20 rule. Daily orders for replenishment and non-stock items received at the distribution centre are picked by highly automated methods, and loaded in delivery sequence. Organization of the delivery centre is thus a key feature of the system. Another is the basic sales and production planning process. This is coordinated by Kao's integrated market intelligence system, which tracks sales by product, region, and market segment [29]. Planned and actual sales are monitored daily, and production/distribution plans revised if difference above a given percentage arise. Minimizing finished goods stocks between manufacturing and retail, reducing retail stock replenishment times, and improved customer service are key performance measures.

While the automotive and electrical/electronic sectors have been major targets for Japanese competition so far, many other segments will follow. Kao has set

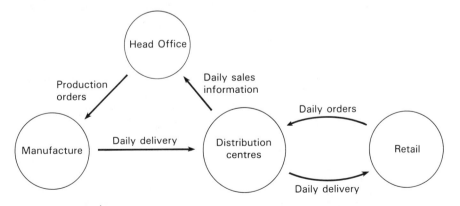

Figure 1.7 Integrated manufacturing and delivery system at Kao

up its US headquarters in Cincinnati, Ohio – the traditional site of the headquarters of Procter and Gamble, its huge American rival.

■ Lean production

JIT concepts, which started in manufacture, have spread to all functions of a business and to all industries. In Japan, JIT has developed into a total management system from marketing through to delivery. It has diffused through suppliers and distributors. It has provided Japanese companies with a formidable competitive advantage over their Western rivals. If you are competing against a Japanese company, you are competing against JIT. A recently completed study of the world motor industry [30] sponsored by the Massachusetts Institute of Technology (MIT) calls the results 'Lean Production'. Lean manufacturers can offer cars which take half the engineering man hours to design, half the man hours to assemble, and with double the model range and with 30% the number of defects in comparison with mass-production rivals. This results in the sort of divergence between Japanese and Western results indicated in Table 1.1. For US you can read European, too: in fact, the evidence is that US car plants are introducing lean production faster than their European counterparts. The threat is that Western manufacturers who do not pursue lean production will be overwhelmed by a burgeoning array of new products with shorter concept to job one and delivery lead times and with much shorter life cycles. Nissan has been offering six suspension choices on the Cefiro in addition to 'normal' offerings. It is also experimenting with fashion cars with low volumes like the Pao and the S-Cargo. Tariff barriers, import quotas, and local content rules have delayed the full force of the threat – so far. But the battleground is changing – from high-volume, low-variety, make-to-forecast manufacture to the speed and flexibility necessary to respond to changing consumer tastes and to competitor activity. Although based on the automotive industry, the MIT report emphasizes the applicability of lean production to all other manufacturing industries. In Japan, it was perfected by Toyota, but spread rapidly to all other industries.

Table 1.1 Comparison of typical figures from a study of car assembly plants

	Best	Japanese transplants	European
Man hours per car	13	21	36
Defects/car	0·3	0·3	1·0
Repair area	4	6	14
Inventories (days)	0·1	1·5	2·1
Teams as % of workforce	80	67	1
Absenteeism (%)	4	5	12

Source: Womack *et al.* [14]

■ JIT and the manufacturing strategy

While there are a few excellent applications in the United Kingdom, surveys have come up with disappointing conclusions about the reasons for pursuing JIT by most UK manufacturing companies. Voss and Robinson [31] surveyed 123 UK companies in 1986, and concluded the following:

■ Despite widespread intentions, there is very little real action taking place.
■ Only 8% of responding companies stated that they were conducting a major JIT programme.
■ Many companies were focusing on easy-to-implement techniques, and were neglecting core JIT techniques which would yield far better payoffs.

A summary of results from this survey is shown in Figure 1.8. A more recent survey of over 130 manufacturing companies of comparable size and industry representation in the United Kingdom and the USA was undertaken by Billesbach *et al.* [32]. It shows the following results:

■ A significantly higher degree of JIT activity in the USA than in the United Kingdom. It was concluded that US companies started the adoption of JIT about 2 years earlier on average than UK companies.

	Implementing or planning to implement some aspects of JIT
Yes	53.0%
No	47.0%

	Formal programme for investigation and implementation of JIT
Yes	15.9%
No	84.1%

	Nature of JIT effort	
	% of total	% of those implementing or planning to implement
Nil	59.2	14.3
Experimental	10.6	20.0
Ad hoc modification of existing systems	9.8	18.6
Major JIT programme	8.3	15.6

$n = 123$

Figure 1.8 The extent of JIT application in the United Kingdom – results of a survey conducted in July 1986

■ Employee training and development in the USA was directed at all levels of the company, whereas in the United Kingdom it was focused almost exclusively on top and middle management training courses. UK companies provided on average less than 20 hours/year on training of factory personnel, while US companies averaged between 20 and 40 hours/year. Further, the number of UK companies providing no shop-floor training at all was much higher (22% of companies) than was the case for US companies (4%).

■ US companies have a greater strategic emphasis on JIT: it was concluded that UK companies suffer from a significant lack of knowledge and education in the management of JIT activities.

A summary of these results is shown in Table 1.2. Both surveys imply that UK companies are comparatively loath to commit themselves to long-term strategies of improvement, and tend to go for short-term advantages without investing in infrastructure.

Such conclusions show that the majority of UK companies have a lot of catching up to do on the route to world-class manufacturing performance, and are consistent with a much wider concern about the state of British manufacturing industry [33].

The starting point for improvement – as indicated above – is setting a strategy. This could be for the next 5 years, or (in the case of Daimler Benz) 35 years. The usual initial area of impact of JIT is the manufacturing function, but this book also addresses the key contributions of design and distribution. Individual functional strategies are subordinate to the overall business strategy as follows:

Business strategy
— Marketing strategy
— R&D strategy
— Manufacturing strategy
— Information systems strategy
— Etc.

Table 1.2   JIT US/UK survey [31]: summary of results

Percentage of companies	USA	UK
Using JIT	90	75
Using consultants	77	19
With operator involvement in problem solving	69	48
Using operator inspection	88	74
Giving line stop authority	68	39
With operator maintenance	40	23
With paid suggestion schemes	38	47
Average training (hours/year)	20–40	<20
No. of responses	68	64

Each strategy needs to be consistent within itself, with other business strategies, and with the corporate strategy. Each strategy forces us to answer two key questions:

1. Where do we want to be in x years' time?
2. How are we going to get there?

Once developed, a strategy becomes the core set of beliefs and attitudes which are reinforced by behaviour at all levels of the organization [34]. It is regularly reviewed against the changing business environment.

A company which is developing its manufacturing strategy must start by considering customer needs in the market place and competitor activity.

Hill [35] gives us an excellent framework for developing manufacturing strategy in terms of supporting products in the market place better than competition. Manufacturing and marketing strategy issues are linked by identifying how products win orders in the market place, and by using such order-winning criteria to become the task for manufacturing to achieve. This helps us to answer the question 'what are the (few) key tasks which manufacturing must do really well?' Competitor activity is typically addressed by benchmarking the performance of our company (on a range of measures) against that of the toughest world-wide competitors, including sister companies [36]. Such measures might include product cost, inventory (months supply), defects per 100 units, product development time, and order-to-delivery lead times. Data comes from sources like trade associations, publicly quoted information, and tear downs.

The relationship of JIT to manufacturing strategy development can be considered in terms both of its impact on customer needs and of matching – or improving on – competitor activities. Table 1.3 shows how JIT benefits can be used to provide different forms of competitive advantage. For example, improvements in flexibility help to make the facility more responsive to changes to customer demand, and shortens lead times. The links can also be looked at in the reverse way. A company which has already decided on the major aspects of its manufacturing strategy can match this strategy to the

Table 1.3   JIT and competitive advantage

JIT capability	Competitive advantage derived from JIT capability
WIP reduction	Lower-cost manufacture
	Reduced order to delivery lead time
Increased flexibility	Responsive to customer demands: volume, short lead time, product change
Raw materials reduction	Lower-cost manufacture
Increased quality	Higher-quality products
	Lower-cost manufacture
Increased productivity	Lower-cost manufacture
Reduced space requirements	Lower-cost manufacture
Lower overheads	Lower-cost manufacture

particular capabilities of JIT. Examples of how this can be done are shown in Table 1.4 [37]. A competitive strategy of rapid response to customer needs can be supported by the JIT capability of flexibility and WIP reduction, and so on.

One popular misconception of JIT is that it is limited to the flowline/large-batch environment of the automotive industry. Historically this is where JIT began in Japan, and it was in this industry that most early adopters in the West started too − as evidenced by most of the industry examples used so far in this chapter! Even within the automotive industry, however, there exists such a variety of batch sizes and output volumes that it is difficult to prescribe what constitutes 'repetitive' manufacture. Once an automotive company has started along the JIT route, there seems to be no area or section which does not benefit from JIT principles like the elimination of waste. JIT applies very well to the toolroom (jobshop) as it does to the assembly line. Techniques for eliminating waste can be applied to good effect outside manufacturing as well, such as in sales and distribution. It is simply that there is a difference in emphasis on which techniques are used in the pursuit of excellence. In industries where there is already a high element of flow in manufacturing, such as food processing, one can often find that many JIT techniques are already in place. However, such companies cannot ignore the need to make further improvements in areas like supplier development, the reduction of finished product inventories, and greater responsiveness to major customers like the supermarket chains.

Figure 1.9 illustrates the suitability of JIT for a range of process choice environments. Those at the centre of the diagram are prime candidates for JIT manufacturing. Those at the top left or bottom right will be suitable for selected applications. In the case of jobshops, such applications may include total quality, workforce flexibility, and the promotion of flow in manufacture. In fact, the message is similar for all types of manufacturing:

■ JIT is about the pursuit of excellence in manufacturing. A company can never be satisfied until no further improvement is possible. As yet, no company in the world has achieved this state. So the term 'implementation' does not apply to JIT: JIT will never be totally implemented.

Table 1.4 Company strategies and JIT

Competitive strategy	JIT capability supporting strategy
Rapid response to customer needs	Flexibility
	WIP reduction
Compete on quality	Increased quality
Compete on price	WIP reduction
	Raw material reduction
	Increased productivity
	Reduced space requirements
	Lower overheads
Rapid product change	Flexibility

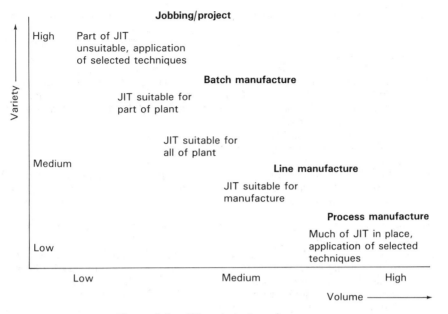

Figure 1.9 JIT and choice of process

- JIT has the power to provide a holistic approach to the improvement process. Individual projects like the introduction of MRP II (Manufacturing Resource Planning), or a major investment in new plant, may at best be only partial solutions, at worst an irrelevant waste of time and money, unless part of the overall JIT improvement process. There is no systems solution, no instant process improvement which will at a stroke propel a company into world-class performance.

So a more accurate term for JIT is a strategy [38]. It is a strategy which absorbs all aspects of operations management. No wonder that so many JIT 'implementations' have failed when they concentrated on reductions on work-in-progress or on exploiting suppliers ('just-in-time delivery'). While initial applications may be limited while a company tests out JIT concepts in a pilot setting, it soon becomes mandatory to develop an overall improvement strategy, and to pursue excellence across a broad front.

■ References

1. See for example *MITI and the Japanese Miracle: The Growth of Industrial Policy, 1925–1975*, Chalmers Johnson, Stanford University Press, 1982 and references therein. Also *Kaisha: the Japanese Corporation*, J. C. Abbeglen and G. Stalk, Basic Books, New York, 1985 and *The Enigma of Japanese Power*, Karel van Wolferen, Papermac, Basingstoke, 1989.

2. See for example 'Toyo Kogyo Ltd (A)', Harvard Business School Case no. 682–92, 1982.
3. 'JIT in the factory', Y. Nakayama, *CBI Conference on Just-in-Time*, Birmingham, 1986.
4. *Toyota Production System*, T. Ohno, Diamond Publishing, Tokyo, 1978.
5. 'Toyota Production System and Kanban Production System: Materialisation of Just-in-Time and Respect-for-Human System', Y. Sugimori, K. Kusonoki, F. Cleo and S. Uchikawa, *International Journal of Production Research*, **15**, no. 6, 1977, pp. 553–64.
6. Chalmers Johnson, *ibid.*, p. 286ff.
7. 'Detroit's big three', *The Economist*, April, 1990.
8. See for example *Fortune*, 11 November 1985, p. 36.
9. 'Just-in-Time v. Just-in-Case Production/Inventory Systems', D. O. Neshman and L. F. Smith, *Production and Inventory Management*, **23**, no. 2, pp. 12–21.
10. *Lee Iacocca: an Autobiography*, L. Iacocca, Sidgwick and Jackson, London, 1985.
11. 'Ford's perspective of the Japanese challenge', W. Harahan, Ford Motor Company (unpublished).
12. See for example 'GM is tougher than you think', *Fortune*, 10 November 1986. Also 'GM: What went wrong', *International Business Week*, 16 March 1987 and 'GM hasn't bought much peace', *Business Week*, 15 December 1986.
13. 'Car manufacturing joint venture tests feasibility of Toyota methods in the US', *Industrial Engineering*, March, 1986.
14. *The Machine that Changed the World*, J. Womack, D. Jones and D. Roos, Rawson Associates, New York, 1990.
15. *Working for Ford*, H. Beynon, Pelican, Harmondsworth, 1984.
16. 'AJ and beyond', G. Guthrie, *Production Engineer*, May, 1987, pp. 29–31.
17. See for example, *The Dunlop Story*, J. McMillan, Weidenfeld and Nicolson, London, 1989. Also, 'How Sumitomo changed Dunlop Tyres', *Long Range Planning*, **22** (3), 1989, pp. 28–33.
18. *JIT: A Global Status Report*, C. A. Voss and D. Clutterbuck, IFS, Bedford, 1989.
19. *Restoring our Competitive Edge: Competing through Manufacturing*, R. Hayes and S. Wheelwright, Wiley, New York, 1984.
20. C. Voss, *ibid.*, pp. 90, 91.
21. Integrated Manufacture, Ingersoll Engineers, IFS, Bedford, 1985.
22. See for example *Manufacturing Strategy*, T. Hill, Macmillan Education, Basingstoke, 1985.
23. 'The managerial challenges of integrated manufacturing', C. A. Voss, *International Journal of Operations and Production Management*, **9**, no. 5, 1990, pp. 33–8.
24. *Operations Management: Improving Customer Service*, R. J. Schonberger and E. Knod, Richard Irwin, Homewood, IL, 1991.
25. J. C. Abbeglen and G. Stalk, *ibid.*, p. 46.
26. M. Porter, *The Competitive Advantage of Nations*, Macmillan, London and Basingstoke, 1990.
27. H. Yamashina, *Proceedings of the Second International Conference on Just-in-Time*, IFS, Bedford, 1987.
28. 'Time: the next source of competitive advantage', G. Stalk, *Harvard Business Review*, November/December, 1989, pp. 42–6.
29. 'Kao in Singapore', J. D'Cruz, IMEDE Case no. 389-019-1, 1989.
30. J. Womack, D. Jones, and D. Roos, *ibid.*
31. 'The application of just-in-time techniques in the United Kingdom', C. A. Voss and S. J. Robinson, *International Journal of Operations and Production Management*, **7**, no. 4, 1987, pp. 46–52.

32. 'Just-in-time: A US/UK survey', T. Billesbach, A. Harrison, and S. Croom-Morgan, *International Journal of Operations and Production Management*, **11**, no. 10, 1991, pp. 44–57.
33. 'Industry's bleak future', *Management Today*, April, 1991.
34. R. H. Hayes and S. C. Wheelwright, *ibid*.
35. T. Hill, *ibid*.
36. *Benchmarking*, R. Camp, ASQC Quality Press, Milwaukee, WI, 1989.
37. 'JIT in the manufacturing strategy', C. A. Voss and A. S. Harrison, in C. A. Voss (ed.) *Just-in-Time Manufacture*, IFS, Bedford, 1987.
38. 'A framework for JIT implementation', J. Bicheno, in C. A. Voss (ed.) *Just-in-Time Manufacture*, IFS, Bedford, 1987.

2 Just-in-Time Philosophy and Core Techniques

So far, just-in-time has been referred to as an operations strategy for the business. In this chapter, we go on to develop this theme, and to show how JIT/TQ is comprised of a central set of beliefs which form the fundamental philosophy. The second section of the chapter (page 51) goes on to describe some of the most important techniques which support the JIT/TQ philosophy and enable it to be put into practice.

At the heart of the Japanese style of management is a set of beliefs. It is almost unnecessary for a Japanese manager to set up a foreign transplant armed with a set of company manuals which tell him or her how to do things. He or she can figure things out for themselves! One of the core beliefs is in the excellent company – one which will become a world leader over time. The rate at which excellence is achieved depends on the rate at which a company can improve relative to its competitors, and continue to improve faster than they can. From an operations point of view, this translates into a company which produces only as needed by the customer; immediately the customer need is made known; with perfect quality; and with no waste.

Another central belief is that we cannot achieve such excellence by good management alone. It is excellent people who make an excellent company [1]. Achieving an excellent company requires that company members develop to their full potential, so that they can contribute towards and handle the more exacting tasks which result from improvement. Even more importantly, they contribute their creativity towards further improvements. If only some of the people are involved, then only some of the problems will be solved. The excellent company fires on all cylinders!

Supporting these beliefs are three basic elements: the elimination of waste, total quality, and people preparation. The three basic elements form an overlapping set of virtuous circles, as depicted in Figure 2.1. JIT techniques are needed for the elimination of waste, total quality is needed to develop the organization, and its people need to be prepared to grasp the new challenges and opportunities which are created. In this sense, JIT/TQ is directed towards

Figure 2.1   Basic elements of the JIT/TQ philosophy

people preparation: it is the company members themselves who must absorb the new philosophy and new techniques. It is the company members who must be leaner, stronger, and fitter than members of competitive companies. It is like the team which always comes top of the football league: the players are better trained and more skilful than those of other teams. People are assets which grow over time. JIT/TQ philosophy and supporting techniques are directed at facilitating this growth.

Three key elements of JIT/TQ are crucial to understanding the philosophy involved, so we will go through them in some detail here.

■ First basic element: the elimination of waste

Waste is defined as any activity which does not add value. When Cummins Engine at Daventry in the United Kingdom began their JIT work they carried out a study of how long it took for a number of products to work through the factory [2]. The study used the simple ASME (American Society of Mechanical Engineers) symbols to classify each activity which an engine went through during the course of manufacture as follows:

| Transport | Inspect | Delay | Operation | Storage |

Of these classifications, only the operation activity is value added: the rest are one type of waste or another. Results showed that, at best, an engine was only being worked on for 15% of the time it was in the factory. At worst, this fell to 9%, which meant that for 91% of its time, the engine was adding cost, not value! Only the operation activities are value added; the rest are various forms of waste. Although already a relatively efficient manufacturer in Western terms, Cummins were alerted by the results of this exercise to the enormous waste which still lay dormant in their operations, and which no performance measure then in use showed up. The aim over time is gradually to reduce the non-value-added activities and to enrich the value added.

Toyota identified seven wastes, which have been found to apply in many different types of operations – both service and production. Figure 2.2 illustrates and summarizes these seven wastes. They are as follows:

1. **Overproduction:** Producing more than is needed by the next process is the greatest source of waste according to Toyota. This source of waste builds on the JIT definition above, where we referred to 'producing instantaneously', that is at the moment when the customer requires our 'product' (which could be a component, drawing, or data). Working ahead of the next operation is very common in UK industry. It is 'safer' to have a nice, comfortable buffer between you and the next operation: that way, you will not get blamed for stopping the line! Unfortunately, this causes scheduling problems, double handling, lead time delays, extra space requirements, and lack of responsibility for quality as well as extra work-in-progress (WIP). Persuading people to think differently is not a simple task, and depends on advances on the organization development front, which is one reason why total quality is so important.

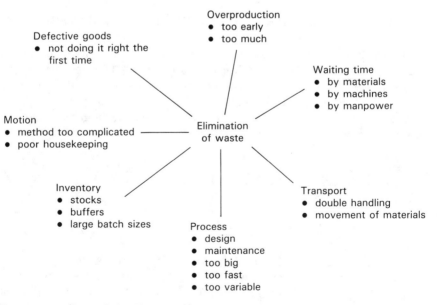

Figure 2.2 Elimination of waste: JIT basic element 1

2. **Waiting time:** We have typically been very aware of waiting time as a source of waste. Machine efficiency and labour efficiency are two popular measures widely used in UK industry. What is more difficult to expose is the real amount of waiting time, because it is often disguised by operators who are kept busy producing WIP which is not needed at the time. Industrial engineering standards allow for machine operators to stand idle while their machine is in cycle, and call it 'attention time'. Waiting time by materials is not measured so often, and can produce some startling results, as the Cummins example above shows.

3. **Transport:** While transport clearly does not add value to the product, we have a tendency to build it into our processes as some sort of 'given'. Powered conveyors become a kind of 'automated waste'! Double and triple handling of WIP from various storage points becomes the standard practice, and there is no need to worry about the number of fork lift truck drivers who are needed, or the extra storage space. Raleigh Industries, who manufacture bicycles in Nottingham, found to their amazement that a cycle frame travelled a total flow distance of 6·5 *miles* at the start of their improvement programme. So layout improvements by bringing processes closer together, and in transport methods and workplace organization, become important drivers of the reduction of waste.

4. **Process:** The process itself may become a 'given' source of waste. Deburring operations often reflect poor component design, or poor dye maintainence, and so could be eliminated. Some processes are themselves

Figure 2.3 Pallet for offcuts from the guillotine at Millard Manufacturing

waste. Arnie Zink of **Millard Manufacturing** in Omaha, Nebraska, described the bending of offcuts from the guillotine so that they would fit into a pallet as 'black work'! He had redesigned the pallet so that it could take long strips, thus eliminating the bending operation (see Figure 2.3). Many improvements over time can lead to considerable reductions in process time, and to better delivered quality. This would be reflected in a reduction in what had previously been classified as value-added time itself!

5. **Inventory:** Once you have become converted to JIT/TQ beliefs, then inventory becomes an evil. You can soon distinguish the excellent company from the average one, because there simply is not much inventory around the place! In an average company, inventory is used to hide production problems like equipment breakdowns, lengthy setup times and large batch sizes, and poor coordination between processes. Cushioning ourselves from the effects of such problems, we unconsciously ensure that they survive. It is only by tackling the causes (like the problems listed above) that inventory can be reduced as a consequence of our actions. It is a bad mistake to remove the inventory and expect the problems to look after themselves!

6. **Motion:** A favourite saying of John Wolfson, former chairman of the British Institute of **Management**, is 'don't confuse motion with progress or you'll become a busy fool'! The same applies in industry. An operator may look busy because she or he is looking for a missing box of parts, or going to the supervisor's office to collect another job card. The value

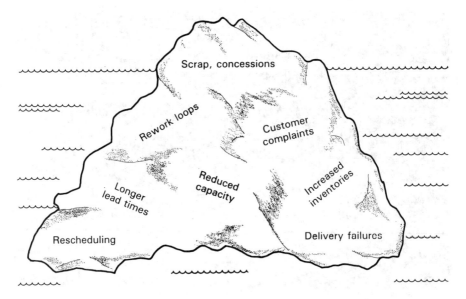

Figure 2.4 The non-conformance iceberg

added is actually non-existent. Simplification of work by improved jigs and fixtures is a rich source of reduction in the waste of motion. Often, our industrial engineers have been very good at spotting such improvements, but have ignored the savings which the operators have themselves subsequently made. So again, not all of the improvements have been reflected in company performance.

7. **Defective goods:** Our accounting systems are typically quite bad at telling us what is the true cost of the waste of defective goods. For example, what is the true cost of defects which get out into the field and which cause customers never to buy again? Does improved quality really lead to improved market share? Traditional accounting systems do not begin to address such difficult questions, and yet an understanding of them is very important to a company's competitive position. So why are quality measures only seldom found on a company's monthly report to headquarters, yet financial measures abound? Within the company, quality measures are often too limited as well. Scrap notes tell us the material and maybe part of the labour cost involved. But disruptions to the production control system, extra expediting actions, and the failure to deliver as promised are invisible. Figure 2.4 shows this effect as an iceberg. While scrap costs and numbers of concession notes may be visible, most of the true costs are hidden below the water line. Total costs of quality are much greater than traditionally has been considered, and it is correspondingly more

For each section, ask:
● who is the supplier, who is the customer?
● what are the core requirements?
and carry out process flow charting.

For example, how does the paperwork system operate for goods-inward transactions? Is the process route jumbled (diagram A), or does paperwork flow (diagram B)?

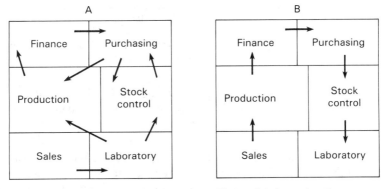

The goal: information time = zero

Figure 2.5 Waste in administration and service departments
(Source: IBM UK)

(A) Old system

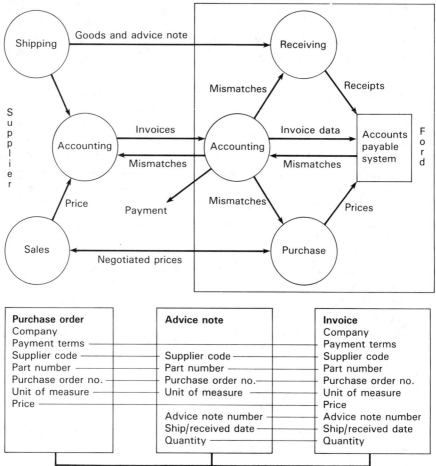

Figure 2.6a Simplification of a System: Ford's Evaluated Receipt System: Old Method

important to attack the causes of such costs. Total 'costs of quality' (in reality, the costs of un-quality) have been put at 15–30% of cost of sales [3].

An eighth waste which is sometimes added to the list is Western in origin: the waste of human potential (Dr Deming). We have tended to manage our businesses without much input from the workforce. The waste in terms of lost opportunities is incalculable.

The concept of waste applies equally well to administration and service departments. Each department needs to define what are its core tasks, who are

(B) New system

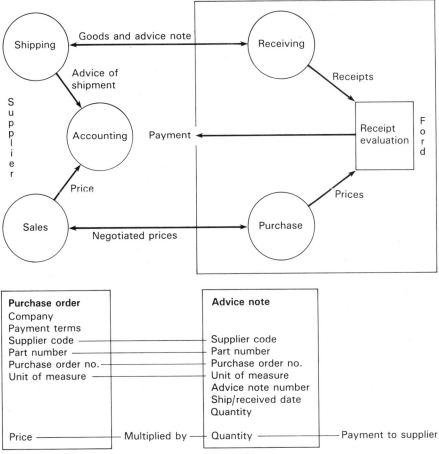

Figure 2.6b Simplification of a System: Ford's Evaluated Receipt System: New Method

its suppliers and customers for each task, and to conduct an activity value analysis of the way in which they are carried out (Figure 2.5). Think about the way in which goods are ordered in your company, for example. A purchase requisition may first be raised (46 copies in one company!), followed by the purchase order and by various amendments to order. The supplier responds with an acknowledgement to order, delivery note, and invoice. Internally, we raise a goods received note, remittance advice, and cheque. And that is if things have gone smoothly! At an Electronic Data Interchange conference in 1987, Xavier Dereppe of GM Europe (Passenger Cars) presented a computer printout which detailed all transactions involved in ordering and shipping a batch of goods from the USA to Europe. He pulled it out as he went up the steps of the hall, a distance of perhaps 50 yards, and still had not exhausted the pile before he reached the far wall! Ford in the UK have done something about this wasteful bureaucracy. Their solution is called evaluated receipt settlement, and the dramatic reduction in the flow of paperwork before and after improvement is shown in Figure 2.6.

■ Second basic element: total quality

It is a pity that total quality (TQ), like JIT itself, has been open to many interpretations [4]. 'Total quality control', 'total quality management', and 'total quality leadership' are examples of the variety of terms which has been used to emphasize various aspects of this basic element of the route to excellence. Do not be put off by the confusing array of terms, and recognize that it is the 'total' term (everyone and every process is involved) which is key. Control is embedded within, and driven by, the organization. 'Quality' refers to everything we do as a quality company in terms of providing goods and services which meet customer requirements, the way that company members interact together, and what the company expects from its suppliers. The fact is that TQ is fundamental to becoming an excellent company, and is often expressed as the twin of JIT and written as JIT/TQ. The two strategies complement each other. While many books have been written about TQ itself, the following are key aspects which we need to emphasize here. They are summarized in Figure 2.7:

1. **Management leadership:** Becoming a quality company demands that management ensures that the company advances in the correct direction for

Figure 2.7 Total quality: JIT basic element 2

the future. Consistency over time becomes a key challenge. Leadership is needed, not supervision. Deming said: 'We are in a new economic age. Western management must awaken to the challenge, must learn their responsibilities, and take on leadership for change' [5]. The new economic age he refers to is what Ford UK would have called 'After Japan' (AJ).

2. **Integration of effort:** Ishikawa's famous phrase 'the next process is the customer' powerfully expresses the need to integrate all processes in the company as a series of customer–supplier relationships. We must find out who is the next stage for each activity which we perform, and set out to serve that customer by finding out what his or her needs actually are. Deming talks of the need to break down barriers between departments [6], and to develop teamwork. Again, this is a massive task for companies steeped in traditions such as the distinction between full-time staff and hourly rated.

3. **Prevention:** The prevention of defects is the basic philosophy of modern approaches to quality control. It is far better to find defects during the process than in the products of that process. Defects are better detected at source than at some later, downstream activity. This is the foundation for statistical process control (SPC), which aims to eliminate special causes of variability and to ensure that the process remains under control [7]. Process capability studies aim to ensure that a process is capable of holding the required tolerances. Eventually, there comes a point when the process cannot further be improved, and the next round of process investment needs to be considered.

4. **Detection:** The detection of defects is still necessary on the route to the excellent company. Charts and checklists of current interest and value which monitor process performance are far more important than posters of a lion which exhort shop-floor people to believe that the 'customer is king', however well intentioned the message! Once detected, defects must immediately become the focus of problem-solving activities between the processes involved. Visibility of problems and internal customer feedback are essential supporting mechanisms. Samples of good and reject parts on display help in training and in problem solving. Use of error-proof devices (*poka-yoke*) aims to ensure that only conforming parts are used in, or produced by, the process.

5. **Ownership:** Responsibility for the accuracy of a process and its output rests with the person who is carrying it out, not with a third party like inspection or rectification personnel. At the Nissan plant at Washington, England, teams are expected to be their own quality assurers. If a defect is found at final test, the car is returned to the station at which the part was fitted, and left for the team to rectify. Responsibility implies that people are trained to carry out their jobs accurately, and to solve problems which affect the work they do. Training should cover the seven tools for

41

Check sheets

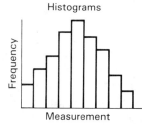

Check sheet		
Age groups of participants		
Age group	Participants	Total
15–19	ЖЖ II	12
20–24	Ж III	8
25–29	Ж Ж II	12
30–34	Ж	5
35–39	IIII	4
40–44	IIII	4
45–49	I	1
Total	46	46

Help to analyse data systematically

Cause and effect diagrams

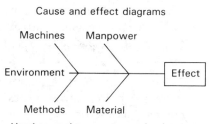

Used to analyse causes and subcauses
which may impact on a given problem

Histograms

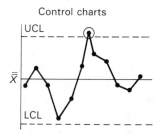

Shows shape and spread of a set of data

Pareto analysis

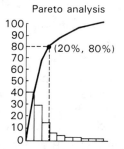

Helps to prioritize sets of data
from most important to least

Control charts

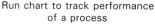

Run chart to track performance
of a process

Scatter diagrams

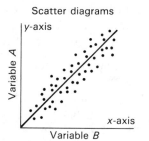

Shows relationship between
two variables

Process charting

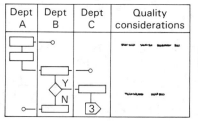

A pictorial route map of
all the steps in a process

Figure 2.8 Seven tools for quality control

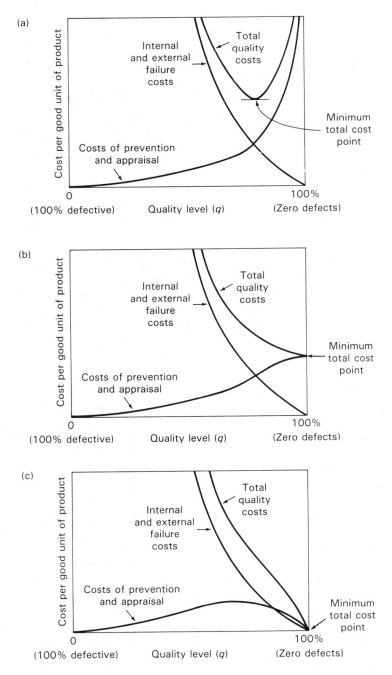

Figure 2.9 Three views of quality costs: (a) traditional model; (b) total cost minimum at zero defects (adapted from Arthur M. Schneiderman, 'Optimum Quality Costs and Zero Defects: Are They Contradictory Concepts?' *Quality Progress*, **19**, no. 11, November, 1986, p. 29); (c) effects of improvement through simplification (Source: adapted from K. J. Schonberger and E. M. Knod, *Production and Operations Management*, Business Publications Inc., Homewood, IL, 1991)

quality control illustrated in Figure 2.8 – check sheets, cause and effect diagrams, histograms, Pareto analysis, control charts, scatter diagrams, and process charting. We should attack the problem, not the person – so another of Deming's principles comes into focus: drive out fear [8]. It must be safe for people to participate. This is a very difficult but essential message to get across to Western managements. Once savings have been proposed, the pressure is on to reduce heads. Further, exhorting people to improve matters over which they have little or no control is an example of the double standards into which we sometimes get ourselves. I was dismayed to see a notice which exhorted operators to 'do it right the first time' at an engine assembly line in the United Kingdom. You could hardly cross the gangway for the scores of engines which had material shortage tickets on them!

6. **Continuous improvement:** This is an obvious area of overlap with JIT. The company develops a 'habit of improvement' – what is OK this year is not OK next year. Defects which were first measured in percentages are measured in tenths of a percentage, then hundredths, then parts per million, then parts per billion.... The ultimate goal is zero defects: then and only then are we confident that all processes are totally under control. As we get closer to that ultimate goal, so each defect becomes a mine of information about what can go wrong with the process. Perfection is always worth pursuing. This is a major departure from Western thinking, where we have used fixed acceptable quality levels (AQLs) for sampling and have regarded quality costs as going through some sort of minimum (Figure 2.9(a)). By implication, it is not worth spending more on prevention and appraisal once that minimum has been reached. But what if quality costs actually reduce overall as we approach zero defects? Figure 2.9(b) proposes this case, and Figure 2.9(c) takes the argument a stage further by proposing that prevention and appraisal costs actually reduce towards zero as the zero defects goal is neared. Many companies are coming to believe in this proposal – that zero defects is *always* worth pursuing, even if there appears to be no immediate payback in the actions taken. Such actions emphasize that quality comes 'first, second, and third'. Improvement towards the zero defects goal is led by teams, which can be both quality circles (6–8 voluntary members, led by the foreman, select problems themselves, meet on a regular basis) and small-group improvement activities (temporary, membership and problems selected). Progress results from installing more and more improvement ideas (Juran calls this 'project by project improvement' [9]). So it is important to ensure that many ideas are being generated and installed by maintaining a high visibility of numbers of projects.

A foundation of TQ was used in Japan before JIT developed. This may become a logical way for a company to develop now, and was used by IBM UK as the route to the introduction of their Continuous Flow Manufacturing

44

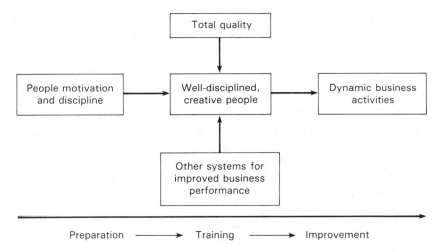

Figure 2.10 People motivation and discipline: the first step towards an excellent company

(JIT). The sort of management commitment and organization development necessary to get TQ under way provides a fertile breeding ground for JIT to follow in its wake. Murata and Harrison [10] go further by stating that TQ itself may have to follow the basic preparation of the people (Figure 2.10). In many organizations, it is necessary to start with a basic overhaul of people motivation and discipline, starting off with doing the job correctly under management guidance, and going on to take pride in simple tasks like tidiness and even saying 'good morning' in an enthusiastic way. This is consistent with a basic theme of doing the simple things right, and gradually doing them better. We need to dig down far enough to ensure that the foundations are sound.

Finally, a word on standards. Inspectors in many UK companies have fallen into the role of purveyors of concessions: you go to them if you have made a non-conforming product, and they tell you that it can go through. We have got to get a lot tougher about what is conforming product. The Japanese MD of GEC–Hitachi (as it then was) in South Wales was making one of his frequent tours on the shop floor when he spotted a television cabinet which had been scratched. Calling over the nearest person, he demanded a sledge hammer and, in front of everyone, demolished the offending set! While it may have cost £300 of parts, it acted as a strong and lasting message that – in this company – we insist on compliance.

■ Third basic element: people preparation

Making full use of our people's capabilities is the starting point for this element of the JIT/TQ philosophy. We want to hire the whole person, and not waste the incalculable value of that person's brain, senses, and potential. In this way, we can approach what has been referred to as 'respect for human system'.

'I work only for the money' is just as much a sign of poor company health as a bald statement that 'this company exists to make a profit'. O'Toole [11] criticized the American emphasis on relating work with pay. He proposed that work should be redefined as 'an activity that produces something of value for other people'. While company members still think of work as only pay related, we will be in poor shape to make full use of their capabilities. This is still a basic failing in most Western companies. Behaviourists have been trying many ways to pinpoint how people in Western companies can be motivated. Hertzberg [12] proposed that pay is a potential dissatisfier (hygiene factor) rather than a satisfier. Other approaches are needed to motivate people: involvement, recognition, responsibility, and growth. Our sad lack of progress in this area prompted Konosuke Matsushita, founder of the giant Matsushita Electric, to taunt Western managers with the view that 'we will win and you will lose' (Figure 2.11). A new management response is needed, based on people preparation which includes the following aspects, as illustrated in Figure 2.12:

1. **Discipline:** Work standards which are critical for the safety of company members and the environment, and for the quality of the product, must be followed by everyone all the time. A company which allows such rules to be flouted will not survive in the long term, for its members have no respect for the way in which the company is managed. Unnecessary and unfair rules should be abolished, so that we are left with only the critical ones. In this way, members are not overburdened with rules and learn to respect the key standards which everyone follows. Discipline is the critical essence of a manufacturing company [13].

2. **Flexibility:** It must be possible to expand responsibilities as much as people are capable. This applies equally to managers as it does to shop-floor personnel. Barriers to such flexibility, such as grading structures and restrictive practices, must be confronted and removed. True flexibility is only gained over time as a result of a consistent, long-term programme of

A secret is shared

We will win and you will lose. You cannot do anything about it because your failure is an internal disease. Your companies are based on Taylor's principles. Worse, your heads are too. You firmly believe that sound management means executives on one side and workers on the other, on one side men who think and on the other men who can only carry out work.

We have passed that stage. We are aware that business has become terribly complex. Therefore a company must have the constant commitment of its employees to survive. For us, management is the entire workforce's intellectual commitment at the service of the company – without self-imposed functional or class barriers.

Figure 2.11 A secret is shared (Source: Konosuke Matsushita)

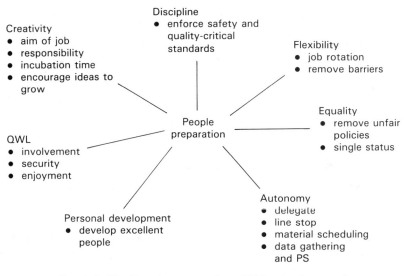

Figure 2.12 People preparation: JIT basic element 3

training people in new skills. The benefits are greatly enhanced flexibility of the facility as a whole.

3. **Equality:** Unfair and divisive personnel policies must be ditched. Traditional UK companies have been extraordinarily divisive in terms of 'perks' for different grades of personnel. 'Staff car parks' and dining rooms have been slow to disappear, in spite of the influence of the subsidiaries of American companies. Japanese subsidiaries are taking the egalitarian message even further – to company uniforms, consistent pay structures which do not differentiate between full-time staff and hourly rated staff, and open-plan offices. Even the manager's tie is regarded as a potential barrier!

4. **Autonomy:** Another principle is to delegate increasing responsibility to people involved in direct activities of the business. In a sense, management's task becomes one of supporting the shop floor, so that the organization pyramid becomes inverted (Figure 2.13)! Such autonomy is manifest in a JIT/TQ company by such activities as the following:
    ■ Line stop authority: if a quality problem arises, or he or she cannot keep up, an assembly line operative has the authority to stop the line. It is the line which is run by people, not the other way round!
    ■ Material scheduling: parts are made to well-known rules, notably, do not produce more unless the customer needs more. Many routine aspects of material scheduling can thereby be delegated away from the central production control system.
    ■ Data gathering: data relevant to shop-floor performance monitoring is gathered and used by shop-floor personnel. Data extracted for the central finance system, which takes weeks to process and return to

47

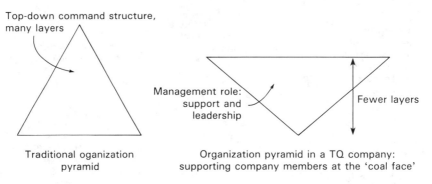

Figure 2.13 Traditional and total quality views of the organization pyramid

the foreman, is waste. By the time it gets back to the shop floor, memories have become vague, and/or defensive positions have become established!

■ Problem solving: shop-floor personnel get first crack at solving problems which affect the work they do. Only if they need help from experts should that help be sought and provided.

Delegation for running and improving the workshop to shop-floor personnel is the main feature of Toyota's Respect-for-Human System [14].

5. **Development of personnel:** Over time, the aim is to create more company members who can support the rigours of being an excellent company. Murata and Harrison [15] distinguish three levels of quality of work:

■ Repair level: reacts to problems, cannot foresee the future. Runs round with a bucket of water putting out fires. Asked to do something, and simply 'does it'.

■ Prevention level: can foresee potential problems, or the requirements of other company members, and reacts in advance.

■ Improvement level: not only foresees potential problems, but also proposes solutions so that the problems never recur.

The excellent company has a richer mix of people at the improvement level than the average company. Partly, this is achieved by long-term personal development of company members.

6. **Quality of working life (QWL):** It is nothing to be ashamed of that we need to use well-worn ideas from time to time. Many JIT/TQ concepts fall into this category. Because they have been used and discarded in an isolated sense does not mean that such ideas do not work in an overall process of improvement.

■ Involvement: company members respond better to the change process if they are involved in the way decisions are made:

participation + involvement = commitment

expresses the value of involving people in this process; they become committed to the outcome.

■ Security: deliberately setting out to achieve security of employment may seem pie in the sky in today's business environment. But there are several policies which can help to facilitate this aim:

  • maintaining a 'hard core' of permanent employees, perhaps based on length of service and merit;
  • subcontracting work in boom periods, which can be brought back in house when there is an order famine;
  • maintaining a business strategy which is based on growth;
  • ensuring that all company members – including directors – take a reduced working week and reduced pay during a crisis;
  • any combination of the above.

  Short time and redundancies need *not* be the first reaction to difficult trading conditions. Such policies typically have an awful effect on morale, and take a long time to overcome.

■ Enjoyment: work need not necessarily be a bore. Is it possible to achieve the goals set by GE of the USA (Figure 2.14)?

QWL also extends to ensuring that our people have adequate facilities like hygienic snack areas, well-appointed locker rooms and toilets, and good production equipment. How often do you see battered seats patched up with tape, poor lighting, and Dickensian toilets in UK factories?

7. **Creativity:** This is one of the indispensable elements of motivation. Most people get a kick out of not just doing the job successfully, but also improving it for next time. This attitude needs to be nurtured and encouraged by sensitive management. In the past, improvement activities have been regarded as 'none of my business'. To compete today, it is essential that everyone's contributions to solving problems and improving methods are harnessed. If only some of the company members are involved, then only some of the problems will be solved. Kondo [16] proposes four steps for making work more creative:

■ Work instructions should make it clear what is the *aim* of the job. More often, we focus on the methods of carrying out the job, without

General Electric
1989 annual report

We want GE to become a company – where people come to work every day in a rush to try something they woke up thinking about the night before. We want them to go home from work wanting to talk about what they did that day rather than trying to forget about it. We want factories where the whistle blows and everyone wonders where the time went, and someone suddenly wonders aloud why we need a whistle. We want a company where people find a better way, every day, of doing things; and where by shaping their own work experience, they make their lives better and your company best.

Figure 2.14 General Electric annual report

making its purpose clear. Apart from the discipline of safety and quality standards, company members should be encouraged to devise their own methods to achieve best the aims of the job.

■ Foster the development of people's sense of responsibility for what they do. People naturally tend to shirk such responsibility, blaming others. Managers can foster ownership of problems by refusing to accept excuses: help people to identify the key point of the problem.

■ Give time for the creation of ideas. Often, an incubation period will help in the generation of fresh means to solve problems. We need to encourage such periods, perhaps by allowing time for the team to meet.

■ Let the ideas grow and come to fruition. Early in their life, new ideas are easily rubbished. Sensitivity is needed to help them to grow.

The positive feedback from installed new ideas is a great motivator, helping to improve the self-confidence of the team. How does creativity fit in with the first point – discipline? Kondo argues that creativity and standardization are not mutually exclusive, but on the contrary mutually complementary. By standardization, he refers to the *aim* of the job, leaving company members free (other than for quality and safety critical activities) to use their own ingenuity to develop improved methods.

People are an investment which grows over time. But the very process of continuous improvement invokes another powerful motivator – the Hawthorne effect. Motivation comes from recognition. Schonberger describes the Hawthorne studies at Western Electric as 'the second major event in the history of manufacturing management' [17] (the first being scientific management and the third JIT/TQ). So the rewards of continuous improvement are highly geared: the company benefits not only from the improvement itself, but also from the boost in motivation which recognition brings. Yet achieving this energized state is not a quick and simple task. Many companies have greatly underestimated the time and resources necessary to prepare management and workforce. So many things must be changed across a broad front. Hall describes it as 'rebuilding the thought patterns of an old organisation' [18]. It is not easy, and requires great determination and far-sightedness on the part of the top team.

JIT/TQ has become the most widely used Western term to describe Japanese management approaches. In a sense, this is unfortunate because the term encourages the view that JIT is simply an inventory reduction programme based on getting suppliers to deliver 'just in time'. Many other terms have gained currency in the West, such as 'Zero Inventories' (American Production and Inventory Control Society and its British counterpart), and 'Short Cycle Manufacture' (Ed Heard, [18]). IBM and Philips use the term 'Continuous Flow Manufacture', and Amot Controls 'Value Added Manufacture'. Some of these terms are improvements on JIT and emphasize key aspects like flow, and lead time reduction. But the similarities are more important than the differences: a philosophy of doing the simple things well and gradually doing them better, put into practice in an organization culture which makes improvement part of everyone's job. The philosophy becomes the attitudes and beliefs shared by company members. It becomes manifest by a complex, interlocking series of tools and techniques. Setting out to cherry-pick from JIT/TQ is doomed to a few short-term gains and long-term failure. You want to eat the elephant? Do it a bit at a time, making progress every day [19].

■ Supporting tools and techniques

The engine room of JIT/TQ is furnished with a series of tools and techniques which are the weapons for cutting out waste. They are often called 'core JIT techniques'. There are many of them, and they follow on naturally and logically from the overall JIT philosophy. Indeed, starting from the philosophy, it should be possible to re-invent the core techniques! Fortunately, that is not necessary because we now have a wealth of documented and working examples to consider.

Because of their diversity, organizing the techniques into groupings is not easy. One approach is to group the techniques into three areas:

1. In-company JIT: conversion of the business into a JIT processing facility.
2. Inter-company JIT: extension of JIT systems to relationships between customers and suppliers.
3. Supporting mechanisms: systems, procedures, and policies which support JIT/TQ.

These areas and the most commonly used JIT techniques they encompass are shown in Figure 2.15. Many of these techniques are not new; many have Western origins. But combined together into an overall improvement strategy they provide an organization with a formidable springboard for advancing competitiveness.

Inclusion of techniques like MRP (Material Requirements Planning) and EDI (Electronic Data Interchange) needs some comment. While MRP has been broadened in recent years to form an integrated approach to manufacturing planning and control systems, it must still be viewed in the context of the overall JIT/TQ strategy. Furthermore, the groundwork aspects of JIT/TQ, like simplification and people preparation, are fundamental for an organization to exploit fully the advantages of MRP.

Another way of presenting JIT/TQ techniques in a structured fashion is due to Bicheno [20]. Techniques are sorted into groups called 'JIT1' and 'JIT2' as a guide to implementation (see Figure 2.16):

■ JIT1 techniques are concerned with the fundamental preparation of the organization for competitiveness. The aim is to provide a flexible,

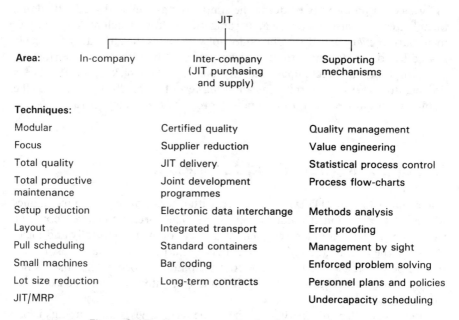

Figure 2.15   Key areas and selection of techniques

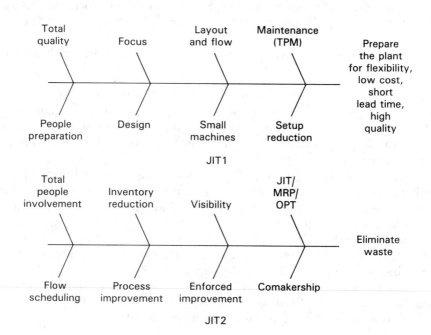

Figure 2.16   JIT1 and JIT2 (Source: after Bicheno [20])

low-cost, high-quality facility with short lead times. The techniques in this stage are applicable to the operations activities of all organizations. They are universal best practice.

■ JIT2 is concerned with running the facility according to the JIT/TQ ideals of producing instantaneously with perfect quality and no waste. The techniques in this stage usually need a foundation of JIT1 techniques in place to be thoroughly effective. The applicability of these techniques needs to be considered in relation to the product's position on the volume/variety grid in Figure 1.8.

Progress can be visualized as a cyclic series of developments between JIT1 and JIT2. It is not necessary to have JIT1 fully in place before starting JIT2 techniques. For example, setup reduction (JIT1) may help to cut batch sizes and buffer stocks (JIT2). This in turn may help to improve layout (JIT1), and hence to provide improved opportunities for visibility (JIT2) [21]. Each improvement opens up horizons for a further round of improvements. We achieve a 'virtuous cycle', whereby each advance stimulates further progress. A brief summary of core JIT techniques, arranged according to JIT1 and JIT2, follows.

JIT1

Total quality and people preparation

These form the basic preparation of the organization and its people. They are so fundamental to implementing JIT that we have described them above as 'basic elements'. No further explanation is necessary here.

Design

Studies in automotive and aerospace companies have shown that design determines 70–80% of production costs [22,23]. Design improvements can halve the product cost through quantum changes in the number of components and subassemblies, and better use of materials and processing techniques [24]. Achievements like this would not be remotely possible by manufacturing efficiency improvements alone. So design strategy must form part of the overall JIT/TQ strategy, and design for JIT is the most fruitful area for product cost improvement. Because of its fundamental importance, Chapter 4 is devoted to this subject.

Focus

The concept behind focus is that simplicity, repetition, and experience breed competence [25]. Focus within manufacturing is:

■ learning to focus each plant on limited, manageable sets of products, technologies, volumes, and markets;

■ learning to structure basic manufacturing policies and supporting services so that they focus on one explicit manufacturing task instead of many inconsistent, conflicting implicit tasks.

Many plants have moved away from focus by extending the product range, by repeated expansion on the same site (leading to more bureaucracy, distant relationships, and cumbersome systems), and/or by lack of responsiveness to new product and process technology [26]. Refocusing means limiting the manufacturing task to a single set of consistent, non-compromised criteria which can be achieved [27]. The focused plant will always outperform the non-focused plant. Possible approaches to focus are as follows:

■ Focus within the plant: by regrouping products into 'plants-within-plant', each with its own identity, and internally consistent plans and policies. A special case of plant-within-plant is cellular manufacture, where a facility is dedicated to a family of components or subassemblies.
■ Product focus: general-purpose plant focused on the ability to manufacture diverse products. This can be particularly useful when there is a wide product range, and there is a need for a flexible manufacturing response.
■ Process focus: each facility is dedicated to the manufacture of a defined, limited set of products.

Focus considerations include volume, product/market, and process split. An example of volume focus is provided by Albion Pressed Metal, a supplier of pressed parts to the automotive industry. The company began their JIT journey by carrying out a Pareto analysis of their product range: 86% by sales value came from less than one-third of the part numbers (see Figure 2.17)! The

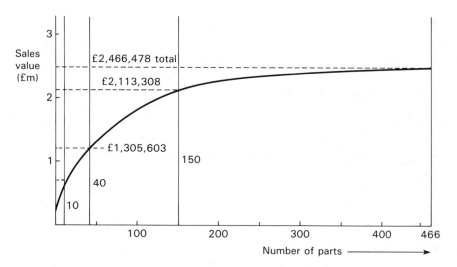

Figure 2.17 Product range Pareto analysis at Albion Pressed Metal (based on October to December sales)

company refocused its business on to volume presswork, and greatly reduced its customer base. It went on further to focus its manufacturing operations by major markets, using the plant-within-plant approach.

Layout and flow

This is a continuous drive towards shorter process length, achieved by moving machines and processes closer together whenever the opportunity arises. Thereby, the waste of transport is reduced and greater coordination of operations is achieved. Also, there is no room for work-in-progress! To facilitate improvement, machines are not 'permanently plumbed in', and may even be on wheels!

JIT layout follows logically the concepts of focus, a point developed by Burbidge in his excellent book *Production Flow Analysis* [28]. The grouping of parts by product family is one of the applications of group technology (GT). Once product families have been identified, we can group the machines necessary to produce that family into a cell. Ideally, it should not be necessary for parts to leave the cell until they have been finished, and to flow round the cell in batches of one. A 'U'-shaped layout of the cell provides minimum walking distance and proximity between load/unload areas. Easier access to specific product lines for material deliveries can be achieved by the 'many gate' facility of having multiple access points. Material handling is improved by small containers and gravity feed of parts to and from the lines. Further development of these ideas is contained in Chapter 5.

Small machines

The principle behind this technique is that several small machines, possibly permanently set up, are used instead of one large machine. Home-grown, inexpensive equipment is used to modify general-purpose machines so that they perform more reliably, are easy to maintain, and produce better quality over time (often by means of error-proof devices). This demands that in-house engineering skills are available, and can be utilized to modify the machines for the introduction of new models inexpensively. Small machines are easily moved too, so that layout flexibility is enhanced. The risks of making errors in investment decisions are reduced because small machines are by definition low investment, often written off. A further advantage is that 'mastery of fundamentals comes first' [29], so that we learn fully about quality, maintenance, and operating disciplines before moving on to the next level of improvement. Another is Schonberger's 'economy of multiples' [30], which refers to the advantages of multiple small production facilities against single, large-capacity equivalents. The sunk cost of a large machine means it needs to be operated continuously, and inhibits change. BS and W Whiteley, the Yorkshire-based manufacturer of pressboard, went broke largely as a result of a decision to maintain high utilization of the expensive calendarizing plant. A downturn in the market meant that stocks of finished goods piled up, which greatly worsened cash flow. The company had become locked into a high-investment, high-throughput strategy from which it could not escape.

Applications of the small-machine concept include use of bench-top flow solder machines in printed-circuit machine manufacture, dedicated to specific product lines. This avoids the use of large, central flow solder facilities which create queues and extend lead times. A legitimate tradeoff is increased capital investment (perhaps with underutilized capacity) for reduced investment in work-in-progress (and shorter lead times). The small-machine technique reinforces the focus concept by facilitating the development of dedicated product lines.

Total productive maintenance (TPM)

The objective is to increase equipment up time towards the ideal of zero breakdowns. Maintenance is a much-neglected area of UK manufacturing, and is frequently operated on a 'run to breakdown' basis because no better policy has ever adequately been considered. Early experiments with preventive maintenance (PM) proved costly in terms of administration, spares stockholding, etc. Maintenance trades proved to be the last bastion of restrictive practices, with a wide range of trades and demarcation barriers. Comparative studies show UK-based factories of multinationals showing up especially badly as a result of maintenance-related problems, such as lack of development training for maintenance craftsmen and inadequate maintenance windows leading to excessive overtime. As long as production operators regard maintenance as 'not my problem', PM can never work. Only if we can answer the question 'what can everyone do to help prevent breakdowns?' constructively can we start to make progress. TPM challenges everyone in the company to take a personal involvement in the task of achieving zero breakdowns. The operator's task becomes one of:

■ cleaning (which is also a form of inspection) and housekeeping;
■ proper machine operation, often with instruction from the maintenance craftsman;
■ developing an enhanced awareness of potential problems through monitoring machines for noise, smell, vibration, or other signs of impending trouble;
■ carrying out routine maintenance activities such as changing oil and low-voltage repairs.

These new duties are illustrated in Figure 2.18. The maintenance craftsman's task changes to:

■ training operators in correct machine operation and care;
■ repairing equipment which is deteriorating to prevent major breakdowns;

What can everyone do to prevent breakdowns?

Figure 2.18 Total productive maintenance

■ identifying potential future problems and finding permanent solutions.

Once basic improvements have been made, and company members are working together with a common aim, then more sophisticated maintenance methods like computerized maintenance scheduling systems and condition-based monitoring stand a far higher chance of success. Chapter 7 is devoted to the key area of maintenance.

Setup reduction (SUR)

The time for a setup is defined as the time taken from the last good piece from the last batch to the first good piece from the next batch. Reducing setup times is key to improving flexibility without losing capacity, and hence to reducing inventories and lead times. Problem solving, improved methods, training, and practice all make big differences to what can be achieved. SUR is an excellent opportunity for having shop-floor teams take ownership of the projects, and be responsible for making the improvements work in practice.

SUR is the means by which Cummins Engine at Daventry first convinced themselves of the power of JIT. Setup time on the head face drill (a CNC machine tool on the block line) was 17 minutes. The operator team reduced this time to just 8 seconds, and spent less than £100 in doing so! The methods which they used were fine applications of the lessons of simplicity, and are described in Chapter 6. Within a few months all setup times on the block line were down to less than 5 minutes. Batch sizes were cut from about 80 (2 weeks' production) to 1.

JIT2

Total people involvement [31]

Building on the foundations of people preparation (page 45), we are here talking about the 'whole person' concept. Company members devote all their abilities to the benefit of the company as a whole. They are trained, capable, and motivated to take full responsibility for all aspects of the work they do. In turn, they are trusted to carry out these responsibilities with autonomy for their own 'plant-within-plant'. This is manifest by such actions as the following:

- Selection of new recruits.
- Dealing directly with suppliers over schedules, quality issues, delivery information, etc.
- Self-measurement of performance and improvement trends.
- Spending improvement budgets (SP Tyres at Washington delegates 25% of capital budgets to sections in the factory to spend as they see fit).
- Planning and reviewing work done each day through communication meetings.
- Dealing directly with customer problems and requirements.

It is doubtful about how much can be achieved with TPI in the West. Most companies are still struggling to get some of the basic people preparation policies to work. Others are jumping the gun and trying to introduce more advanced ideas before their people are prepared, or before managers' attitudes have changed. Quality circles are a case in point. Circles clearly can work at various stages in a company's development, but their chequered history in the West implies that they should follow, not be a motor for, people and company preparation. While some mistakes are allowed on the road to excellence, ideas that get tired are worse than no ideas!

Flow scheduling

The aim is to create the conditions whereby parts do not stop at all during the manufacturing process, but flow in an orderly and continuous way throughout (the goal of IBM's 'Continuous Flow Manufacture'). Measures of success include the ratio of value-added time to total time (flow factor), and the total flow length for parts or subassemblies. Improvement of all such measures should be shown over time. Achieving flow means that we must recognize the importance of timing, and make the most of regular cycles in manufacture. Lucas Engineering & Systems [32] distinguish between:

- runners (products or key features produced every day, every week);
- repeaters (products or key features produced regularly but at longer time intervals);
- strangers (products or key features produced irregularly).

It should be possible to reduce the variability of timing intervals for producing runners and repeaters. The aim is to synchronize processes concerned with parts and subassemblies for such products so that they appear to take place on a 'drumbeat' or pulse which governs material movements. Better to derate faster operations than to have them produce more than can be handled in the same time by the next process! Assembly and component manufacture can be linked by cards or signals (*kanban*) to order more from the previous process. This is the basis of 'pull scheduling', which seeks to ensure that preceding operations only supply and make as much as is needed by succeeding operations. The ultimate 'drumbeat' is set by the final assembly schedule. Batch sizes are kept to a minimum throughout by means of a concept called 'mixed modelling', which is illustrated in Figure 2.19. Two key supporting concepts to flow scheduling are the following:

1. Tightly coupled logistics: the gradual and deliberate synchronization of operation times and material movements.
2. Undercapacity scheduling: scheduling for less than a full shift's work to leave time for maintenance and improvement activities, so that people are not constantly struggling to meet tight work quotas.

Flow scheduling is further described in Chapter 8.

Inventory reduction

JIT/TQ is not an inventory reduction programme in itself. But reduction of work-in-progress (or rather, work *not* in progress!) is often one of the most visible benefits. (A more descriptive term to emphasize the dramatic reduction of work-in-progress is 'RIP' – Raw materials and In Process.) There is often a fairly close relationship between reduction in WIP and reduction in lead time, because a new batch of parts does not have to struggle through queues of WIP on its way through manufacture. Lead times can be affected by

Mixed model production:
- This is about reducing the time interval between models to the shortest possible.
- This way, finished product inventories are kept to a minimum. Regular schedules for components can be passed on to suppliers.
- For example, the week-by-week production schedule for a given range of three products (A, B, and C) is as follows:

200A,   120B,   80C

Instead of being made in large batches to match total schedule requirements, the schedules could be divided by 40 to give very small batches:

5A,   3B,   2C

A further reduction could be made by building in the sequence:

AABABCABCA

and repeating this pattern throughout the day.

Figure 2.19   Mixed model production

'invisible inventories' too [33]. There are delays prior to manufacture caused by ponderous order entry systems, and lengthy requirements for technical specifications. After manufacture, problems in despatching goods to customer premises and in receiving payment also amount to delays — sometimes very serious delays — in the value-added chain.

Progress in the reduction of batch sizes depends on progress in setup reduction, otherwise we lose capacity. But the benefits of reduced batch sizes are:

- reduced production lead times;
- earlier recognition of defects, and less rework;
- less work-in-progress;
- improved flexibility (fast response to changes in mix, etc.).

These advantages apply both to internal batch sizes and to external (purchased) batch quantities.

Buffer stocks (for example, prior to bottleneck operations and prior to assembly) represent the degree of nervousness we have that supply may be interrupted. Reducing buffer stocks depends on reducing that nervousness by improved scheduling accuracy, reducing the likelihood of breakdowns through TPM, improved quality, and so on. A virtuous cycle is created, whereby such improvements result in reduced lead times, so that more buffer stocks can be cut, which further improves lead times and so on.

Process improvement

Part of Taguchi's concept of the 'loss function' [34,35] (the loss imparted to society from the time a product is shipped) is that all deviations from a nominal value are waste. There is a real value in progressing from a standard deviation (SD) of one-sixth to an SD of one-twelfth. According to Taguchi philosophy, the customer's loss as a result of performance variation is roughly equal to the square of the deviation from target value. This loss function may be simply defined as:

$$L = K(d)^2$$

where d = percentage deviation from target value T

K = loss constant (£) made up from traditional quality costs: prevention, appraisal, internal and external failure

L = loss to customers (in £) resulting from variation by percentage d from the target T

Taguchi's quality loss function is illustrated in Figure 2.20(b). It is compared with the equivalent Western concept of quality loss (Figure 2.20(a)), where losses are only reckoned if they occur outside customer tolerance limits $(T \pm t)$, and are limited to the total value of the part. The Taguchi loss function argues that quality losses begin immediately the value of the variable (for

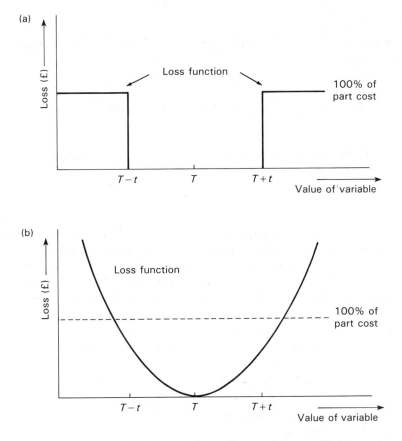

Note: T = target value of variable; $\pm t$ = tolerance limits specified by customer

Figure 2.20 Taguchi loss function: (a) Western interpretation of quality loss; a step function 1 − 1 loss = 0 if value of variable is within $T \pm t$; (b) Taguchi interpretation of quality loss: a quadratic function 1 − 1 is only zero if value of variables = T, and can be greater than 100% of part cost

example, length) differs from target T, and increase in line with d. Taguchi philosophy also argues that there is no limit to losses imparted to society as a result of poor-quality goods and services.

The concept of quality loss applies to any point in the product's life, not just at delivery. Losses to society are caused not only by defects (results outside tolerance range) but also by variability (any deviation from nominal value). A bottle of cough mixture leaks because the cap diameter is on the high side, and the bottle neck is on the low side. The basic cause is tolerance stackup. Another virtuous cycle, aimed at improving the loss function, is:

- control the process (get it to operate consistently within current capability);

then

■ improve the process (improve process capability so that variability is reduced);

then

■ get it back under control (operating within the new control limits)

....

Process data collection, the collection and immediate use of data at the workplace, is a key facilitator here.

Visibility

The JIT/TQ factory is characterized by the easy visibility of processes, problems, and improvement projects. Gone are the well-intentioned but meaningless posters. Instead, charts and check sheets of current interest and value abound. Examples of visibility are shown in Figure 2.21. The accent is on shortening the control loop by extracting and using data as it happens. The emphasis is on simple and concise wording, with as much pictorial and graphical display as possible. Each display highlights one key point only [35]. Problem conditions (for example, breakdowns and defects) are often signalled

Improvement measures
- flow factors
- flow distance
- defects, scrap, yield

Process issues
- causes of delay
- stoppages (coloured light system)
- control charts (SPC)

Improvement activities
- Pareto and fishbone charts (current projects)
- PM and setup reduction checklists

Display room
- samples of products and components
- samples of defectives
- samples of competitive products

Visual controls
- *kanban* boxes, squares
- plans, schedules
- impending material shortages
- on wallcharts, not in computer!

Layout
- open-plan offices, no partitions
- avoid pallet stacks, cabinets >5 ft high

Control
- management by walking about

Figure 2.21 Visibility

by coloured lights or buzzers. Such conditions demand immediate action. 'Management by walking about' becomes far more effective than attempting to supervise by using last week's figures.

Enforced improvement

This is the determined and ongoing war on waste. The famous analogy of the ship and the rocks, shown in Figure 2.22, illustrates the principle. In the past, we have covered up our problems (rocks) by means of a sea of inventory. Enforced problem solving is about getting rid of those problems, and gradually enabling the water level to come down. Deliberately taking out inventory is a much more risky affair, because the likelihood is that the system will collapse (the ship will sink!). But inventory withdrawal may be tried out on an experimental basis in order to find out where the key problems are. This may simply amount to withdrawing a *kanban* card or part of a buffer, and should be carried out by the team concerned.

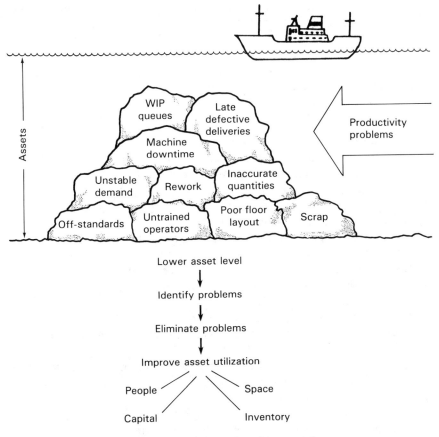

Figure 2.22 Enforced problem solving

JIT/MRP/OPT

There is no need to regard these approaches as being mutually exclusive, in spite of many early attempts to do so! Brief descriptions of the impact of each system on manufacturing planning and control are as follows:

- **JIT pull scheduling:** This uses 'demand pull' by final product, downdated to subassemblies and component manufacture by means of cards or signals (*kanban*) which instruct preceding operations to make more. It normally uses simple, visible systems of control and scheduling (typically FIFO – First In, First Out). It is excellent for control, but not for planning material requirements. Other aspects of JIT/TQ philosophy attack all forms of waste, and demand continuous improvement. The potential impact of pull scheduling is entertainly shown in the video 'Stockless Production', available from Hewlett-Packard, which has become a JIT training classic.

- **MRP (material requirements planning):** This is a computerized materials management system aimed at minimizing inventories by working out time-phased material requirements from the master production schedule (MPS). Modern 'closed loop' versions of MRP allow the MPS to be updated for actual achievement. While it is an excellent system for planning material requirements (hence its name!), in practice it is very difficult to enforce MRP disciplines at shop-floor level. Although designed as a 'pull' system of control, it becomes a 'push' system where parts are pushed through from the early stages of manufacture.

- **OPT (optimized production technology or theory of constraints):** This is a philosophy combined with a computerized system of shop scheduling and capacity planning. OPT aims for dependable due date performance by sequencing parts to defined rules (as yet unpublished). Better use of limited capacity is achieved by finite scheduling of bottleneck operations, and by use of increased process batch sizes – produce more of a high-priority part once it has been set up on a bottleneck machine. Greater throughput speed is achieved by cutting down on transfer batch sizes – move partial batches on to the next work centre instead of waiting until the whole batch has been finished. Central to the OPT philosophy are the following concepts:
  - Drum: the drumbeat of the master production schedule is established by finite forward loading of the (normally very few) major bottlenecks in the plant.
  - Buffer: time buffers (as distinct from stock buffers) are used to 'immunize' bottlenecks from variability in flow (due to such causes as breakdowns, wrong forecasts, and absenteeism).
  - Rope: tying a notional 'rope' to the first (gating) operation so that input of raw materials is controlled by the rate at which plant constraints can produce.

These concepts are held to be applicable to all manufacturing environments. OPT believes in removing constraints to increased throughput in all parts of the organization [37]. Other methodologies are used in manufacturing planning and control (MPC) systems. JIT/TQ has many important things to contribute to the MRP and OPT examples quoted above:

■ JIT1 preparation is always of value. The introduction of basic disciplines and motivation are fundamental to the success of any MPC system.
■ The number of transactions on MRP can be greatly reduced by JIT simplification activity. Fixed lead times and scrap rates are anathema to JIT!
■ The capacity of bottlenecks on OPT can be increased by setup reduction. Reduction of transfer batches is consistent with JIT batch size reduction and flow scheduling techniques.

There is no reason why different approaches to MPC systems should be regarded as inconsistent with, or as separate from, the overall JIT strategy. The key point is to develop an integrated approach which is best suited to the particular company situation. These points are further developed in Chapter 8.

Comakership

The supply chain ideally consists of a series of buyer—supplier relationships, each link dependent on preceding and succeeding links for smooth movement of scheduled material. Overall, there is a key role to be played by the original equipment manufacturer (OEM) who is competing in the retail market at large. The OEM's task is to forecast that market as accurately as possible and pass on the knowledge to its comakers, and to react to market changes (for example, by new product development) quickly and accurately. So the OEM has a key role to play in orchestrating its comakers.

We used the word 'ideally' above. The reality is still very different in most European supply chains, where significant progress in such areas as ending adversarial relationships and substituting them with cooperation between buyer and supplier, and minimizing paperwork (specifications, purchase order routines, and so on), has been slow and faltering [38]. Many suppliers to the automative industry think that JIT stands for 'Japanese Inspired Terror', because OEMs have used demands for JIT deliveries as a means to pass costs and inventories down the supply chain! Such an interpretation of JIT supply is very short-sighted and potentially very damaging. Comakership is placed in JIT2 to emphasize the point that progress must first be made in developing excellence *internally* before going on to develop further excellence in the supply chain. Poor material schedules and expediting 'hot lists' are a lousy foundation on which to attempt to build tight inventory controls with your suppliers!

Developing a series of cooperative buyer–supplier relationships down the supply chain requires a long-term strategy of change to be implemented. Some of the key tasks are as follows:

■ Supplier reduction programmes, aimed at leaving only a few good suppliers. It is easier to have close, cooperative relationships with suppliers if there are fewer of them! Also, the variability of quality characteristics can be more closely controlled. Long-term commercial contracts (often not designed to be legally binding) help to cement the new relationships.

■ For the remaining preferred suppliers, supplier quality assurance (SQA) and training help to improve delivered quality, making it possible to reduce goods-inward inspection. 'Real time' schedule updates using EDI (Electronic Data Interchange) make it possible to facilitate shorter response times and more frequent deliveries by the supplier.

■ Further improvements at the supplier are rewarded by the possibilities of greater schedule flexibility, and by 100% conformance quality and part count accuracy. Deliveries can be scheduled to shorter time windows ('time spot deliveries').

Industry-wide cooperation is something we have not seen much of in Europe, apart from a few limited examples like EDI standards. In North America, the Automotive Industry Action Group (AIAG) is a not-for-profit organization which seeks to promote the competitiveness of the American automotive industry as a whole. It sets out to achieve this through a wide range of activities such as training, and setting standards for areas like bar codes, pallets, and data transmission. Perhaps the nearest equivalent are the 'clubs' being set up by Japanese manufacturers such as Nissan and Canon. The aim is to encourage the sharing of knowledge and expertise between club members, and to share common problems. Comakership is examined in more detail in Chapter 10.

■ Conclusion

The above presentation helps to show the very wide scope into which the JIT/TQ strategy can develop, and the apparent complexity which the relationships between techniques can seem to develop. But in essence, the concepts are based on simplicity: there is nothing awe inspiring about that! The result of putting into place many complementary techniques, each helping to reinforce what has already been done and also to develop progress further, makes the structure composite and therefore hard to explain (and to copy!). It is this which makes JIT/TQ such a formidable competitive weapon: the whole is stronger than the parts.

■ References

1. *How to Make Japanese Management Methods Work in the West*, K. Murata and A. Harrison, Gower, Aldershot, 1991.
2. 'Setup time reduction: Making JIT work', D. L. Lee, in C. Voss (ed.) *Just-in-Time Manufacture*, IFS, Bedford, 1987.
3. See for example *Quality is Free*, P. Crosby, McGraw-Hill, New York, 1979.
4. 'The total quality management maze', M. Foster and S. Whittle, *The TQC Magazine*, May, 1989.
5. *Out of the Crisis*, W. Edwards Deming, MIT Center for Advanced Engineering Study: Cambridge, MA, 1987, p. 23.
6. W. E. Deming, *ibid.*, p. 62.
7. See for example *Guidelines to Statistical Process Control*, Anon., Society of Motor Manufacturers and Traders, 1986.
8. W. E. Deming, *ibid.*, p. 59.
9. *Juran on Planning for Quality*, J. M. Juran, Free Press, New York, 1988.
10. K. Murata and A. Harrison, *ibid.*
11. *Work in America*, J. O'Toole *et al.*, MIT Press, Cambridge, MA, 1973.
12. *The Motivation to Work*, F. Hertzberg, Wiley, 1969.
13. K. Murata and A. Harrison, *ibid.*, p. 54.
14. 'Toyota Production System and Kanban Production System: Materialization of Just-in-Time and Respect-for-Human Systems', Y. Sugimori *et al.*, *International Journal of Production Research*, **15**, no. 6, 1977, pp. 553–64.
15. K. Murata and A. Harrison, *ibid.*, p. 44.
16. *Human Motivation*, Y. Kondo, 3A Corp., Tokyo, 1989.
17. *World Class Manufacturing*, R. Schonberger, Free Press, New York, 1986, p. 4.
18. See for example *Playing the Competitive Game for Keeps*, E. Heard, Manufacturing Technology International, 1990.
19. Remark made by L. Bertain.
20. *Implementing Just-in-Time*, J. Bicheno, IFS, Bedford, 1991.
21. J. Bicheno, *ibid.*
22. 'Design for economic manufacture', J. Corbett, *Annals of CIRP*, **35**, no. 1, p. 3, 1986.
23. 'Manufacturing by design', D. Whitney, *Harvard Business Review*, May/June, pp. 83–91, 1988.
24. J. Corbett, *ibid.*
25. 'The focused factory', W. Skinner, *Harvard Business Review*, May/June, 1974.
26. 'Every factory has a life cycle', R. Schmenner, *Harvard Business Review*, March/April, pp. 121–29, 1983.
27. W. Skinner, *ibid.*
28. *Production Flow Analysis for Planning Group Technology*, J. Burbidge, Oxford Science Publications, 1989.
29. *Attaining Manufacturing Excellence*, R. Hall, Dow Jones/Irwin, Homewood, IL, 1987.
30. R. Schonberger, *ibid.*, p. 77.
31. R. Hall, *ibid.*
32. *Minicomputers and Microcomputers in Engineering and Manufacture*, J. Parnaby *et al.*, Collins/Blackwell Scientific, Oxford, 1986. See also 'A Systems Approach to the Implementation of JIT Methlolodologies in Lucas Industries', J. Parnaby, *International Journal of Production Research*, **26**, no. 3, 1988, pp. 483–92.
33. R. Schonberger, *ibid.*, p. 51.

34. *Introduction to Offline Quality Control*, G. Taguchi and Yu-In-Wu, Central Japanese Quality Control Association, 1979, p. 2.
35. 'Taguchi's quality philosophy', R. Kackar, *Quality Progress*, December, 1986, pp. 21–9.
36. K. Murata and A Harrison, *ibid*., p. 41.
37. *From the Cost World to the Throughput World*, E. Goldratt, Manufacturing Technology International Europe, 1991, p. 21.
38. 'For JIT read jitters', *The Economist*, 16 February 1991, p. 87.

3 | Design for JIT

The JIT philosophy of producing instantaneously with perfect quality and no waste can be applied to all areas of design, manufacture, and sales/distribution. From the customer perspective, savings in time and cost are equally valuable, whatever the source from which a saving comes. When Toyota engineers had succeeded in squeezing much of the waste out of manufacturing, they turned their attention to sales and distribution, where delays and inventories still choked the order processing system [1]. The eventual result was a 4-day processing time from confirmed customer order to delivery. Dealers became part of the Toyota family, the essential link between customer and producer. A policy of 'aggressive selling' ensured that customer orders were known in advance, and that customer preferences could be built into the product development process [2]. This policy gave additional perceived product leadership in satisfying customer requirements. But the last 10 years have seen the development of an even more impressive competitive advantage. While Japanese cars used to win orders on high accuracy with low cost, they are starting to win orders on superior product ranges and frequent new product launches leading to an image of innovation. Lessons had already been learned of the effectiveness of this strategy in the domestic market from the Honda/Yamaha motor cycle wars already referred to [3]. The recently published MIT survey [4] summarizes three telling figures. In comparison with average Western practice, average Japanese practice delivers:

- Development lead times for a new car which are 25% shorter;
- half of the design man hours per model;
- half of the assembly man hours per car.

Much of this has been achieved by applying JIT/TQ principles to design and development processes. Following research into automotive, computer, and electronics companies, Blackburn [5] has summarized Western new product development practices by comparing them with conventional batch

Table 3.1 Comparison of Western and Japanese practices in manufacturing and new product development: (a) Western; (b) Japanese

(a) Western

Process parameters	Conventional batch manufacturing	Conventional (Western) new product development
Batch sizes	Large-batch production; transferred in large batches	Information processed and transferred in large batches
Layouts	Jobshop	Functional by department
Process flow	Sequential activities	Sequential
Scheduling	Centralized scheduling	Centralized control
Employee involvement	Low	Low
Supply relations	Little coordination with suppliers	Low involvement with suppliers in design of components
Quality	High defect ratios: rework	Numerous engineering changes; rework
Automation	Islands of automation; isolated robots or transfer devices	Isolated systems (e.g. CAD systems with negligible integration)
Lead times	Long	Long

(b) Japanese

Process parameters	JIT manufacturing	Japanese new product development
Batch sizes	Small-batch production; transferred in small lots	Information processed and transferred in small batches
Layouts	Product layout	Grouped by project team
Process flow	Coordinated activities	Overlapping activities; simultaneous engineering
Management	Localized control; high level of employee involvement	Local control; management by project team
Supply relations	Close coordination with suppliers	High involvement with suppliers in design of components; technology and information exchange
Quality	Low defect rates	Few engineering changes
Automation	Integrated systems; automation follows process simplification	Automation of information flows: integrated CAD/CAE/CAM
Lead times	Short	Short

Source: Blackburn [5]

manufacturing. His model is shown in Table 3.1, together with an equivalent model for Japanese new product development compared with JIT manufacturing. For example, Western development processes are compared with large 'batches' of information, which are produced separately and passed on to the next stage in series. The Japanese equivalent requires information to be

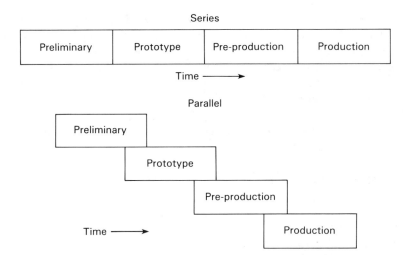

Series

Preliminary	Prototype	Pre-production	Production

Time ⟶

Parallel

Figure 3.1 Parallel versus series approach to development

passed on to the next stage in the smallest workable units so that downstream processes can begin work earlier. The comparison is illustrated in Figure 3.1.

Design/development processes are a far greater driver of product costs and quality than manufacturing. Studies of 2,000 components at Rolls-Royce [6] showed that 80% of total costs were determined by design. The converse of this conclusion is that there is no point in developing manufacturing technology in an attempt to overcome the shortcomings of the product design.

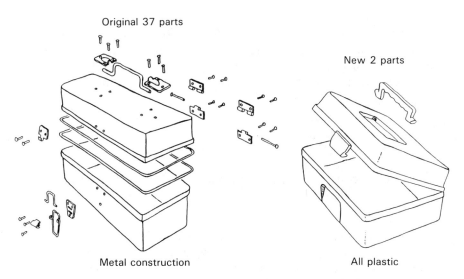

Original 37 parts

New 2 parts

Metal construction   All plastic

Figure 3.2 Lunch Box: a case for product redesign
(Courtesy Lucas Engineering and Systems)

This is brought home by the comparison between designs of a common-or-garden lunch box shown in Figure 3.2. There is no way in which the beautifully engineered metal version will be able to compete on cost with the plastic alternative (unless it is needed for a very hot climate!). Companies which are focusing on manufacturing costs are neglecting the major cost driver of the business. As Whitney put it, 'design is a strategic activity, whether by intention or default' [7].

Companies which set about reducing product development lead times grow the following competitive advantages:

- Latest technology improvements, such as ceramic engine valves, can be incorporated.
- New legislative changes, such as new 'Euro-Standards', can be incorporated.
- 'First mover' advantages which can shape new legal requirements can be built in, such as the 'flip-up' roll bar by Mercedes.
- Competitors can be bombarded with a burgeoning range of new designs which more accurately reflect current consumer tastes.

Such advantages, combined with low-cost designs and flexible manufacturing support, can be overwhelming in the market place.

■ Traditional design process

Design processes of course can vary widely from one firm to another. But in order to illustrate some of the difficulties which can emerge in a traditional approach to product design, the model shown in Figure 3.3 will be used. The four stages are typical of design in a repetitive manufacturing firm [8].

1. Preliminary design

Ideas for new products can come from many different sources. In the case of tyres, these can be grouped as follows (see Figure 3.4):

- **Innovation:** Research work is typically a fruitful but long-term source of new product ideas. But research projects need skilled management and a supportive culture to overcome the many hurdles to product launch; otherwise, lengthy delays and cancellation of promising projects can easily become the outcome.

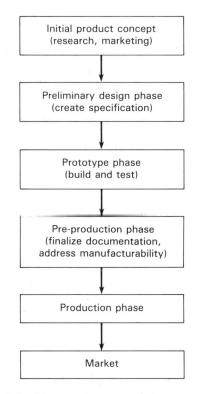

Figure 3.3 Phases of new product development

- **Marketing requests:** Customer needs are identified and development projects initiated. These can be at varying levels of complexity. A new size in an existing range takes less development time than a new pattern in a size which already exists. A new pattern in a new size requires going 'back to the drawing board', trial building, etc.

- **Product changes:** There is always a need to improve existing products, whether as a result of competitor action or customer problems. Improvements in load carrying or speed of operation lead to the need to change existing products.

- **Product transfer:** The transfer of existing designs from one factory to another may not be a straightforward task because of the need to develop new or modified processes. Lack of availability of requisite materials may lead to the need for further design and development work.

Whatever the source, a product specification must be formalized. This can be a hazardous task. Specifications can be subjective in nature, and demand

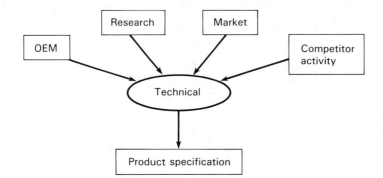

Figure 3.4 The input of ideas

conflicting requirements. For example, one territory may require traction and wet grip, another low-noise pattern, and a third regular wear performance. The design dilemma becomes one of meeting all three requirements without compromise in a single design. Ideally, three different designs are required, but would not be entertained because of the excessive development and mould costs. Volumes and target dates are difficult questions to answer, and so are usually described by marketing by means of unclear statements like 'as soon as possible'. The debate does not involve manufacturing because it is felt that, at this stage, final product details are hazy and it is too early to find out about manufacturability.

2. Prototype

Once the specification has been approved, the development process can start. Continuing the tyre example, an initial step is to determine the ability of existing tyre constructions to meet the need, and what gap needs to be bridged. Technical drawings for the tyres are converted into mould drawings, costed, and scheduled for manufacture. The mould manufacture lead time is several months. Meanwhile, detailed development continues. Delays can – and often do – occur because financial clearance has not been given for all or part of the work. Although update meetings are held from time to time, development tends to be done in isolation: so it is easier for the designer to start from scratch. This can mean that products, components, and designs proliferate. The main sources of information and ideas are colleagues within the design group. Suppliers and manufacturing are generally excluded from the process.

3. Pre-production

Once the new design has been through its final review and the necessary paper-work completed, it is passed to manufacturing. The design has to be converted into a set of shop-floor process specifications. Some would describe this part of the sequence as 'throwing it over the wall'. It is up to manufacturing to work out how to produce the design in a cost-effective manner (and to make up the delays which have already put the project behind schedule!). Development work so far has produced an interdependent set of decisions which it is too late to question for fear of unravelling the whole design [9]. So pleas for improvements in manufacturability are resisted. After all, this was not part of the original product specification! The new tyre design meets some additional problems here. The pilot quantities required for evaluation purposes (typically only three) disrupt production schedules. While high-priority tyres gain rapid progress, lower priorities have to wait. If they are to be produced on equipment which is only available occasionally, then the wait may be months.

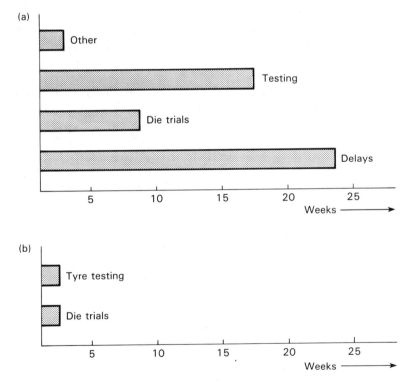

Figure 3.5 Monitoring of tyre development projects: (a) worst case, total development time = 50 weeks (18 weeks testing: 8 tyre sets; 8 weeks of die trials: 10 die trials; 24 weeks of delays in between); (b) ideal JIT style, total development time = 4 weeks (2 weeks of die trials and samples: 2 max; 2 weeks of tyre testing: 2 sets max.; zero delays)

If the tyre does not meet specification, then further design iterations may be needed.

4. Production

Once the product is performing to specification, the design and process standards can be produced and authorized. Pilot production may now start, with manufacturing being left to run things very much by itself. But the various problems which were identified during the pre-production phase are starting to trickle through the complex authorization process. They appear as engineering change orders (ECOs), which cause disruption, recalls, and rework. In the case of tyres, a further stage is that of final proving to test for handling, noise, and comfort, which could become a source of further change orders.

The overall timescale from concept to volume launch can be very lengthy, but when analysed, a major factor turns out to be delays. Figure 3.5 illustrates what may happen in an extreme case. Such a monitoring provides a useful record of how time was used up on the project, and hence some of the opportunities for improvement.

The development process for a more complex product (a vehicle) is illustrated in Figure 3.6. Downstream departments request changes to information released by preceding activities to improve the function and assembly of the vehicle. ECOs are launched by upstream activities on to downstream, and as programme timing becomes more critical, pressure mounts to clear designs for production. Sometimes the full development stage is rushed or bypassed. Parts must go into production in a less refined state, and manufacturing is left with poor designs which are difficult to produce to normal

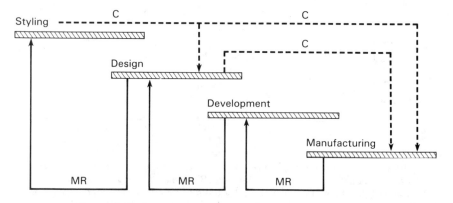

Figure 3.6 Product development process: C = change;
MR = MOD requests

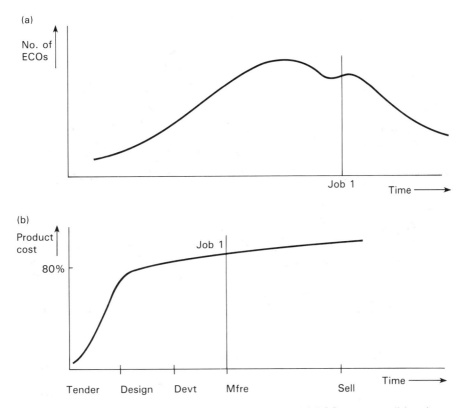

(a)

No. of ECOs

Job 1

Time ⟶

(b)

Product cost

80%

Job 1

Time ⟶

Tender   Design   Devt   Mfre   Sell

Figure 3.7 Comparing the timing of numbers of ECOs in a traditional design cycle with the building of product cost: (a) typical profile of ECOs (modification) in traditional engineering: (b) profile of development of product cost

quality levels. One consequence is a rush of ECOs near the realization stage of the programme, which is when project costs are at their highest (Figure 3.7) [10].

The same pressures typically occur for make-to-order (MTO) designs. Figure 3.8 shows major activities for the design and manufacture of a power transformer. A delivery date has been agreed with the customer beforehand, and an estimated manufacturing cost is being worked to. In reality, all of the major costs are determined at the design stage. But manufacturing involvement is limited to attendance at 'design review' meetings, which are used mainly to inform downstream activities about design details and progress. So although it appears that most of the major activities are manufacturing related, it is design who hold the purse strings and who have greatest influence on whether it is possible to make the contract to time and cost objectives.

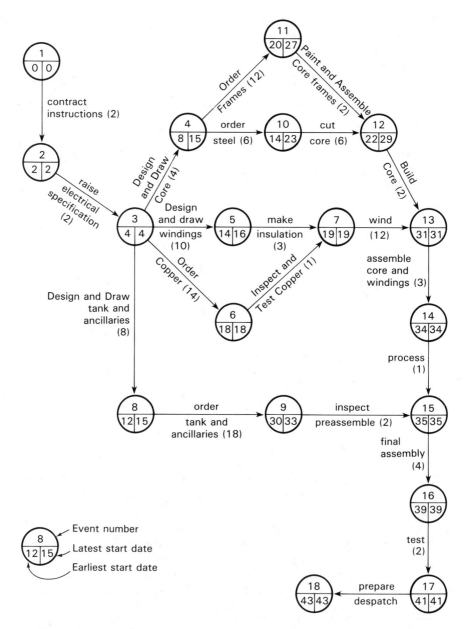

Figure 3.8 Outline network for the design and manufacture of a power transformer

■ Modern design process

An increasing number of companies report that the most effective route to improved designs is provided by multi-disciplinary teams. Design for manufacture (DFM), concurrent engineering, simultaneous engineering, overlapping problem solving [11], and parallel engineering are all equivalent terms which used to describe the processes involved. We will use the umbrella term 'DFM' here, for which the Lucas definition [12] is:

> the focusing of design team effort on the cost effective use of parts and processes to produce on time, high quality products that meet customer and business requirements.

DFM ensures that manufacturing and other concerns are catered for by means of multi-disciplinary teams and parallel engineering. Such an approach seeks to ensure the following:

■ Lower product design and development costs through the elimination of waste and early allowances for potential downstream problems.
■ Shorter time to market because downstream activities can start earlier.
■ Reduced product cost because design proposals are questioned at source, not when it is too late.
■ Improved product quality because manufacturing processes are considered alongside designs.

However, Lucas experience shows that it is not sufficient to reorganize different functional representatives into teams. Designers still see themselves as creators of ideas, and paperwork still gets passed between members for vetting. A key change is for team members to focus on the downstream implications of what they are doing, for example to think about how easy it will be to assemble the proposed design. (Such considerations seem to come naturally to small companies. John Partridge, the brilliant proprietor of Sonardyne Ltd, told me how he used to assemble his new designs for underwater transponders in the garden while a colleague stood over him with a stopwatch!) In a large company, focus on end objectives is needed to help provide common aims for the teams. So goals for cost, quality, and delivery need to be set at the product specification stage. Extra effort at this stage in defining markets, how the new product will win orders, volumes, competitive benchmarks, performance, specification, product cost, and production methods pays dividends. Once agreed, the product specification should be frozen to help assure rapid introduction. Design teams should be given a high level of autonomy in order to achieve product specification goals. In particular, the top team should resist the temptation to interfere or to change the goal posts. The opportunity is to change the organization's culture by breaking down barriers and delegating complete authority for innovation and implementation. This is very much in line with the total quality objective of control being embedded within the organization.

Possible limitations on the use of DFM are very large-scale design projects (such as aerospace), great leaps in innovation (such as a new discovery), or the inventions of a genius [13]. DFM teams need a suitable range of tools and techniques to help them achieve their aims. Tools and techniques encourage informed decision-making.

■ DFM tools and techniques

There is currently a considerable range of tools and techniques available to facilitate DFM objectives. Some of these (like value analysis) have been around a long time. Others (like Lucas Design for Assembly) are of more recent origin. All need to be viewed in the context of the staggering technology improvements now available to the designer, such as greatly improved surface-modelling software and virtual reality (allowing a computer to map a user's body and senses directly into a digital world, so removing the user interface with the computer environment) [14]. Such techniques are beyond the scope of this book, but will no doubt impact on DFM in the future. Here, we provide a brief description of some of the DFM tools and techniques in current use, and indicate how they fit in with the design and development process.

1. Value engineering (VE)

The aim of this technique is to achieve new component designs which maintain the key functions of the assembly while providing best value to the customer. 'Functions' implies what the assembly does, not what it currently is. Usually, the team carries out a systematic problem solving routine as follows:

- Collect information (current design, proposed assembly method, component costing and process method). Carry out a Pareto analysis by cost.
- Make functional definitions of the 'A' and 'B' category items.
- Create alternatives: the team brainstorms new ideas, and then selects the most favoured ones.
- Develop the proposed new method.

An example of the result from a VE exercise is shown in Figure 3.9. VE is preferred to value analysis (VA), which is carried out on components which are already in production, because it is closer to the design process, and therefore has greater potential impact on time and cost.

2. Boothroyd Dewhurst

This is a software-based system which sets out to simulate the assembly process

To apply value engineering techniques to analysing the current design of the compressor bracketry.

To achieve a new component design that would maintain the key functions of the assembly at the best value to the company.

The team were to utilize the current mounting faces on the engine and there was no potential to modify the compressor mounting points, as this was a proprietary part.

The existing component count	= 43 parts
Comprising 7 special parts and standard fixings	
Assembly labour cost	= £1.704
Usage volumes:	
compressor bracketry	= 801 units/wk
	= 36,500/annum
Total annual cost of units and labour	= £302,200
Revised condition following VA	
Component count	= 11 parts
comprising 3 special parts and 8 std	
Assembly labour cost (est.)	= £0.577
Total annual cost	= £206,500

Results of exercise:
74% saving in parts (43 to 11)
32% saving in cost (£302,200 to £206,500)

Figure 3.9 Summary of results from a value engineering exercise

and to question the use of every part by asking three basic questions [15]:

1. When the part is in operation, does it move with respect to all other parts already assembled?
2. Must the part be made of material which is different to that of all other parts already assembled?
3. Must the part be separate from all others already assembled in order to allow for the assembly or disassembly of other parts?

If the answer to any of these questions is no, then the part is classified as non-critical. The part is then identified for further investigation and possible deletion. So parts are reduced to a minimum, and the remaining parts assessed for ease of manufacture. It is a useful way of comparing alternative designs, assessing improvements, and of gaining an early understanding of assembly costs.

3. Lucas Design for Assembly (DFA)

Lucas DFA [16] feeds off the product specification. The initial design is then analysed by means of a three-stage process:

1. Functional analysis, which categorizes parts into:
    *   A parts (demanded by the design specification);
    *   B parts (needed to meet the proposed design solution, for example to perform fixing and locating duties).

    The aim is to reduce the number of B parts to less than 40% of the total.
2. Handling analysis, which uses a knowledge base to assess the cost of handling every part, and sets a target cost of handling per category A part.
3. Fitting analysis, which determines a cost of assembling every part, and sets a target for assembly cost per category A part. Cost indices have been developed for gripping (ease of pick and place) and insertion (ease of fitting). This step ensures that manufacturability is considered at an early stage in the product development process.

The product is then redesigned to improve the performance measures, and finally validated (Figure 3.10). Lucas DFA is claimed to reduce part counts by typically 30%, assembly costs by typically 40%, and overall product costs by 35%.

4. Quality function deployment (QFD)

QFD [17] is one of a number of techniques which are aimed at building customer needs into the product from the start. This is typically done by listing

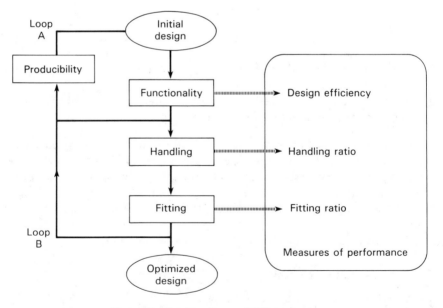

Figure 3.10 The Lucas DFA procedure

customer requirements ('voice of the customer') down the left-hand side of a matrix, and the design requirements (outputs) along the top columns of the matrix. The body of the matrix can then be used to identify relationships between inputs and outputs, so that priorities and any mismatches can be shown. Further additions to the matrix can be made to relate design requirements with each other, to provide units of measure, and to compare competitor benchmarks. A simplified example is shown in Figure 3.11. QFD is described by Lucas [18] as a four-phase process:

- QFD 1: relates customer and design requirements;
- QFD 2: relates component characteristics to the key design requirements from phase 1;

		Design requirements: Door close effort	Door open effort	Internal handle operation	External handle operation	Max. noise on slamming	Does not leak	Seal compressibility	
Customer requirements	Shuts easily	●		△	△			○	
	Does not leak						●		
	Quietness					●		△	
	Opens easily		●					○	
Units of measure		75 ft lbs	85 ft lbs	7 lb max.	10 lb max.	80 dB	4 minute water test	100 H lbs	
Competitor benchmarks	Better								
		×			×			×	
				×			×		
			×						
	Worse					×			

Figure 3.11 A much simplified QFD worksheet for some of the factors which affect the design of a car door

- QFD 3: relates proposed manufacturing process characteristics to key component characteristics from phase 2;
- QFD 4: relates proposed operational control characteristics to the key manufacturing process characteristics from phase 3.

A proposed relationship between the four QFD phases, product and process design, and other tools and techniques to aid design is shown in Figure 3.12. Although the benefits of QFD are less easily measured than DFA, Lucas report

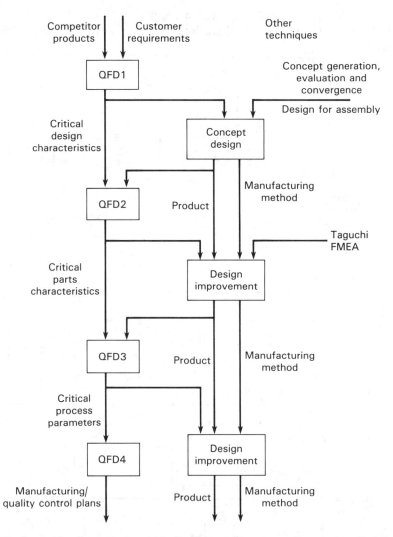

Figure 3.12 The relationship of QFD stages 1 to 4 and the design process, shown without feedback loops (Source: Lucas Engineering and Systems)

that QFD is a useful enabler for DFM teamwork, and helps to ensure that the 'voice of the customer' is heard during the DFM process.

5. Taguchi optimization

The basic Taguchi philosophy of 'loss to society' was explained in Chapter 2, page 60. But Taguchi methodology is intended to be operational in nature, to have a strong practical thrust. The basis for this approach is that productivity and quality should be built in to a product at the design stage, and not simply as a discipline during manufacture. This is fundamental to DFM. 'Taguchi methods' is the trade mark of the American Supplier Institute, which has done most to promote Taguchi methodology in the West.

The first Taguchi principle is that of parameter design. Then methods of manufacture which most closely achieve these design parameters are considered. The aim is to produce exactly at the nominal design variable. In practice, the starting point for Taguchi methodology is statistical experiment design. This is largely based on the work of Sir R. A. Fisher around 1920 in the analysis of variance (ANOVA) methods for agricultural research in the United Kingdom. Systematic ('all at once') experimentation is often necessary in agriculture because of the length of the growing cycle. ANOVA methods aim to test a number of variables in the minimum number of experiments. For example, four variables to be tested at three different levels would require 3^4, that is 81, separate tests for all possible combinations to be tried out. Taguchi's 'L9 orthogonal array' limits the number of tests to only nine, provided that the variables are independent, that is they do not react with each other [19]. The value of such a reduction is that the overall cost of systematic testing can be greatly reduced, and the best design found at minimum time and cost.

6. Knowledge-based engineering (KBE)

KBE is a major new technology which enables users to capture information which defines design intent. This is achieved by building a 'smart' model from engineering rules which specify how products and processes are defined. The technology enables users to complete work in a shorter period with fewer design man hours. A major attraction is its ability to capture the engineering expertise of an organization, a critical issue with current demographic trends. KBE provides a foundation for DFM by providing a model which retains knowledge from many different company disciplines. Two KBE systems will be briefly described here.

1. Intelligent Computer-Aided Design (ICAD)

This is a rule-based system, and so requires a high level of expertise to operate. Manufacturing and material processing data is created in rule form. In addition, rules can be written which place a working envelope around a component. If another component encroaches into that space buffer, then the whole part flashes on the screen. This can be used to simulate dynamic assembly. In particular, at the concept stage of design, it can confirm that press feasibility has been achieved, and can help to construct changes where necessary. So it is well suited to concept design and to facilitating frequent product changes.

2. Variation Simulation Analysis (VSA)

The traditional method of finding the effect of tolerance buildup on component assemblies is to add up all the tolerance in one direction and subtract them in the other. For example,

panel joint tolerance	± 2 mm
component tolerance	± 3 mm
normal gap between the two	8 mm

So the resultant gap variation would be ± 5 mm on the nominal of 8 mm. This approach, called tolerance stacking, uses the extremes of the process range. These extremes might never occur, and so the approach leads to conservative designs and limited quality improvements. VSA is a mathematical technique which gives a statistical prediction of the assembly tolerance of part assemblies. It assumes that processes are in statistical control, and that detailed process performance data is available. It uses dimensions taken at random for all components of an assembly, and repeats over 1,000 assemblies to give a typcial spread of assembly tolerances. VSA can identify critical subassemblies and processes which have an adverse effect on the final assembly accuracy. Such problem areas are targeted for quality planning and special action.

KBE systems typically involve high costs of initial inputs, and of updating. They are therefore not really suitable for small companies.

Tools and techniques, such as those listed above, rely on a clear and professionally managed design process for full effectiveness. An overall design strategy needs to be developed and its company-wide impact emphasized. Which techniques fit in with this strategy will depend on the character of the product [20]. VE, Boothroyd and Dewhurst, and Lucas DFA all build on the multi-disciplinary team approach. Boothroyd and Dewhurst and Lucas DFA tend to be limited to components for bench-type assemblies, and concentrate on reducing the number of support parts. VE has a broader application to assemblies at all levels, and seeks to find a better 'value' alternative for the most expensive items. ICAD and VSA are specialist activities which need to be carried out by experts. Outputs from such KBE systems need to be fed into teams at the appropriate stage. A suggested model showing where the best features of each technique link in with stages in the design process is shown

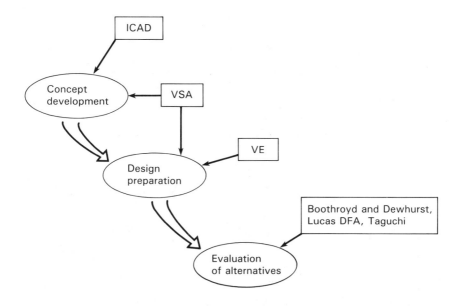

Figure 3.13 Suggested areas of the design process matched with major strengths of DFM techniques (Source: L. Gill, Jaguar Cars)

in Figure 3.13. An important consideration is the speed at which people in the organization can learn: mastery of techniques in an ordered sequence is preferable to attempting to skip key learning steps and introduce sophisticated technology when the business benefits are unclear [21].

■ Product diversity

Meeting the need for burgeoning product ranges would appear to lead us down the road of part number proliferation. But this in turn will cause extra costs and complexity in the manufacturing costs. No concrete studies have been published to show this relationship, but internal company studies based only on material handling and ordering costs suggest a figure close to £1,000 for each extra class C or D part [22]. In reality, many more costs are associated with part number proliferation, which Lucas have described as 'a major cost driver'. Figure 3.14 suggests that we have an iceberg here, with poor visibility of the true cost and time penalties involved. So the challenge is to produce product diversity with minimum parts count.

Modular designs are one way in which companies have traditionally reacted to this challenge. Starr [23] described the principle as one of designing, developing, and producing the minimum number of parts that can be combined in

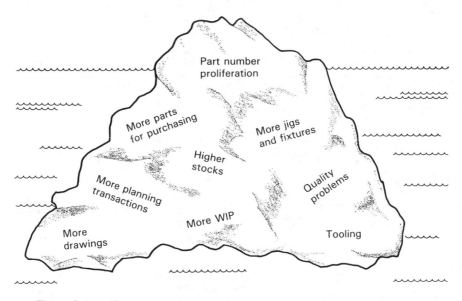

Figure 3.14 The part number proliferation iceberg: what is the true cost of an extra part?

the maximum number of ways to offer the greatest number of products. Producing complexity (a wide product range) from simplicity (a limited number of standard modules) is consistent with JIT philosophy. Designing in modules allows subassemblies to be distinguished clearly. It permits assembly work to be focused, rather than to be a complex, high-variety task on one line. It facilitates make/buy decisions. 'Standard' production runs are facilitated, with variety being added late in the process. Modular designs also help to support cellular manufacturing and focus. Purchasing can issue the 'base' specification earlier, with variations being added later on.

Beware of focusing on part cost as the justification for using extra part numbers. Two examples serve to illustrate this principle:

1. Marketing decided that it was necessary to have the switch in the internal light on the Range Rover on the left for left-hand-drive vehicles. This was a simple thing for the designers to achieve: the switch was turned through 180°. However, this meant that the wiring, which ran up the 'A' post, had to be lengthened. A new part number was commissioned and drawn. Production only used the new left-hand-drive version of the wiring harness, and simply cut off 3 inches to make the right-hand-drive version! Result: stock of the left-hand-drive harnesses was rapidly exhausted. The part has now been redesigned as a single item, and the extra 0.5p written off as being inconsequential in relation to assembly costs!
2. Intel Corporation [24] posed the question 'why order eight resistor values when one costs only one cent more?' The question was directed at the need

to stock a wide range of parts which all carry out the same function, and which are held only to make a small piece part saving. This saving is more than offset by the cost of the extra part numbers involved.

Several technology advances have helped the quest for part number reduction. Two applications are described here to show the possibilities:

1. Rexel Engineering in South Wales are delighted with their decision to change the method for producing the wide range of small pressed parts used in the manufacture of staplers. Previously, this was carried out on a combination of pierce and blank presses, transfer tools, and second-operation (forming) presses. Although larger presses and new toolroom equipment were needed, the introduction of progression tooling soon paid for itself in terms of reduced parts and hence WIP [25]. Further benefits such as reduced space requirements and throughput times followed (Figure 3.15). Progression tooling helped Rexel to reduce the number of parts in its most popular range of staplers from 250 to 120.

2. The advent of CNC punch and blank machine tools has provided designers with a whole new world of possibilities for fabricated parts design. Smart designers are looking for opportunities to reduce the complexity of manufacturing tasks instead of proliferating new designs which take ages to plan and set up. Figure 3.16 shows a redesigned hopper to collect dispensed granules in a Sankey Vending drinks machine. The hopper was previously made from four shaped parts which had to be welded and then painted. The hopper is now made from a single punched and blanked component which is simply folded to shape and painted. Eight part numbers have been reduced to two. A small step in itself, maybe. But as

Before: pierce blank and forming tools

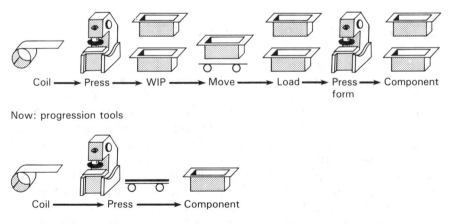

Coil ⟶ Press ⟶ WIP ⟶ Move ⟶ Load ⟶ Press ⟶ Component
form

Now: progression tools

Coil ⟶ Press ⟶ Component

Figure 3.15 Reduction in process complexity through progression tools
(Source: J. Cameron, Rexel Engineering)

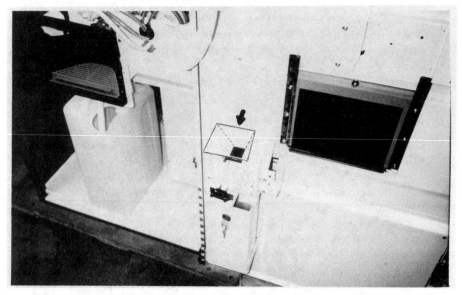

Figure 3.16 Redesigned hopper at Sankey Vending: hopper (arrowed) is now made from a single punched and blanked component

part of a comprehensive drive to produce simpler, more manufacturable designs many small steps become a large one.

So part number proliferation is worth confronting at the tactical level. A greater impact can be made if part number reduction and simplification is part of the design strategy. DFM is one contributor; group technology (GT) is another.

■ The strategic importance of GT

Group technology is a set of manufacturing techniques which enables us to exploit the basic similarities of parts and of manufacturing processes. Families can be classified by size, shape, manufacturing or routing requirements, or by volume. At the heart of this classification is a coding system. Various coding systems have been proposed which use similarities in design or manufacture to propose families of parts. One of the applications of such coding systems is to reduce the variety of parts. The costs of setting up a system of classifying and coding can be recouped quickly (typically within 2 years), and design costs consistently reduced thereafter [26]. An example of what can be achieved is provided by GEC Distribution Transformer Co. in South Africa [27]. This company previously designed practically all new contracts specifically to customer order. A new bill of material and process design had to be drawn up for each job, and in turn had to be individually interpreted on the shop floor. Enquiries had to be individually estimated: a 'strike rate' (conversion of tenders into contracts) of 10% would mean that 90% of a valuable design engineer's time was wasted on preparing tender estimates for which no value was received by the company. The company achieved a substantial improvement in its competitive position by making the following changes:

■ A database of standard options was designed, which avoided as far as possible the limiting of end products available to the customer. This file is referred to as the options master, and is not the same as a modular bill of material in that all processes (such as paint colour and customer test requirements) must be included. The options master was not limited to part coding alone, but ensured that due consideration was given to the assembly sequence within predetermined cells. This essential set of considerations ensured that manufacturing interests were included, a 'design for JIT' approach.

■ Tenders could now be designed from the options master by the commercial engineer. A list of available options offered to the potential customer, called the options configuration, is prepared from the customer's tender specification. Standard tender prices of all components reside on the system, so that a 'roll up cost' is simultaneously prepared.

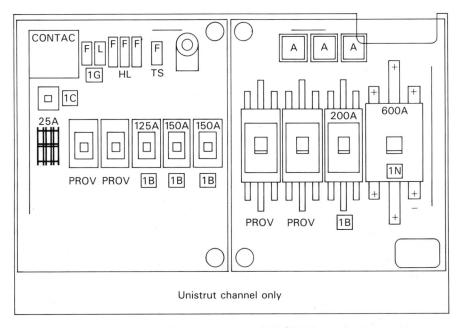

Figure 3.17 Example of the extent of CAD/CAM integration, with a panel using a unique combination of standard back panel holes and door cutouts

- If the tender is successful, then the options configuration becomes the works order. Because design and manufacturing information are strictly compatible, no further processing is necessary. Information on the options configuration has been sorted by work centre, and so can be used to load bottleneck operations and hence to provide basic scheduling data.

A few parts still need to be designed to specific customer order. These are usually panels and compartments which must carry specific instruments. Again, design and manufacture have been closely linked. The panel is designed by CAD using a unique combination of standard holes and door cutouts (Figure 3.17). It is produced by moving pictures of the chosen instruments into the correct position on the screen. The tape for the CNC punch and blank machine is prepared automatically from CAD data, together with accompanying planning information.

The above illustration shows how GT can be used not only to facilitate development of a coherent design strategy, but also to act as the essential link between design (CAD) and manufacture (CAM) by the inclusion of planning information in the design of the options master. The challenge is to include computer-aided process planning (CAPP) in the way that GT is put to work.

■ The timing of diversity

A critical issue is the time at which derivatives are created in the manufacturing process. The later this take place, the shorter that customer lead times can be. Toyota defines the ratio between two lead times in order to promote progress [28]:

P = lead time for a product (the total lead time from ordering of raw materials through to delivery)
D = expected customer lead time

The lower the $P:D$ ratio, the more closely it is possible to assemble to known customer demand, and at the same time reduce the period for which customers have to wait. Where P is greater than D, and a major competitive factor for the product is delivery speed, then it is essential that product design aims for standarization early in the manufacturing process and that options are added as late as possible. Thereby, it is possible to avoid either high stocks of WIP (to cover many options) or lengthy lead times. Further, precise customer requirements are more accurately known then. The design concept can be illustrated by means of a 'mushroom chart', an example of which is shown in Figure 3.18. Here, Rexel are aiming to achieve a 48-hour lead time to customer by designing staplers so that uniqueness is left until the last possible minute of manufacture [29]. Trigger times for parts (both internal and bought out) will need to be sufficiently short to support this lead time objective.

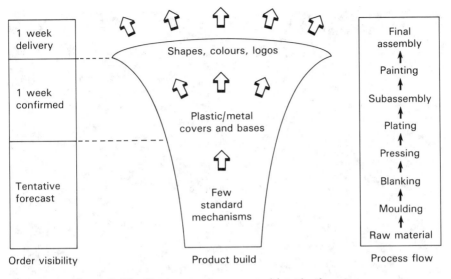

Figure 3.18 Product variety created late in the process
(Source: J. Cameron, Rexel Engineering)

Massey Ferguson decided to design the CX tractor so that it would be available in virtually any specification that the customer might want. This was achieved by designing variety into every feature of the tractor (wheel size, lighting, power takeoff, cab, transmission, etc.). Unfortunately, this meant that variety was also designed deep into the manufacturing processes, and an incredible number (theoretically 10 followed by 19 noughts) of derivatives was possible. There was a real danger that the bill of materials processor on the former MRP system would be unable to cope with the burgeoning demands being made on it. Manufacturing, which had been laid out to handle large volumes and low variety, found it extremely difficult to meet the new demands for increased variety. Responsiveness became one of the tradeoffs. Many of Massey Ferguson's efforts in recent years have been directed towards overcoming the difficulties caused in manufacturing.

Forced with similar market demands – high-variety, low-volume automotive products – the Japanese manufacturer of construction equipment, Komatsu, tackled the factory first [30]. Once a JIT manufacturing system is in place, a company can use the advantages to reduce costs or increase variety (or both). Komatsu chose the latter course to scale up its operations against its US-based competitor, Caterpillar. Even by 1981, Komatsu had the wider product range. But the strong relationship between design and manufacturing processes was clear from our visit to the Komatsu factory at Osaka [31], where 200 different varieties of construction equipment were made in small quantities. Variety for the revolving frame excavators, for example, was delegated to many subassembly cells which held only half a day's inventory and which

Figure 3.19 The final assembly line at Komatsu Revolving Excavators: variety is delegated to flexible cells (to the right of the assembly line in this photograph)

fed directly into the main assembly track. Figure 3.19 shows how the subassembly cells fed into the track, which is in the foreground in the photograph.

■ Structuring the bill of materials

Traditionally, the task of structuring the bill of materials (BOM) has fallen to design engineers who had little idea of how the product would be assembled. So decisions about the BOM would be based on design features, which became the 'subassemblies' by which the product was structured. This often led to different versions of the BOM (design and manufacturing versions for a start). Compromises also included the labelling of design subassemblies as 'phantoms', and creating new part numbers for physical manufacturing subassemblies. But improvements in process design open up a host of new possibilities in a JIT environment as follows:

■　Very short P times mean that physical subassemblies are no longer so important. Subassemblies can be made to order and delivered to final assembly only as needed. Ultimately, they do not need separate part numbers, nor do they need to be inventoried [32].

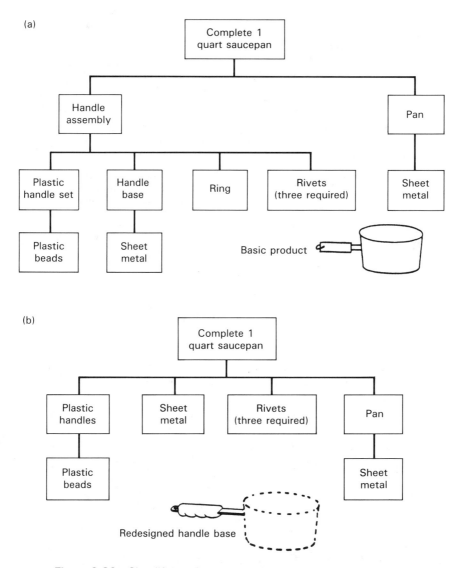

Figure 3.20 Simplifying the product structure through redesign:
(a) original; (b) simplified with redesigned handle base (Source: adapted
from T. Vollman *et al.*, Manufacturing Planning and Control Systems,
Irwin, 1989)

■ Therefore, less and less structure is needed in the BOM. Subassemblies can
be called up for final assembly using an unstructured parts list via assembly line broadcasting.

■ Therefore, fewer levels are needed in the BOM and fewer part numbers.
This greatly reduces the number of transactions on MRP.

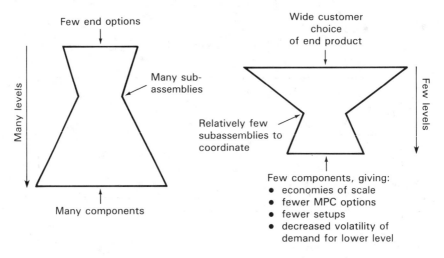

Figure 3.21 Preferred changes in the shape of the bill of materials for an assemble-to-order product

Improvements in product design can be used further to accelerate this virtuous cycle. Figure 3.20 shows the BOM before and after product redesign [33]. By redesigning the handle base and ring on different options, it was possible to make the base handle common without reducing the number of options available to the customer. The BOM has now been reduced to three levels, and three part numbers eliminated. It is no longer necessary to keep stocks of the handle assembly. A further substantial reduction in MRP transactions is possible. If the pan could be redesigned, yet more reductions in both stocks and MRP transactions could be made. The sort of preferred changes in the shape of the BOM are shown in Figure 3.21 for an assemble-to-order product. A wider choice of end options has been achieved with fewer subassemblies and fewer components.

■ Supplier relationships

DFM is perhaps not so good at conveying the need for early involvement of suppliers in the design and development processes as simultaneous engineering. But the same principles apply as to the early involvement of manufacturing: the earlier that suppliers are involved in the design process, the more impact they can make on reducing costs and improving quality. Figure 3.22 contrasts the way in which suppliers were traditionally involved with the way we would like now [34]. Formerly, their involvement was late and sporadic, with several small-scale projects late in the product design phase. Traditionally, British Original Equipment Manufacturers held design expertise 'in

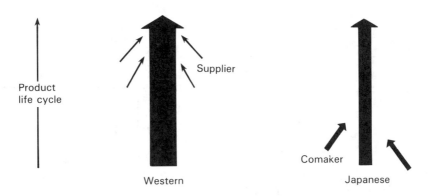

Figure 3.22 Contrasting roles of traditional suppliers and comakers in the product life cycle (Source: N. Deverill, Electrolux)

house', and issued detailed design specifications. Suppliers therefore had little or no room to innovate. The aim now is to involve them early by means of a few major projects. Comakers should be used as experts in their own area, and entrusted with the necessary information about future product plans. 'Open specifications' allow comakers to innovate and improve quality from broad requirements stated by the original equipment manufacturer (OEM) in the product specification.

■ Project management

New product development projects can be birds of passage across the functions of an organization in spite of cross-functional design teams. A further strengthening of the process of new product development is necessary. Such strengthening is provided by the appointment of a project manager (PM) to oversee the whole of the design and development process from product specification to volume production. The PM needs to have sufficient 'clout' to be seen as the person to whom DFM team members report on a day-to-day basis during the life of the project. Too background a role means that the PM is not taken sufficiently seriously to enable him or her to peform the essential task of planning, integrating, and monitoring. The PM's job is to achieve project objectives to time and cost. Actions taken to bring Ford's much-vaunted Lincoln Town Car back on programme included an enforcement of a freeze date for engineering change orders 9 months prior to job 1, and prototype build being shifted to the future assembly plant to familiarize personnel with the car early in the development process [35]. Both the launch manager and the project manager were senior personnel. At 41 months, the Town Car was the fastest Western new car development.

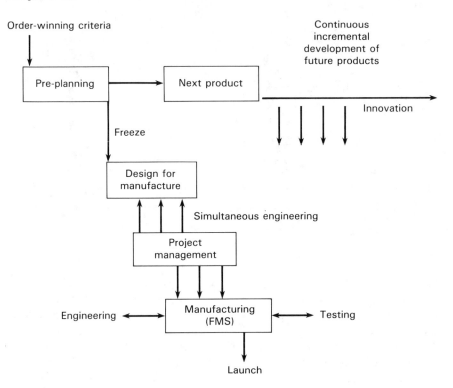

Figure 3.23 Proposed model for the new product design and development (Source: M. Evans, SP tyres)

A proposed model for new product design and development places the project manager linking the DFM teams with manufacture, process engineering, buying, and other areas concerned with implementation of the new project (Figure 3.23). Criteria for products to win orders in the market place are built in at the pre-planning stage, so that it is clear what objectives are being aimed for in the activities which follow. The new product specification is subsequently frozen to allow rapid design and process development to take place, facilitated by the PM. Flexibility in manufacture helps to facilitate process development, prototyping, and launch.

■ Conclusion

A sound design strategy is necessary for converting product specifications into excellent products. Multi-functional teams help to put such a strategy into practice by reducing design lead times, and by improving quality and manufacturability. It is impossible to get too close to the initial design concept. Such teams become the new product champions, aware of and responding to the pressures of the external market. As their role evolves, they become major drivers for change in the organization. So the teams need to be given a high level of autonomy to enable them to react quickly. Some of the tools and techniques of design for manufacture are a departure from the basic JIT feature of simplicity. But it is essential for the excellent company to learn how to make best use of available methods to innovate designs with new materials and processes. Excellence in manufacture is heavily dependent on excellence in design. As before, the starting point is to do the simple things well, and gradually to learn the relevant, more specialized tools and techniques. The key constraint becomes how quickly the organization can learn: Progress Equals Our People's Learning Experience [36].

■ References

1. See for example *Study of Toyota Production from an Industrial Engineering Viewpoint*, S. Shingo, Japan Management Association, Tokyo, 1981.
2. *The Machine that Changed the World*, J. Womack, D. Jones, and D. Roos, Rawson Associates, 1990, New York, p. 66.
3. *Kaisha, the Japanese Corporation*, J Abbeglen and G. Stalk, Basic Books, 1985, New York, p. 48.
4. J. Womack *et al.*, *ibid.*, p. 118.
5. *Time-based Competition: The Next Battleground in American Manufacturing*, J. D. Blackburn, Business One Irwin, Homewood, IL, 1991.
6. 'Design for economic manufacture', *Annals of CIRP*, **35**, no. 1, p. 93, 1986.
7. 'Manufacturing by design', D. E. Whitney, *Harvard Business Review*, July/August, 1988.
8. 'Design for manufacturability: Product development in JIT manufacturing', K. L. Rowe, MSc Thesis to Alfred Sloan School of Management, MIT, 1986.
9. D. E. Whitney, *ibid.*
10. *Integrated Product Development*, M. Andreason, M. Myrup, and L. Hein, IFS, 1987.
11. 'Overlapping problem solving in product development', K. Clark and T. Fujimoto, in K. Ferdowes (ed.) *Managing International Manufacturing*, North Holland, Amsterdam, 1989, pp. 127–52.
12. Brian Miles, Lucas Engineering & Systems.
13. 'Managing the new product development process: How Japanese companies learn and unlearn', K. Imai, I. Nonaka and H. Takeuchi, *HBS Colloquium on Productivity*, March, 1984.
14. *Virtual Reality: Theory, Practice and Promise*, ed. S. Helsel and J. Roth, Meckler, London, 1991.
15. 'Making it simple – DFA', G. Boothroyd, *Mechanical Engineering*, February, 1988, pp. 28–31.
16. 'Design for assembly: A key element within DFM', B. Miles, *Proceedings of Institution of Mechanical Engineers*, **203**, 1989.
17. 'Quality function deployment', L. P. Sullivan, *Quality Progress*, June, 1986, pp. 39–50.

18. 'Training for DFM', Paper presented at the Institution of Mechanical Engineers DFM Seminar, April, 1990.
19. For further explanation and a review of Taguchi optimization, see *Taguchi Methodology within Total Quality*, A. Bendell, G. Wilson, and R. Millar, IFS, Bedford, 1990.
20. D. Whitney, *ibid.*, p. 85.
21. 'Success and failure in advanced manufacturing technologies', C. Voss, in B. Hunley (ed.) *Proc. 3rd European Conference on Automated Manufacture*, Birmingham, May, 1985, IFS Bedford.
22. Source: Jaguar Cars (unpublished).
23. 'Modular production: a new concept', M. Starr, *Harvard Business Review*, **43**, no. 6, pp. 131–42, 1965.
24. Information given to JIT US Study Tour by J. Manders, Manager, Device Bank, March, 1988.
25. 'Becoming globally cost competitive in the office products industry through JIT', J. Cameron, *Proc. 4th International Conference on JIT Manufacturing, October, 1989*, IFS, pp. 237–44.
26. 'GT and productivity', N. Hyer and V. Wemmerlov, *Harvard Business Review*, July/August 1984.
27. 'Implementation of JIT and CAD/CAM in the distributor transformer industry', D. Peles and R. Wallis, Electricity South Africa.
28. *A Study of the Toyota Production System from an Industrial Engineering Viewpoint*, S. Shingo, Productivity Press, Cambridge, MA, 1989.
29. J. Cameron, *ibid.*
30. J. Abbeglen and G. Stalk, *ibid.*, p. 117.
31. IFS JIT Study Tour to Japan, March, 1988.
32. 'The impact of JIT on bill of material structuring', K. Balcerak and B. Dale, *BPICS Control*, October/November, pp. 17–19, 1986.
33. *Manufacturing Planning & Control Systems*, T. Vollman, W. Berry and C. Whybark, Irwin, Homewood, IL, 1988.
34. Source: N. Deverill, Electrolux (unpublished).
35. 'Town Car Odyssey', J. Risen, *Los Angeles Times*, 8 October 1989.
36. J. Cameron, *ibid.*

4 Invest in People

In Chapter 1 we referred to the JIT/TQ basic element of people preparation, and to the 'whole person' concept incorporated into total people involvement in JIT2. Here, we examine supporting personnel plans and policies which help facilitate these aims, in particular the development of a teamwork approach to running and improving the factory. Wickens [1] describes three key personnel policies which were abstracted from Japanese management methods and used as a model for Nissan's new plant at Washington in the United Kingdom.

1. **Teamworking and commitment**: Everyone works in the same direction. Deming [2] describes this as convincing a 'critical mass' so that the thinking of most people is in line with the wanted company culture. It is not simply about group working or interdependence.

2. **Quality**: There is absolute commitment at every level that quality is the prime objective. It is not simply about introducing quality control circles (QCCs).

3. **Flexibility**: All jobs should be expanded as much as possible, to the extent of employees' capabilities. It is not simply about being able to move people around from one job to another.

Wickens calls these policies the 'Nissan Tripod' and they are illustrated in Figure 4.1. Each of the policies has a key role of play, so each must be in place for the structure to stand. In particular, they emphasize the fundamental need to root such concepts into the culture of the organization. The tripod represents the basic management beliefs.

Faced with the undoubted need for major changes over the next few years, companies can act in a range between two extremes roughly represented by the following two statements:

1. We still manage it in the traditional way by issuing instructions, monitoring progress, and taking corrective action where necessary. Basically,

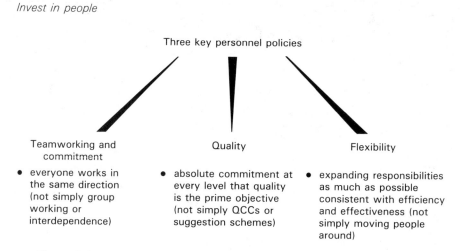

Three key personnel policies

Teamworking and commitment	Quality	Flexibility
• everyone works in the same direction (not simply group working or interdependence)	• absolute commitment at every level that quality is the prime objective (not simply QCCs or suggestion schemes)	• expanding responsibilities as much as possible consistent with efficiency and effectiveness (not simply moving people around)

Figure 4.1 The Nissan tripod (Source: *The Road to Nissan* by Peter Wickens © 1987 with permission of Macmillan Ltd)

management will decide what to do, although we will communicate our plan, and perhaps consult over details.

2. We will do it the TQ way by letting our people identify and solve problems which affect the work they do. We will give them the tools through training, and help progress change by personal involvement and commitment.

The first refers mostly to management supervision of change. The second refers to leadership of change, with much of the responsibility for action being delegated to people 'at the coal face' of the organization. In an increasingly turbulent business environment, the second option becomes the only one that can be used to prepare the business for immediate response to new challenges and opportunities. We can no longer afford to wait while a decision is sent up the organization for authorization: the opportunity may have gone by the time it comes back. People must be trained and empowered to deal with such challenges and opportunities. How far this concept can be applied depends on how far the process of expanding responsibilities can be accomplished. Often the costs involved, and the relatively long-term gains associated with such a route, put off the management of the day. It is simpler and quicker to get results by managing the traditional way. Maybe results are currently quite good, so why change a successful formula? The latter attitude was graphically illustrated at the Morgan Motor Company by Harvey-Jones [3]. Here, the management of a specialist manufacturer of sports cars with a 10-year waiting list (!) was terrified of change. In spite of most unprofessional management practices, the company had come to believe in its own success. Yet Toyota, described as 'the best car marker in the world', is permanently dissatisfied, even with exemplary performance [4].

■ Beliefs and company culture

Company culture results from the execution of a set of policies which in turn are based on a set of beliefs or values. Ford Motor Company's Mission Statement and Values are reproduced in Figure 4.2 [5]. Values for Japanese companies often appear vague and informal in comparison – the motto for Yuasa Battery Company is also shown in this figure as an example. The true beliefs are often not specifically recorded, and actually manifest themselves in the management decisions which are made, and how they are made. Such manifestations can sometimes appear to be quite confusing and contradictory, resulting in very variable degrees of commitment to the company on the part of employees. Beliefs need to be sufficiently robust to withstand management

MISSION

Ford Motor Company is a worldwide leader in automotive and automotive-related products and services as well as in newer industries such as aerospace, communications, and financial services. Our mission is to improve continually our products and services to meet our customers' needs, allowing us to prosper as a business, and to provide a reasonable return for our stockholders, the owners of our business.

VALUES

How we accomplish our mission is as important as the mission itself. Fundamental to success for the Company are these basic values:

People – Our people are the source of our strength. They provide our corporate intelligence and determine our reputation and vitality. Involvement and teamwork are our core human values.

Products – Our products are the end result of our efforts, and they should be the best in serving customers worldwide. As our products are viewed, so are we viewed.

Profits – Profits are the ultimate measure of how efficiently we provide customers with the best products for their needs. Profits are required to survive and grow.

MOTTO (Japanese Parent)
Toward contributing to the richness of
humanity and the world through the
attainment of a creative enterprise group

COMPANY POLICY (UK Subsidiary)
1. To achieve wider recognition within the international battery market for the excellence of our company
2. To respect the individuality and promote the development of all members of our company
3. To stengthen our contribution to the community

Figure 4.2 Ford mission and values statements (Source: Q101), and
Yuasa Battery motto and objectives

changes: the culture becomes more important than the individual who happens to be at the helm. It is difficult to see how TQ will survive in a Midlands organization which has seen three MDs in the last 4 years. The first began to implement a TQ programme based on Crosby, the second replaced this programme by one based on Conway's teachings, and the third has not yet made up his mind what TQ programme he will favour!

Under JIT/TQ, the tools and techniques are secondary to the beliefs, as we noted in Chapter 1. The most fundamental belief is in the potential of the individual. In a sense, beliefs develop in line with the progress which has been made. As buffer stocks are reduced, and the operation works on a shorter fuse, the problem at a process becomes the problem for the factory as a whole. The individual who is operating the process cannot be left to struggle by him or herself while the whole factory waits, so team working is a natural consequence of JIT disciplines, and becomes an essential part of company culture. Because problems are now much more exposed, improvement activities are needed to ensure that they do not recur, so continuous improvement fits in naturally too. Given strong management leadership, we have a fertile ground for growth in feelings of responsibility and commitment [6]. But a precondition is to harken to the advice of Dr Deming in his 14 points for management [7]. One of the key issues is to 'drive out fear' from the organization, otherwise people will not feel free to participate in improvement activities without worrying about the impact on their own or a mate's job. Sherkenbach has described fear as 'a highly leveraged commodity' – one act of criticism wipes out ten of praise [8]. He also pointed out that fear impacts upon most of the other 14 points. Some radical rethinking is needed in this highly sensitive area for Western management. Cummins Engine in the USA gave people who thought up ways to eliminate their job favourable early retirement terms. One Western company which seems to have achieved lack of fear of the consequences of improvements activities is The Paul Revere Insurance Company. Here, a department eliminated its own work, but the ten people concerned were redeployed [9]. Driving out fear can be achieved. But on 'brownfield' sites (those with long-standing employment histories) with entrenched, traditional attitudes it is a lengthy, uphill task. Traditional values have often set manager against manager, department against department, customer against supplier, and management against union [10]. The starting position may be that a skilled fitter is not trusted to withdraw £10 of parts from stores without the foreman's signature on a requisition form. By contrast, it was amazing to see how much some Japanese companies have achieved in making it safe for people to participate. At Yamaha Grand Pianos, operators were wearing 'Challenge 90' badges on their uniforms, to show their support for a campaign to improve labour productivity by 30% in 2 years.

As indicated above, it is through the manifestation of what and how decisions are made that actual beliefs are revealed. This is the practical side of culture making. In a JIT/TQ company, we are leading a shift from an authoritarian environment to one of joint responsibility, open communication, and

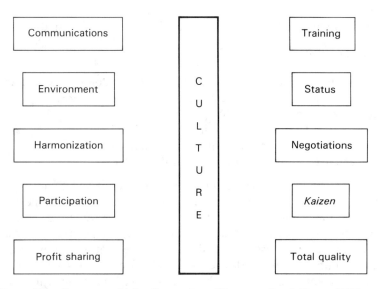

Figure 4.3 Features which affect culture (Source: after I. Sloss, SP Tyres)

joint problem solving. Features which affect the new culture are shown in Figure 4.3. The shift is gradual, and each stage needs to be accepted and adjusted to. The sequence shown in Figure I.1 proposes that implementation is started off at stage 2 by introducing basic disciplines like tidiness and cleanliness, and developing a sense of ownership before progressing. Ownership could perhaps be further promoted by creating team leader positions further to encourage group problem-solving activities. Then we can move on to improvements in process control.... Each stage needs to be planned and managed. There will always be obstacles and setbacks. British managers have been criticized for giving up too soon when faced with obstacles, and for avoiding the pain and discomfort that is associated with change [11]. The energy which should be directed at solving the problems which accompany change is often squandered in covering up the consequent lack of positive actions and failures which result. Murata's concept of 'intention and reflection' [12] is useful here. You will never achieve change without the strong intention to do so. Every day should have its purpose, and then we can reflect on the progress made and the problem points. Reflection is more than a recognition that something has gone wrong. It is deliberately putting pressure on yourself to come up with a better plan. Self-satisfaction is the enemy of improvement.

■ Conditions of employment

Conditions of employment are the starting point for development of an

105

excellent company culture. Company members need to feel that:

- they are treated equally in terms of car parking, eating facilities, toilets, and so on;
- they are involved in decisions to which they can contribute, and are kept informed about areas of the business where they cannot;
- there is equal opportunity for promotion;
- there is fair day's pay for a fair day's work;
- there is a fair pay structure and benefits package;
- the benefit of improved company results is shared.

The aim is to get rid of 'them and us' relations. Terms and conditions which continue to promote such relations must be phased out. Corrupt incentive schemes, 'job and finish' measured daywork schemes which put a ceiling on improvement, and staff/hourly rated terms which differ on matters like normal hours worked and on absenteeism/sickness entitlement are all examples.

Small numbers of job grades help to create the conditions where flexibility, quality, and teamwork can flourish. So Nissan UK determined to have only two job titles: manufacturing staff and technicians [12]. This broke with tradition in the UK motor industry, where Ford UK had as recently as 1985 reduced the number of manual worker job titles to 52 (from 516). Nissan UK also decided not to have job descriptions (hence avoiding the non-value-added activities of job evaluation) which were felt only to limit what people do. This meant expanding the jobs as much as possible to encompass tasks like quality responsibility, housekeeping, and cleaning. Nissan also built responsibility for improving quality, safety, and productivity into the everyday job through *kaizen* (continuous improvement) teams. There are only five levels between manufacturing staff and MD (seven levels in total). Another unusual feature of the Nissan UK pay structure is that the same terms apply to all levels. Thus all personnel are on annual salary contracts with performance increments related to achievement of objectives.

Harmonization of terms and conditions in a brownfield situation has the additional complexity of getting rid of former bad habits and resetting the course towards excellence. But given clear goals and strong determination, it is possible to make progress over time, as Ford UK have done. Making the necessary structural changes to terms and conditions is one thing, but attitudes and behaviour have to follow in its wake. This is a challenge for management at all levels.

■ We are all in the same boat

With harmonized terms and conditions of employment it should be an easier task to develop shared goals with company members. Some of the old bad practices like laying off hourly rated personnel first when there is a downturn in business will no longer be possible. People are an asset which grows over time, so redundancy is a means of letting hard-won experience go to waste. It should be a last reaction to hard times, not the first. A downturn is an opportunity to carry out more improvement activities and is a challenge for everyone to reduce costs. If there is a need to cut people costs, then this should be carried out 'across the board', and the same reduction should be applied to everyone. For example, Hewlett-Packard cut the pay of all employees by 10% during a business downturn in 1985.

One company calculated that there was a differential in material costs between the United Kingdom and Japan: in the United Kingdom, material prices are inflating at $+3\%$; in Japan, they are inflating by -3%. The difference -6% of material costs $-$ would be greater over 1 year than the whole of the company's direct labour budget! And it is not a good idea to take people out in advance of making progress on such major improvements on the grounds that we want to have as lean or leaner structures than competitors. The very means by which we can develop those improvements is lost. So altering foreman ratios from 1:25 to 1:70 leaves no time for improvement activities to be carried out. Some of the bad old management ways die hard....

■ Teamwork

Once product flow (cellular manufacture, product flowlines) has been determined, it is logical to focus people as well into work teams, led by a supervisor or team leader. While overall team leadership is provided by the supervisor, individual projects can be and often are led by team leaders or specific team members. The associated cultural shift is from individual to team decisions. Decisions are made through a process of concensus seeking through canvassing ideas and opinions from all team members. Japanese sources call this process *nemawashi*, or watering the roots. The team needs facilities to meet, and it needs available time to do so. The Nissan solution is to have designated team rooms, where the team can meet for 5 minutes for briefing before the start of the shift, and where breaks, communication, and *kaizen* meetings can be held during the day [13]. Yuasa Battery UK use the first half hour of every shift for the shift supervisor to report on productivity and quality matters, and for improvement project work to be undertaken [14]. The developing close relationship between supervisor and team members helps the organization as a whole to grow. More authority and responsibility are devolved over time, so that better decisions are taken, ownership is encouraged, and potential problems are sorted out on an informal – not a procedural – basis. Instead of being a job which is usually the culmination of many years of service, the supervisor's task becomes far broader and more challenging. Jobs in manufacturing as a whole become more attractive [15].

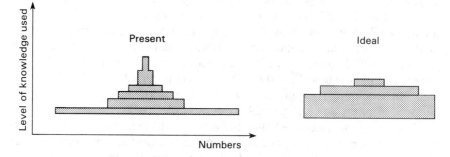

Figure 4.4 Filling in the organization pyramid

Figure 4.4 illustrates the long-term vision of the organization. The starting point is an autocratic structure where a small number of overburdened managers make all the decisions, and the level of knowledge used by junior levels in day-to-day decision making is small. The aim over time is to improve the extent to which the knowledge of all personnel is used, and also to develop that knowledge itself. The result is an organization which has far greater in-depth capability to compete.

Two of the best-known ways of organizing shop-floor personnel for improvement work are quality control circles (QCCs) and small-group improvement activities (SGIAs). Neither of these concepts needs special organizational structures built around them, or special programmes launched. They should evolve naturally from the overall TQ orientation of the company at every level. They also evolve logically from the work teams discussed above. As a problem is thrown up which prevents progress in improvement, what more logical way to deal with it than to develop a team to sort it out? Deming would argue that shop-floor teams are only capable of dealing with the 15% (the trivial many) of problems which can be influenced at that level in the

Table 4.1 Comparison of QCCs and SGIAs

QCCs Effectiveness teams	SGIAs Quality improvement teams
Voluntary participation	Members are management appointed
Teams select the problems	Problems identified by management
Usually, problems are local to team members	Usually cross-functional problems
Teams permanent	Team exists only as long as the problem: members reassigned on completion
Teams present their proposals for solution to management	Proposed solution fed back to quality steering group
Members trained in problem-solving and interpersonal skills	Members trained in problem-solving techniques and interpersonal skills
Emphasis on participation and development	Emphasis on problem-solving process

Notes: QCC = Quality Control Circle; SGIA = Small-group Improvement Activity

organization. (The remaining 85% are associated with the quality system, and require management to sort them out.) A comparison of the main features of QCCs and SGIAs is shown in Table 4.1, and a brief description follows.

■ Quality control circles (quality circles)

QCCs are small groups of people who volunteer to meet regularly to discuss and solve problems which affect the work they do. Usually, circles select the problems they wish to study, have a formal agenda, and have a team leader who is not necessarily the foreman. Members are trained in team-building and problem-solving techniques like Pareto charts, brainstorming, run and scatter diagrams, and fishbone charts. Training and coordination of circle activities is carried out by a facilitator. Normally, teams must present their analysis and solutions to management, and if agreement is reached, the team is involved in implementing the agreed solution. So circles work from the 'bottom up', have a lot of discretion in what they do, and draw on the expertise of those most closely involved in doing the job. Schonberger and Knod [16] argue that team members are best drawn from chains of maker–user pairs working on a given product flow (for example, raw material store, guillotine, weld and paint personnel), rather than from groups who do the same thing (for example, packers or welders).

Ten years ago, QCCs were very popular in the West, and were often described as the secret of Japanese success. The concept seemed so simple – and it is. There is no question that QCCs have achieved excellent savings and quality improvements in Western companies, and that in the right environment they have had a strong effect on morale and motivation. But there have been many calamities and few survivors: notable survivors in the United Kingdom are Mullard, Wedgewood, and Black & Decker. Often the reason for failure was a misunderstanding of the true nature and uses of circles. Gow [17] describes QCCs as a fine-tuning mechanism for companies whose quality record is already very good. Hutchins and Sasaki [18] state that circles are not a stand-alone technique, but an integral part of the Japanese participative management philosophy. One of the most spectacular failures in the United Kingdom was Ford's AJ (After Japan) campaign, of which QCCs were a key part, in 1981. As noted in Chapter 1, Guthrie [19] attributes the rejection of AJ by the Ford unions as due to a basic management misunderstanding of how QCCs work, and that QCCs are a feature of a very different management technique from that practised by Ford.

■ Small-group improvement activities

SGIAs involve groups of shop-floor personnel combined with any necessary technical people who are assigned specific projects to work on. The group regularly reports to management or a steering committee during the life of the project, and is disbanded when the project has been completed. Over time, everyone could be associated with at least one project team. Supervisors are responsible for the SGIA in their own area, and normally lead team meetings. SGIAs encourage cross-communication, and claimed benefits are:

- generation of improvement ideas by production personnel, and involvement in their implementation;
- improved ownership of the process;
- increased morale due to job enrichment;
- improved teamwork by removal of barriers;
- easier implementation of change and improved respect through participation in management-led projects.

The design of SGIAs overcomes the charge which is often levelled at QCCs that too much latitude is allowed to the teams in problem selection. Further, SGIAs promote greater cross-membership because teams are formed around projects rather than the other way round.

■ The changing role of supervision

One of the most important changes which takes place as the organization evolves towards an excellent one is the role of supervisors. Traditionally, the supervisor has been the 'meat in the sandwich', trying to make some sort of

Table 4.2 The changing role of supervision

Traditional role	Modern role
Progress chasing	Complete product schedule
Troubleshooter	start to finish
Discipline	raw material to customer
Paperwork (lots of it!):	Quality:
specifications/standards	'total' product quality
timesheets/incentive scheme	Tidiness, orderliness
personnel records	Maintenance
absentees, overtime, etc.	Training:
Requisitions (lots of them!):	aim: multi-function teams
stores	Communications:
people	team briefings, etc.
equipment, etc.	Continuous improvement:
Measured by:	looks forward 90%
schedule achievement	Facilitation
performance v. budget (costs)	Measured by:
machine utilization	product lead times
overtime, etc.	process control data
	productivity improvement
	reaction speed

order out of the plagues of material shortages and the difficulties and inconsistencies of the industrial relations scene. The job had of necessity a short time horizon: things were always going wrong, and the supervisor was the last line of defence. The left-hand side of Table 4.2 lists many of the principal activities. The modern role of supervision, listed on the right-hand side, is more accurately described as facilitation. It is about creating the right conditions for high quality and high productivity at the workplace. The job is mainly about looking ahead, and managing the improvement process.

■ Conclusion

The success of a business depends fundamentally on the maximum utilization of its human resources. There is an increasing number of companies in the United Kingdom − many of them not Japanese owned − who are leading the way in how this can be achieved. But many more desperately need to start believing that people are the most important asset of the company. A strategy is needed: how do we get from where we are to where we know we ought to be? How do we translate our beliefs into the company culture, or is it all too difficult because HQ always demands jam today? Transformation requires the will and the skill to match what our international competitors are doing. The goad is that we cannot continue as we are, or our manufacturing base will continue to erode as it has done for the best part of this century. Legislation, either pro- or anti-union, pro- or anti-employer, will achieve nothing within the long term. It is within the company that attitudes must first change, led by far-sighted management who are determined to achieve long-term success and survival. In the Introduction, the essential points which need to be encouraged in any excellent organization were indicated − points like teamwork, loyalty, and interest. The Japanese have locked these into company value systems in their own cultural way: there is no reason why Western businesses should not be able to do the same. Wilson [20] calls the management changes 'time-worn universals' − such as the practice of a little more care and thoroughness, a longer-term view, and a greater consideration for the self-esteem of employees. In the long run, we are all in the same boat.

■ References

1. *The Road to Nissan*, P. Whickens, Macmillan Academic & Professional, Basingstoke, 1987.
2. *Out of the Crisis*, W. E. Deming, MIT Center for Advanced Engineering Study: Cambridge, MA, 1982.
3. *Troubleshooter*, J. Harvey-Jones and A. Masey, BBC Books: London, 1990.

4. 'Why Toyota keeps getting better & better & better', A. Taylor, *Fortune*, 19 November 1990, pp. 32–49.
5. Source: Ford Motor Company Q101.
6. *Japanese Manufacturing Techniques: Nine Hidden Lessons in Simplicity*, R. Schonberger, Free Press, New York, 1982, p. 29.
7. W. G. Deming, *ibid*.
8. *The Deming Route to Quality and Productivity*, W. Scherkenbach, Mercury Business Books, London, 1991.
9. 'The Paul Revere (A)', L. Lytle and C. Hart, Harvard Business School, Case no. 9-687-013, 1986.
10. 'Rediscover the power of values', annual lecture to the British Institute of Management, Manchester, 1991.
11. 'The failings of the British style of management', Y. Fujisawa, *Nippon Keizai Shimbun* (*Japanese Economic News*), March, 1985.
12. *How to Make Japanese Management Methods Work in the West*, K. Murata and A. Harrison, Gower, Aldershot, 1991, p. 38.
13. P. Wickens, *ibid*., pp. 87, 88.
14. K. Murata and A. Harrison, *ibid*., p. 22.
15. P. Wickens, *ibid*., p. 162.
16. *Operations Management*, R. Schonberger and E. Knod, Irwin, Homewood, IL, 1991, p. 150.
17. 'Raiders, invaders or simply good traders?', I. Gow, *Accounting*, March, 1986.
18. *The Japanese Approach to Product Quality*, D. Hutchins and H. Sasaki, Pergamon, Oxford, 1984.
19. 'AJ and beyond', G. Guthrie, *Production Engineer*, May, 1987.
20. *The Sun at Noon*, R. Wilson, Hamish Hamilton, 1986.

5 | Do the Simple Things Right

Having started off the process of reforming company culture and of addressing personnel plans and policies, areas must be sought to apply the new thinking. You cannot spend for ever on perfecting mission statements and team-building exercises when so many processes are out of control. In parallel with development of the organization, it is therefore essential to give people things to do. Most often, the best place to start is with the basics. This way, attitudes can be worked on and improvements made at the same time. For example, to what extent do the following attitudes prevail [1]?

- People work only for the money. They tend to switch off at work and do not enjoy it. They are prepared to produce an agreed amount and no more.
- Company rules are not followed and the enforcement of them is not strict.
- Improvement in working practices is none of my business, but should be left to the experts.

People in such companies are simply told to 'do this', and they 'do it' – no more, no less. Most of the time, people in such companies rush around dealing with day-to-day problems. There is no time to sort out the problems on any permanent basis by improvement activities. Replacing such attitudes with motivation, discipline, and creativity is a key part of the challenge of becoming an excellent company. The challenge is a fundamental one and cannot be bypassed, or left until later. A suitable starting point for this aspect of people preparation is housekeeping, safety, and discipline. It is not simply a matter of setting rules such as those shown in Figure 5.1, and expecting workpeople to obey the rules, perhaps backed up with the threat of disciplinary action. Historically, this has not worked. In most machine shops, you can see people who are not wearing eye protection, and on building sites, people not wearing hard hats. This is in spite of prominent notices which instruct them to do so. Such poorly enforced company rules are symptoms of a lack of people preparation. If people cannot do the simple things right, then how can we become an excellent company?

CODE OF COMPANY HOUSKEEPING

G R O U P

The Oleo Group will maintain an exemplary standard of factory housekeeping. The Health and Safety at Work Act 1974 lays down certain duties for both employers and employees. An important aspect is the need for GOOD HOUSKEEPING. This requires continual endeavour on the part of all levels of management jointly with all employees.

MACHINE AND WORKBENCHES

Machine Tools will be kept clean. Not only working surfaces but all parts of machines will be cleaned regularly.

Benches will be kept clean and tidy. Accumulations of dirt, rags, paper, etc. around benches will not be permitted.

"THESE ARE FIRE HAZARDS"

Miscellaneous tools and equipment not in use will be returned to stores.

All materials and work-in-progress will be properly identified and stored in an orderly fashion, including scrap and rework.

Charts and work information will be displayed tidily.

OFFICES

Offices will be kept tidy.

Windows will not be obscured by notices, calendars or any other literature.

Desks and filing cabinets will be kept clear out of working hours.

Components will not be left lying around.

GANGWAYS, STAIRS, FLOORS & YARDS

All gangways will be clearly marked with yellow lines.

All gangways and staircases will be kept clear.

Work-in-progress and raw materials will be restricted to the designated areas and also not allowed to impede gangways.

Floors will be kept clean.

Care will be taken to avoid spillage of coolants and other substances on to factory floors. Spillages should be immediately removed.

Vending machine areas will be kept clean and tidy with ample provision for disposal of used plastic cups etc. in waste bins.

Yards and roadways will be kept clean and tidy.

Cars must only be parked in designated areas.

Particular care should be taken to always maintain free access to fire hydrants.

HEALTH, SAFETY & WELFARE

Food, milk bottles, tea cups will not be left on, or near, or around machines, benches, desks or filing cabinets.

"THESE CAN BE HEALTH HAZARDS"

Ample provision of waste bins will be made at marked locations. Bins should be emptied at the end of each shift.

Toilet and washing facilities will be kept clean and stocked with materials.

Barrier creams will be used where necessary. Dispensers will be kept replenished.

Drinking water fountains will be maintained in good order and kept clean.

Work employees should wear clean, suitable clothing with particular regard to safety and protection from oil.

Where protective clothing is issued for specific jobs it must be worn.

Employees' clothes should not be hung up around machines and benches making the place untidy and a source of possible dangers.

Emergency exits and doors will be kept clear of obstacles.

NOTICES

No unauthorised notices are permitted.

Notices must be placed on official notice boards. Old notices will be removed from these boards.

Writing on walls is not permitted.

Figure 5.1   Code of company housekeeping: a traditional view

Suzaki [2] refers to the direct connection between standards of house-keeping and workplace organization and general management attitudes. You can quickly get a feel for such attitudes by simply looking at housekeeping standards on the shop floor. Slack management attitudes will be passed on to workpeople in the form of poor morale and lack of interest in improvement activities. Workplace organization cannot be delegated to shop-floor personnel while management concentrates on higher matters [3]. The purpose is to develop everyone's attitudes to doing the simple things right and gradually doing them better. This is the key starting point for improvement activities [4]. The need to provide a strong foundation of basic disciplines is therefore at stage 2 in the model for JIT/TQ development on page 4.

Japanese companies widely use the concept of '4S', which refers to housekeeping:

seiri	sorting
seiton	orderliness
seiso	cleaning
seiketsu	cleanliness

A fifth 'S' (*shitsuke*, or participation in the above) is often added (Figure 5.2). The belief is that 4S is basic to an excellent company. Pride quickly develops, encouraged by using high standards of housekeeping as a strong feature of the company to show off on customer visits. Further, 4S forms a logical sequence of progress: improve workplace organization by sorting and orderliness,

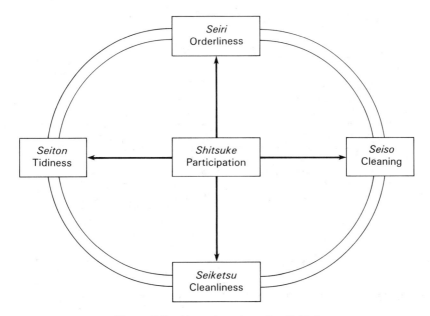

Figure 5.2 Housekeeping: the 5 'Ss'

then clean it and keep it clean. The concept is shown in a poster from the Washington factory of SP Tyres (UK) in Figure 5.3. The comparison with Figure 5.1 is interesting. A major difference is not shown in the two posters: in the Japanese subsidiary, the emphasis is on responsibility by the company member for his or her own area: the poster is there mainly to show off to visitors.

In this chapter, these basic processes will be examined by splitting housekeeping into tidiness (*seiri* and *seiton*) and cleanliness (*seiso* and *seiketsu*), followed by safety and discipline. The aim is always to develop the right attitudes and to promote involvement, rather than to attempt to impose rules.

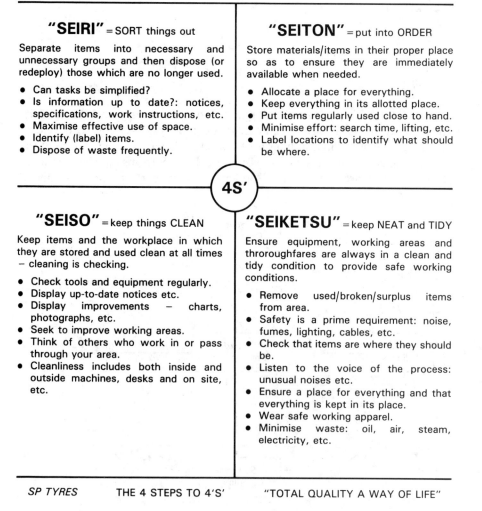

"SEIRI" = SORT things out

Separate items into necessary and unnecessary groups and then dispose (or redeploy) those which are no longer used.

- Can tasks be simplified?
- Is information up to date?: notices, specifications, work instructions, etc.
- Maximise effective use of space.
- Identify (label) items.
- Dispose of waste frequently.

"SEITON" = put into ORDER

Store materials/items in their proper place so as to ensure they are immediately available when needed.

- Allocate a place for everything.
- Keep everything in its allotted place.
- Put items regularly used close to hand.
- Minimise effort: search time, lifting, etc.
- Label locations to identify what should be where.

4S'

"SEISO" = keep things CLEAN

Keep items and the workplace in which they are stored and used clean at all times – cleaning is checking.

- Check tools and equipment regularly.
- Display up-to-date notices etc.
- Display improvements – charts, photographs, etc.
- Seek to improve working areas.
- Think of others who work in or pass through your area.
- Cleanliness includes both inside and outside machines, desks and on site, etc.

"SEIKETSU" = keep NEAT and TIDY

Ensure equipment, working areas and throroughfares are always in a clean and tidy condition to provide safe working conditions.

- Remove used/broken/surplus items from area.
- Safety is a prime requirement: noise, fumes, lighting, cables, etc.
- Check that items are where they should be.
- Listen to the voice of the process: unusual noises etc.
- Ensure a place for everything and that everything is kept in its place.
- Wear safe working apparel.
- Minimise waste: oil, air, steam, electricity, etc.

SP TYRES   THE 4 STEPS TO '4'S'   "TOTAL QUALITY A WAY OF LIFE"

Figure 5.3 The four steps to '4S' (courtesy SP tyres UK)

■ Tidiness

Tidiness costs nothing. It is basically a matter of putting things away in the correct places, and is fully achievable. The aim over time is to do this better and better by thinking about how things should be stored for maximum ease of location and shortest access distance. A tough line should be taken on

(a)

(b)

Figure 5.4 Photographs inside a UK factory: (a) fitter's bench; (b) 40-ft container of spare/surplus parts

clutter, so a good starting point is the Lucas [5] term of runners, repeaters, and strangers:

- **Runners:** Parts, tools, paperwork, and so on which are needed every time. These should be positioned at the workplace, clean and ready to go. A good example of this category is the use of standard boxes of fixed quantities of parts held in exact locations.

- **Repeaters:** Parts, tools, and paperwork which are needed regularly. These should be stored close to the workplace in easily identified format (perhaps colour coded for ease of recognition).

- **Strangers:** Parts, tools, and paperwork which are needed occasionally, at irregular intervals. These again should be stored in easily identified form, but at a greater distance from the workplace.

(1)

1. Never leave implements on or under the table or in the drawers

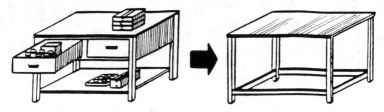

2. Use open shelves so that items are always visible

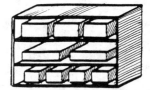

3. Put items of the same kind together

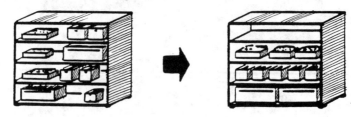

Figure 5.5 Use of space and tidiness (1) and (2)
(Source: Nissan Motor Iberica)

(2)

4. Classify screws etc. by size

5. Use specific tool holders for frequently used tools

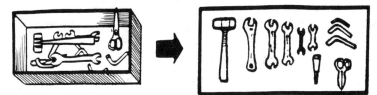

6. Use the space-saving advantages of shelves

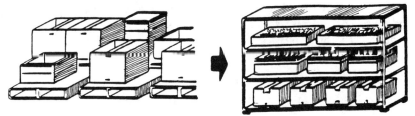

Figure 5.5   *Continued*

A fourth category which is also very important to identify is things not needed at all. This category includes scrap, obsolete parts and fixtures, outdated records and drawings, and computer files no longer used. Such parts and data should be rigorously ditched. Parts are often hoarded 'just in case' they are needed at some (unspecified) future date. A new attitude is needed to recognize the real cost of such a policy. One Midlands company I visited recently makes door furniture. Surplus parts for customer orders were held in stock in case they were ever reordered. Because of the growing number of such parts, a 40-ft container had been installed to store them. The container was already full, and it must have been almost impossible ever to find what you were looking for! A photograph is shown in Figure 5.4 together with a fitter's bench from the same factory.

Paperwork is an excellent target for improvement. Staff should be encouraged to leave clear desks, and to destroy documents, brochures, and catalogues which are more than a year old. Reports can be reduced to a single page (objective, narrative, conclusion, and recommendation) and given a 'destroy by' date. At Mitsubishi Aluminium in Japan, Dr Nakamura was prepared

119

to confront Japanese Industrial Standards in order to reduce the requirement to hold documents for 5 years. 'We believe that the true objective of JIT is to establish an efficient production system rather than an excessive completeness of paperwork', he said [6]. Documents were only subsequently held for 1 year.

Reduction of work-in-progress greatly facilitates tidiness. Large pallets in high-rise racking are gradually replaced by small bins, and by an overall major reduction in parts stored. The tidiness task becomes smaller, more manageable. After Motor Iberica in Spain was taken over by Nissan, an early task was to reduce stocks. Progress was recognized by placing a large flower pot where the stocks had once stood! The campaign was called '100 macetas' (100 flower pots), and is an excellent example of Japanese symbolism. Tidiness was also encouraged by a number of guidelines which are shown in Figure 5.5. For example, spare parts should not be laid out in cupboards where they cannot be seen, but on shelves with labels to make them visible. Dr Nakamura at Mitsubishi Aluminium in Japan referred to this process as 'breathing life into spare parts'! Compare such organization with the problem faced by a maintenance fitter on the night shift who has to find an electric motor from a random pile of various sizes and ratings in a small store room. (The store room is unlit, so the fitter has to use a flashlight!)

■ Cleanliness

Cleanliness costs money, so it is necessary to consider grades. In a company which is in the process industry, these might be:

- 'edible' grade (the highest) for the canteen and the processing/packaging of edible products;
- 'packing' grade for the packing of non-edible products;
- 'process' grade (the lowest) where few people are working.

Such grades would influence the frequency with which walls are washed, floors are mopped, and bins emptied. But underlying such a system for cleanup should be the development of the right attitudes, which should include:

- emphasizing everyone's involvement (for example, if there's a spillage, it gets mopped up immediately);
- cleaning is not to be delegated to 'labourers', but carried out by team personnel;
- cleaning is also a form of inspection, so while a machine is being cleaned down, preventive maintenance checks can be carried out at the same time;
- emphasizing permanent solutions (for example, fix the cause of a hydraulic leak rather than use those revolting granules to absorb its effects).

A striking example of the first two is provided by Murata and Harrison [7]. A locker room was cleaned for 5 minutes each day at Yuasa by the MD and senior managers as an example of flexibility on the part of staff personnel. This example encouraged shop-floor personnel to abandon the attitude that 'cleaning is a cleaner's job', and to clean their own work areas. A similar example was provided by the Japanese MD of SP Tyres: he used to drive round on a cleaning machine when touring the factory to make himself useful!

Standards of cleanup need to be the subject of continuing management attention. Housekeeping audits like those in Table 5.1 help to ensure that everyone is kept aware of the importance of maintaining standards. Involving company members on a rota basis in such audits also helps in this aim. Over time the emphasis should be to increase standards, and to prevent them from falling back. Gradually over time, all standards become 'edible' standard.

Table 5.1 Housekeeping audit
(a) Weekly Scores

		Weeks 17 and 18	
Position	Score	Zone	Area
1	16·5	7	F block cab T244
2	15·7	10	J block finishing
3	15·4	8	Pres shop low bay
4	14·6	9	Car parks/roads
5	14·6	5	Admin. blk offices
6	14·6	2	S block paint shop
7	14·2	4	B stores Saltley
8	13·0	6	F block finishing
9	10·8	3	T block trim & FNL
10	10·1	1	S block BIW
	13·9	Average	LDV plant

(b) Ladder competition housekeeping audit

Position	Score	Zone	Area	Resp. manager
1	127·5	7	F block cab T244	R. Adams
2	123·3	2	S blk paint shop	S. Bogle
3	121·1	9	Car parks/roads	I. Hill
4	114·6	5	Amin. blk offices	P. Groves
5	113·1	10	J block finishing	J. Woodhouse
6	112·6	8	Press shop	P. Henderson
7	104·3	6	F block finishing	R. Bowyer
8	101·7	4	B stores Saltley	G. Nash
9	91·2	3	T blk trim & final	A. Barnett
10	88·1	1	S block BIW	M. Watts
	109·7	Average	LDV plant	

Source: Leyland Daf Vans

■ Safety

Safety is the company's most important welfare provision. Yet in the United Kingdom, it is an area which has been subjected to extensive legislation and frequent hostility between management and trade union representatives. The entrance to the works is adorned with a glass case, dutifully exhibiting a summary of employee rights under the Health & Safety at Work etc. Act and the name of the local factory inspector. Demands to make machinery 'idiot proof' have clouded the need continuously to improve attitudes and knowledge about safety matters. Poor attitudes which need to be addressed include the belief that accidents are inevitable; that a hazardous situation is unsafe for anyone else, but is OK for me; and it is soft to be safe, manly to take risks. Such attitudes contributed to the tragedy at the Chernobyl nuclear power station in 1986, when an unauthorized experiment was carried out using procedures which included several safety violations and operator errors. Complacency, lack of concern for safety rules, and ignorance of the physics of the reactor were some of the major factors involved [8], which proved fatal when combined with a reactor design that was inherently unsafe.

You can set safety rules until you are blue in the face. But the key point is how much progress you can make in influencing people's attitudes and in strengthening their knowledge. Ideally, safe operation should become a value which is shared by all company members, so that safety standards improve over time. Such a shared value can be encouraged by:

- always setting a good practical example of safe operation yourself;
- ensuring that personnel are trained, qualified, and regularly requalified in key safety standards;
- treating safety suggestions seriously;
- setting targets for continued safe operation;
- carrying out joint safety audits with each employee in rotation.

Getting rid of bad habits, such as refusing to wear safety glasses in the machine shop or hard hats on a building site, is not so easy when habits have become entrenched. Over time, bad habits must be confronted and replaced by new habits of safe operation so that company rules and procedures come to be respected. Only in this way will a basis for improvement be possible.

■ Discipline

Without discipline, it is impossible to maintain consistent standards in a manufacturing firm. This applies to standards in crucial areas like quality, safety, and process operation. The more closely we can follow manufacturing standards, set procedures, and rules, the less likelihood there is of errors, defects, and accidents. But trying to impose discipline in an authoritarian, or

'Theory X' manner [9], will not get far in most Western firms today. Rather, people must want to follow the rules, because the rules are actually a set of shared values as in a game of chess or a round of golf. The shared values are achieved by coaching [10], not by orders and penalties. And coaching starts by getting the subordinate to do the simple things right – like tidiness, cleanliness, and safe operation. 'Buying in' to these basic values is the essential starting point to developing an excellent company.

■ Conclusion

Doing the simple things right truly tests the determination of management over time. Good standards may be set for a while, and then drift back after a few months because managers stop enforcing the rules as strictly as they did to begin with. Campaigns are no good: the key point is to involve everyone in the new disciplines so that they become the new norm for the company and it is abnormal to behave otherwise. This cannot be achieved without continuous and visible management leadership, which means much more 'management by walking about' than perhaps was previously the case. The new disciplines are the first and simplest thing to carry out the TQ way – by developing commitment and then supporting company members in taking the initiative themselves (for example, by fixing budgets for storage and cleaning equipment). Introducing basic disciplines will have been successful when all company members are involved and standards improve over time.

■ References

1. *How to Make Japanese Management Methods Work in the West*, K. Murata and A. Harrison, Gower, Aldershot, 1991.
2. *The New Manufacturing Challenge*, K. Suzaki, Free Press, New York, 1987, p. 25.
3. *Attaining Manufacturing Excellence*, R. Hall, Dow Jones Irwin, Homewood, IL, 1987, p. 82.
4. K. Murata and A. Harrison, *ibid*.
5. *Lucas Manufacturing Systems Engineering Handbook*, J. Parnaby (ed.), Lucas Engineering & Systems Ltd, Birmingham, 1991.
6. *Just-in-Time; A Global Status Report*, C. Voss and D. Clutterbuck, IFS, Bedford, 1989.
7. K. Murata and A. Harrison, *ibid*., p. 56.
8. For a psychologist's view, see 'The Chernobyl errors', J. Reason, *Bulletin of the British Psychological Society*, **40**, pp. 201–6, 1987.
9. *The Human Side of Enterprise*, D. McGregor, McGraw-Hill, New York, 1960.
10. R. Hall, *ibid*., p. 86.

6 | Facilitating Flow

In spite of having learned about key elements of lean production over 10 years ago, it is surprising that use of direct labour performance reporting as a major management control tool is still widespread among Western manufacturers today. Figure 6.1 gives a suggested relationship between actual labour costs and management efforts to control costs. The pie chart on the left of the figure shows a typical split of labour, material, and overhead costs in an engineering business. While direct labour is only 6% of total costs, the pie chart on the right suggests that nearly all of the management efforts to control costs have been directed at this comparatively small cost area. The much larger material and overhead costs have received a much lower proportion of management efforts in relation to their size. Direct labour is in fact the value-added element, controlling the processes whereby inputs are transformed into outputs. Yet it has been the subject of most industrial engineering effort (such as time studies and analysis of off-standards) in traditional businesses. Costing systems emphasized that direct labour was a variable cost, and that the task of

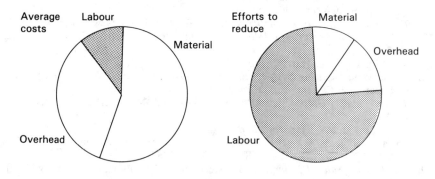

We spend too much effort on squeezing value added

Figure 6.1 Average costs v. efforts to reduce

Product structure
Product life cycle stage

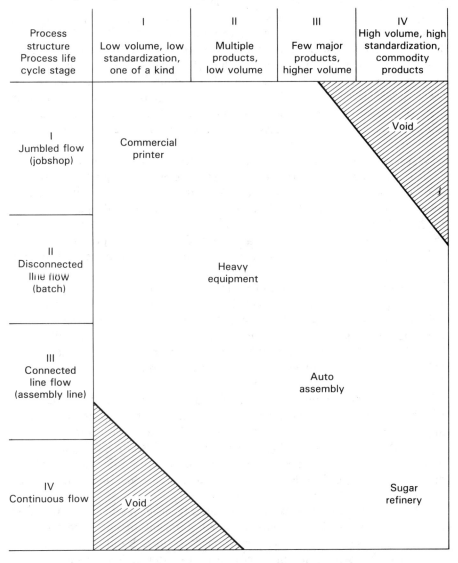

Process structure Process life cycle stage	I Low volume, low standardization, one of a kind	II Multiple products, low volume	III Few major products, higher volume	IV High volume, high standardization, commodity products
I Jumbled flow (jobshop)	Commercial printer			Void
II Disconnected line flow (batch)		Heavy equipment		
III Connected line flow (assembly line)			Auto assembly	
IV Continuous flow	Void			Sugar refinery

Figure 6.2 Matching major stages of the product and process life cycles – the product–process matrix (Source: Hayes and Wheelwright [1] © 1979 The President and Fellows of Harvard College; all rights reserved; reprinted by permission of Harvard Business Review, 'Link manufacturing process and product life cycles', R. H. Hayes and S. C. Wheelright, January/February 1979; and by John Wiley & Sons Inc.)

production management was to reduce variable costs to a minimum. By keeping direct labour busy, the waste in larger cost areas was ignored. Incentive schemes emphasized activity, regardless of whether this activity created inventories which were needed at the time. The more important sources of waste – delays and disruptions which slowed down the movement of parts through processes – have been given lower priority across a wide range of industries. Instead, overheads such as expeditors, inspectors, and cost analysts ('fixed costs') were piled in to make up for the deficiencies of the system.

Figure 6.2 shows a widely used model of volumes by choice of process [1]. As volumes increase along the x-axis, so choice of process is changed from jobshop (low volumes) through small and large batch manufacture to flowline and finally continuous process to handle high-volume, commodity-type products. Western companies in the latter two categories – such as those in food, drink, and household products – have often been comparatively efficient in their manufacturing operations. Food must be processed quickly to preserve freshness, so lead times are short and WIP is low. This is typically achieved by efficient, one-way product flow through a set sequence of operations. The sheer scale of material movements in and out the plant dictate that the manufacturing method must be based on the needs of the product.

Such one-way product flows have not traditionally been used in jobbing and batch manufacture. Here, product variety leads firms to use general-purpose equipment to allow flexibility in process routing. Figure 6.3 illustrates what happens. Processes are divided up into specialist areas (for example, turning), so that workload can be equally shared between the same types of machine, and a specialized foreman and maintenance tradesman allocated. There is plenty of work and machines around, so operators can be kept busy. However, product flows become tangled. Only one routing for a batch of parts is shown in Figure 6.3. If we were to add routings for many more batches, there would be competition for machines, leading to queues of WIP and hence to delays. So a process-type layout like this leads to a high waste of transport and to long lead times. Even the specialization becomes a disadvantage during periods of work imbalances. It is only possible to transfer the few people from milling to turning who happen to be able to do the work. Such firms can learn about improving product flow from firms which are further down the diagonal towards the bottom right of Figure 6.2.

But poor product layouts are not the only problems to be addressed in improving flow. Lack of attention to setups means that it is necessary to produce in large batches, otherwise capacity is lost. Random breakdowns, absenteeism, and poor supplier deliveries mean that it is necessary to keep buffer stocks. Such problem points often apply to flowline and process industries too.

The starting point for facilitating flow is the concept of the focused factory, described in Chapter 2, page 53. If manufacturing is given a set of confused and conflicting tasks, then we will never become an excellent company. Focus is about matching the manufacturing task with the manufacturing

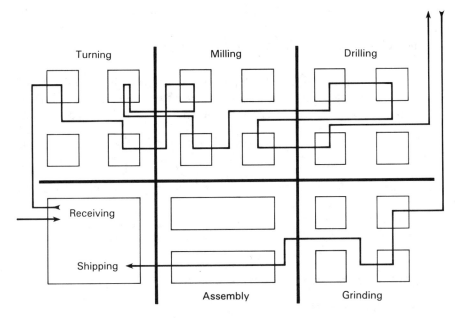

Figure 6 3 Functional layout (maohino typo layout)

capability [2]. The key steps involved are as follows:

Step 1: Translating the business strategy into what it means for manufacturing: to identify how we compete, and hence the key tasks which manufacturing must meet.

Step 2: Examining each element of current manufacturing capability, both structure (capacity, facilities, choice of process, and vertical integration) and infrastructure (systems, procedures, and organization) [3] in relation to manufacturing's key tasks.

Step 3: Developing and implementing a manufacturing strategy which will take us from the current capability identified in step 2 to meeting the key tasks identified in step 1.

This is essentially an iterative process, an example of which is given by Harrison and Bodnar [4]. Here, the Welsh factory of disposable laboratory-ware manufacturer, Bibby Sterilin, was focused into five areas by product. This is called a 'plant-within-plant' approach to focus [5]. The development of a manufacturing strategy for each area was led by the product manager (marketing) and the area manufacturing manager, with other 'central' personnel like the MD and the works accountant allocated to specific teams. Each iteration of the manufacturing strategy produced a deeper insight into the issues, and made more detailed demands on the business and marketing strategies for more specific information. Quite separate priorities for the development of the manufacturing strategy emerged for each focused product area, demanding sensitivity to the needs of the specific manufacturing strategy by product.

The objectives for facilitating flow are to maximize the following:

■ **Flexibility:** The ability of the organization to react to change [6]. In particular, we want to be able to manufacture any product in any sequence. Vollman *et al.* [7] refer to this as 'band width' to handle surge capacity.

■ **Coordination:** The ability to coordinate demand for products at the component level by synchronizing dependent demand items.

■ **Volumes:** The focus concepts of simplicity and repetition are key ingredients of competence. The group technology concept of exploiting the basic similarities between products and processes is also relevant here. As a target to challenge, doubling the volume results in reducing costs by 20–30% [8].

■ **Visibility:** Simple, visible control systems.

■ **Accessibility:** Simple, uncluttered access to processes, tools, and equipment. Work should be able to flow in an unconstrained way throughout the process route.

■ **Discipline:** Things happen the same way, at the same time, every time.

Facilitating flow also means that non-value-added activities like transport, waiting times, and errors are minimized. There is another water analogy here – that of clearing and straightening a water course. The overall throughput may be the same, but now the water flows evenly at all points in the system. The variability has been reduced.

Japanese companies frequently use the term '3-MU' to focus attention on the enemies of flow in a system. The term originates from three words beginning with the letters 'MU' – *muda*, *mura*, and *muri*. *Muda* means waste, *mura* irregularity, and *muri* excessiveness. Relating these meanings to a manufacturing system as follows:

■ *Muda* refers to failure by machines, materials, and manpower to add value to a system. The seven sources of waste described in Chapter 2 describe these in detail.
■ *Mura* refers to failure to achieve consistency. Examples are the erratic arrival of materials which disturbs production flow, and quality resulting from inconsistent standards of work.
■ *Muri* refers to the excessive demands on output as a result of poor quality due to the waste of defective goods are an example of *muri*. Improving flow in manufacture is about squeezing 3-MU out of the system.

■ Operations and processes

Industrial engineers in the West have used process flow charting for many years. As trainees at Procter and Gamble in the late 1960s, we were taught to analyse a film called 'Form X', where an army document spent most of its time in in-baskets or being walked from one side of the camp to the other to collect

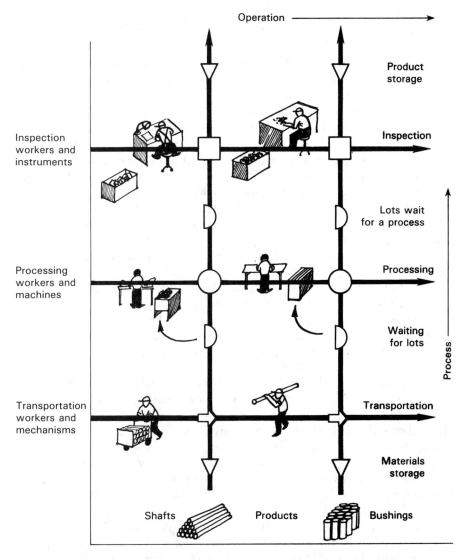

Figure 6.4 Shingo's process/operation matrix (Source: from *A Study of the Toyota Production System from an Industrial Engineering Viewpoint*, Shigeo Shingo, English re-translation copyright © 1989 by Productivity Press Inc., PO Box 3007, Cambridge, MA 02140

signatures. On the other side of the world, the same techniques were being directed at honing the Toyota Production System by another industrial engineer – Shigeo Shingo.

Shingo's ideas were devastatingly simple. He began by defining production as a network of processes and operations [9]:

■ Processes are the chain of events by which raw materials are converted into products.

■ Operations are the chain of events by which workers and machines work on parts or products.

The term network was used because the process chain of events was seen as interacting with the operations chain. Figure 6.4 illustrates how Shingo viewed what happens. The vertical lines are the process chain of events, the horizontal lines the operations. Let us follow a batch of parts through the network. Starting at the bottom of one of the vertical product lines, a batch of parts is received into the factory. It waits in the goods-in store, so there is a storage symbol (a triangle) at that point (see the ASME symbols in Chapter 2, page 33). Next, parts are transported for an operation to take place. An arrow symbol indicates the transport activity, a triangle that the parts must wait in the queue for the operation to be performed. After the operation (circle), parts must again wait (triangle) for inspection (square). Finally, they must wait again (triangle) in the despatch bay.

Shingo teaches us that this is the correct way to look at production. First, we must focus on processes. This can be achieved by drawing a process chart for the full route, and by identifying the sources and causes of waste. (Burbidge's *Production Flow Analysis* [10] is a similar concept.) When we have decided the best way, then operations should be fitted in around them. In the West, we have concentrated on operations at the expense of processes. This has led to a failure to recognize process flow, and to a preoccupation with direct labour and mechanization.

Once this basic method of looking at production has been recognized, the rest follows. JIT production is basically about reducing all of the process activities to zero. Figure 6.5 summarizes what can be done. Starting with operations themselves, it is necessary to identify what functions are required, and how to provide them. Design for manufacture defines such process methods in advance for new products. For existing products, value engineering and value analysis help existing designs and methods to be challenged. Inspection functions are best eliminated by making the operation error-proof, so that defects cannot be made. Error-proofing has been developed into a new art form in itself, and many methods are detailed in book called *Poka-yoke* (Japanese for error-proofing) [11]. Statistical process control has an intermediate role in bringing processes under statistical control and then looking for reduced variability.

Transport functions are best eliminated, too. Transport is waste, so the best layout is where processes are next to each other, with minimum flow

(1) Process, inspection, and transport activities

Processing improvements
- value analysis
- value engineering
- determine what functions are required, and then how to provide them

Inspection functions
- zero defects: the basic goal
- cannot be fully achieved by SQC
- need 100% check at source (*poka-yoke*, defect management, etc.)

Transport
- zero transport: the basic goal
- aim for sequencing processes so that product flows through them
- consider relative difficulty of transport (weight, volume, number, etc.)

(2) Delay activities

Types of delay:
- between supplier and factory
- between processes within the factory
- between factory and customers

Reasons for delays:
- incorrect forecasting and scheduling
- capacity problems
- breakdowns
- defects
- absenteeism
- differences in operating times
- lack of synchronization between processes
- changeovers (setups)
- waiting by part lots

Figure 6.5 Improving process functions (Source: after Shigeo Shingo)

distance between them. In fact, Shingo reckons that Matsushita's production system is better than Toyota's, because their operations are laid out in close sequence. Toyota only operates a *kanban*, or signal system, to tell distant operations that more parts are needed. The better way is to place operations next to each other. That way, operations are most closely coordinated, and transport is minimized.

Finally, delay activities can arise for a number of reasons between the factory and its suppliers; between operations within the factory; and between the factory and its customers. There are many potential causes of this waste. Poor supply chain management leads to incorrect scheduling and forecasting. Ideally, the supplier should make parts at the same rate as the factory uses them, and as the ultimate customer buys them. Any departure from this ideal creates the need for inventory (buffer stocks). Internal inefficiencies such as absenteeism, breakdowns, and lack of synchronization between operations have the same effect.

■ Levelling production

The last paragraph above leads on to the question of synchronizing material movements throughout the supply chain. Synchronizing means getting the timing right. Where work cycles repeat, this is an achievable goal. So it is specially relevant for runners and repeaters. For example, why talk of producing a single batch of 500 parts once per quarter, when what we actually need is 1 part per hour? Like a car, a factory works best when it is operating at constant speed. Works managers often talk of 'rhythm' when the factory is ticking over well and producing a consistent, high-quality output. Levelling production means going for rhythm by squeezing variability out of the system at every opportunity. Achieving level production means balancing cycle times throughout the system by being prepared to:

■ Develop multi-function workers, so that personnel can be transferred from areas of low demand to areas of high demand quickly;

■ Derate machines which are running faster than related operations, and which therefore lose synchronization;

■ Accept that many process operations only need to meet full surge capacity occasionally. Such operations are therefore typically run below this level, and are often shut down.

A master production schedule of 4,000/week for product A, 500/week for B, and 2,000/week for C can be rewritten as a 'mixed model' schedule of 100/hour of A, 12/hour or B, and 50/hour of C, or 8 of A followed by 1 of B and 4 of C. (For an illustration of mixed modelling, see Chapter 2, Figure 2.19.) Large batches which subsequently have to be stored, mixed, and matched in the distribution system are replaced by a uniform output based on 'making a little every day' [12]. It is essential to keep the schedule firm for a recognized period of time in order to balance the work flow. Marketing departments and MDs who constantly tinker with production schedules do not realize the problems they are causing!

The levelled final assembly output schedule then translates to more even requirements for subassemblies and components. So mixed modelling implies that preceding operations must be balanced to support the new levelled schedules of finished product. The aim is to break down manufacture into modules which fit together, so that each work centre operates as if it were part of final assembly. In order to make band width as large as possible (to enable frequent mix and volume changes), rebalancing should become a key issue, with routine rebalancing being undertaken by the supervisor. Recently, it took 2 weeks to make the calculations, reallocate work, and train people in order to rebalance a Midlands transmission assembly line to a new volume: we must do better than this.

IBM defines a 'takt time', the best or pulse of a line similar to the cox of a boat calling out the stroke [13]. The daily going rate (master production schedule) defines the number of machines to be built in any one shift. Performance against this plan is measured on an hourly basis by means of a data collection system. Takt time monitors for each area of operation (module) show current work status. Because output from the test station varies according to yield, the takt time for this station must be continuously adjusted to maintain flow.

Computer simulation and modelling can be very helpful in establishing the rules needed for optimum system performance. Such rules can often be best taught to the shop team by means of simulations using such physical aids as Lego bricks. Typically, team members come up with improvements and ideas which will help put the rules into practice in their environment. Supporting operations must become far more flexible. In particular, batch sizes must be greatly reduced: indeed, the concept of fixed batches at all would best be scrapped. This is the tough but rewarding route to flexibility. The advantages of small batch sizes are as follows:

- Smaller batches get used up more quickly, so that defectives are found earlier and the production of more can be prevented.
- Smaller batches mean that less WIP is needed, and so less space is required. Operations can therefore be more closely linked.
- Material control becomes an easier task, and so many of the routine transactions can be delegated to the shop floor.

This way of looking at batch sizes was proposed by Burbidge [14], who stated that 'ordering should be balanced product sets, and that the best batch quantity is the smallest'. Smaller batches mean in turn that setup times must be reduced, the subject of Chapter 7.

■ Layout and flow

The principle behind layout and flow is to move machines and related operations closer and closer together. This way, the waste of transport is reduced, there is no room for WIP, and operations become more closely coordinated. At each stage of improvement, the new method is analysed and standardized in detail so that discipline is maintained. The cellular manufacturing aspect of group technology is aimed at increasing the possibilities of layout and flow by seeking out component families which can share the same operations. Identification of such families is made easier by a standard classification and coding system which is used throughout the company. Usually, similar process routing is used as the basis for determining logical component families. The necessary machines are then grouped together using operation planning details and planned demand. Demand will first have been levelled, as described in the above section. Ideally, it should be unnecessary for parts to leave the cell until they have been finished. Unfortunately, it is not always possible to achieve this, and 'central' facilities like heat treatment furnaces continue to obstruct cell scheduling. There are ways round such obstacles, such as the use of cold-forged steels and induction hardening to bypass 'central' heat treatment facilities. Results of the grouping process may be quite simple, as in the case of the Raleigh seat cell shown in Figure 6.6. Here, all seat tubes are made in the same cell, although different parts follow different routings around the cell. The layout shows the popular U-shape, which provides minimum walking distance for operators and proximity between load/unload areas. Other groupings come up with quite unrelated products. Cummins Engine at Daventry has a flywheel housing and an engine mounting bracket which share the same cell! The parts are related only in terms of the NC machines which they use.

GT cells have the following advantages over the functional concepts shown in Figure 6.3.

- Lower work in progress;
- Simplified production control;
- Reduced transport distances and space requirements;
- Reduced lead times (2 weeks down to 24 hours at Sandvik Rock Tools for a typical order of 500 parts);
- Improved human relations resulting from the team spirit which develops within the cell setting.

Cellular manufacturing can be an excellent route to reducing costs without major investment. Indeed, the next round of major investment can often be funded from the savings in work-in-progress. This route was used by the American motor cycle manufacturer Harley Davidson to dig itself out of a vicious cycle (performance bad – company does not make money – not

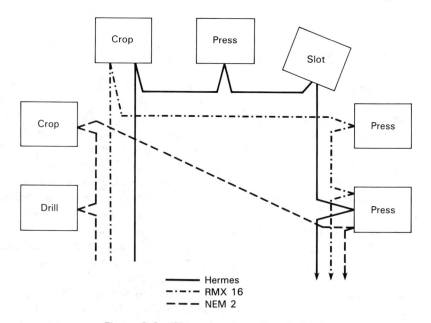

Figure 6.6 The seat tube cell at Raleigh

allowed investment capital − performance gets worse...). So GT can be used as a very effective route to automation: the hard work of grouping parts and simplifying processes has already been done! Figure 6.7 shows a sketch of a cell at Sumitomo disc brakes division. The sketch illustrates the following:

- Close packing densities of the machines to minimize flow distances;
- U-shaped line to minimize operator movement;
- Gravity feed of parts in and out of the cell;
- One-worker multiple machines
- The use of *jidoka* to signal potential problems by stopping the line.

At Albion Pressed Metal there were two 'factories' before re-layout. Parts had to be transported between the two by fork lift (see Figure 6.8). The 528

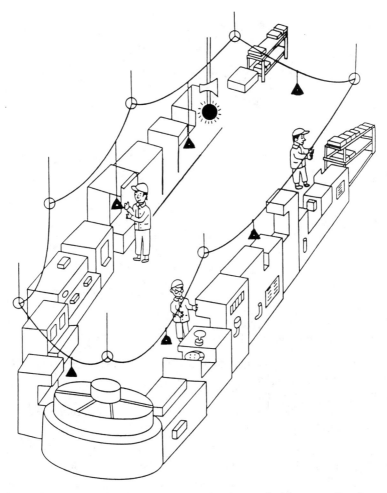

Figure 6.7 Use of *jidoka* in a production cell (Source: Sumitomo Electric)

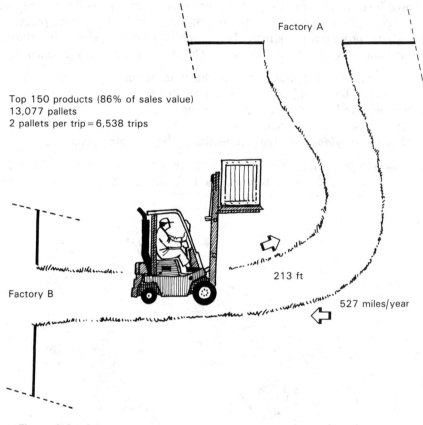

Figure 6.8 Opportunities for improvement – production flow (Source: Albion Pressed Metal)

miles/year of transport waste were eliminated as a result of the move to cellular manufacture.

While cellular manufacture often brings better-than-expected benefits there are some potential disadvantages:

- It may be necessary to duplicate investment between cells so that each cell is independent of other facilities.
- Machine utilization may be lower than the functional layout.
- Cell volume/mix flexibility may be limited, leading to unbalanced loadings from assumptions made when the cells were first laid out.

As an example of the last point, Rolls-Royce has had to replan cell layout because of changes in the mix between military and civil orders. The 'band width' of cell flexibility was insufficient to cater for the extent of the change.

Even where there is great variety in manufacturing, it may be possible to pick out runners and repeaters and put them into a cell. Vickers' tank factory

Figure 6.9   Sprocket cell at Vickers (**Source: Vickers Engineering Ltd**)

in Newcastle upon Tyne is a typical jobshop, currently producing a mix of tanks, armoured recovery vehicles, turrets, and refurbishment work of various kinds [13]. But the drive sprocket (the drive wheel at the back of the tank) for armoured recovery vehicles turns out to be a runner because the part is replaced after every journey. When the factory was transferred from the ramshackle Elswick Works to a new facility further down the Scotswood Road in 1981, the old process layout was replicated. A component which was produced in relatively high numbers, needing just 2 hours of direct labour, had a process route of 6 km and a lead time of 13 weeks! A cell was developed for the part (see Figure 6.9), the process route cut to 240 m, and the lead time to 2 weeks.

■ Implementing GT layout: some practical considerations

At Express Lifts in Northampton, a make-to-order manufactuer of all types of new and reconstructed lifts, work had been put in hand for some time to introduce GT concepts to the wide range of designs. It had also been decided

Table 6.1 Component routing for major family groups

Work centre sequence								No. of components/ major family groups	Actual routing of major family groups
1	2	3	4	5	4	9	10	16	1. Saw, dress, drill, straighten, weld, straighten, spray, assembly
1	2	3	4	5	9	10		2	
1	2	3	4	9	10			24	2. Saw, dress, drill, straighten, spray, assembly
1	2	3	4	10				4	
1	2	3	4	12	9	10		2	
1	2	3	4	13	5	4	9	5	
1	2	3	4	15	5	4	9	1	
1	2	3	5	4	9	10		12	3. Saw, dress, drill, weld, straighten, spray, assembly
1	2	3	5	9	10			3	
1	2	3	8	5	9	10		3	
1	2	3	8	9	10			1	
1	2	3	9	10				7	
1	2	3	12	4	9	10		1	
1	2	3	12	9	10			4	
1	2	3	12	11	10			13	4. Saw, dress, drill, slot, handpaint, assembly
1	2	3	13	5	4	8	10	1	
1	2	4	5	4	10			3	
1	2	5	4	9	10			14	5. Saw, dress, weld, straighten, spray, assembly
1	2	5	10					2	
1	2	10						2	
1	2	13	5	9	10			3	
1	2	13	9	10				1	
6	2	3	4	9	10			1	
6	2	3	6	5	4	9	10	2	
6	2	3	13	5	4	9	10	4	
6	2	4	9	10				4	
6	2	8	5	9	10			3	
6	5	9	10					4	
6	7	3	13	9	10			2	
6	1	5	9	10				3	
6	7	8	5	4	9	10		18	6. Guillotine, trumpf, bend straighten, spray, assembly
6	7	8	5	4	9	10		9	7. Guillotine, trumpf, bend, weld, straighten, spray, assembly
6	7	8	9	10				24	8. Guillotine, trumpf, bend, spray assembly

Note: Work centre routing numbers

Saw	1	Drill	6	Hand paint	11
Dress, markout	2	Trumpf	7	Slot	12
Drill	3	Bend	8	Flame cut	13
Straighten	4	Spray	9	Stud weld	14
Weld	5	Assembly	10	Grind	15

to implement GT cellular manufacture in the Gear Shop as an experiment. This project had been very successful, and benefits included a reduction in WIP of 80%. The company was therefore keen to extend GT cells into other areas of the factory, and to continue to make progress on cellular manufacture before GT design standardization had been completed. One of the areas which was selected was 'F' Shop, part of the fabrication area which makes car frames, safety gear, and associated equipment. Analysis showed that 92% of the forward order load comprised five types of lift. The routings for each of the 198 major 'F' Shop components which go into these types of lift were analysed. The results were shown as processing operations for each component for each subassembly. Routing sequences through the 15 work centres were then analysed on a spreadsheet to make it easy to identify product families. Eight major product families with variations were identified, as shown in Table 6.1. The families did not require the use of all work centres, so flow patterns differed as in the Raleigh example shown in Figure 6.6. Flow patterns were analysed by means of a string diagram, a simplified version of which is shown in Figure 6.10. String diagrams use a useful means of analysing complex movements of many parts. The aim is to determine which operations have the greatest number of transactions between them, and hence the operations which should be placed next to each other. (Many other methods of production flow analysis, including computer simulation packages, are reviewed by Wild [15].)

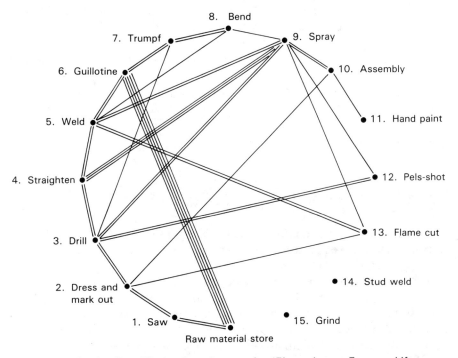

Figure 6.10 Simplified string diagram for 'F' section at Express Lifts

Various alternative layouts were tried until the best from the point of view of minimum material movements was obtained. It is best to check manual results with computer simulation based on the routing file, although manual results often give a good indication. The new layout meant the following:

- Guillotine, trumpf, and bending operations were closer to dressing and marking out. (This move had additional benefits to the subsequent assembly operations.)
- Straight-line material flows were facilitated by means of pillar hoists between major work centres, thus avoiding the use of overhead cranes which are only available intermittently.
- Passage of work between work centres was disciplined by means of *kanban* squares which held a set amount of inventory. The aim was to cut down the WIP by at least half.
- Ideally, the paint spray facility should have been placed next to welding. Safety and logistics (extraction is through the roof) dictated that the facility could not be moved. New methods were therefore investigated to enable some painting operations to take place inside the cell.

As a result of these improvements, flow distances were cut by over 16% for some product families.

This example shows how some tangible benefits can be achieved from a 'bottom up' approach to GT. Inevitably, the new disciplines in manufacture put increased pressure on to pre-shop areas. Deficiencies in planning and stock control became more visible. Opportunities for improved design standardization also became more apparent and urgent issues. Why are there so many components (25) which fall outside the major family groups (8) in Table 6.1? Previously, such issues had been hidden in the jumbled work pattern. Manufacture can therefore be used to bring home the problems and the opportunities. Further improvement depends on the problems being addressed. For example, as we noted in Chapter 2, excellent manufacture is heavily dependent on excellent design.

■ Why did early GT applications fail? [16]

Although GT had its origins in Russia (and was originally translated as 'family planning'!), much of its early development took place in the UK engineering industry during the 1960s and early 1970s [17]. However, it has been Japanese and American companies who have been more recently teaching us about the power of this technique to slash costs, improve lead times, and get closer to customer needs. While some of the early cells are in existence today, most fell into disuse and few ever achieved their full potential. In spite of this, cells often achieved the initial objectives which were set – such as improvements in labour productivity, reduced stock levels, reduced arrears, and improvements in conformance quality. So it is interesting to reflect on some of the major reasons why GT fell into disuse in the United Kingdom [18]:

- Many GT applications were experiments which, although successful, played no part in the overall company philosophy. The applications became 'islands of cell', and the companies guilty of 'technique tokenism'. The effects of this lack of ongoing management leadership are that unresolved problems gradually accumulate, communications become neglected, and disenchantment creeps in. The Hawthorne effect, so vital to harness in the continuous improvement process, gradually fades.

- The physical process of rearranging facilities into a cell often creates many improvements. But this limited view of progress has been referred to as 'shuffling the deck chairs around on the *Titanic*'! It is only the beginning of a learning experience for the organization as a whole. In early applications of GT, those learning opportunities were often wasted. Benefits were limited to the effects of regrouping machines, and few further improvements were made.

- Usually, there were clashes of interest between cell systems and the systems used in the rest of the factory. One of the most common problems was the payment scheme, perhaps based on piecework or measured daywork, which emphasized activity. We now know that activity is not the most important measure of cell performance. Rewards which are based on a person's ability to perform many different operations are often far more relevant.

- Another clash of interest took place over performance measures. While the cell might have been doing great things from the customer perspective, for example reducing arrears and improving quality, the financial reporting system kept churning out reams of irrelevant waffle about performance against budget. Further problems with the accountants in the organization resulted from capital expenditure rules which emphasized 'years to pay off' in terms of headcount reduction. While this may be appropriate for some cost-saving projects, such rules are unsuitable in themselves for projects linked with improved competitiveness, or with the product life cycle.

Such reasons for the failure of early applications of cellular manufacture teach us a number of lessons. First, there is the issue of running an experiment. If an experiment works, meets its objectives, and proves to be a better way of working, then should we not adapt our ideas and extend the experiment to other areas? Some of the old 'sacred cows' of performance measurement may have to be changed at the same time, so that the new cells are encouraged to develop against new measures of business competitiveness.

Then there is the issue of management leadership. If the experiment is successful, the new concepts need to become part of company culture. We need to learn, adapt, and improve. Day-to-day decisions can be delegated more to the cell supervision, in line with the opportunities for greater autonomy which the cell brings. As progress improvement arrives at a plateau, so management leadership must inspire further efforts to lift performance to new heights, rather than letting it drift back to the starting position. Problems highlighted by the experiment – such as band width of volume and mix, difficulties caused by the central production control system, and inappropriate investment rules – need to be handled with sensitivity and knowledge.

■ Facilitating product flow

Figure 6.11 gives a checklist for facilitating product flow in a system [19]. What is remarkable is not so much the headings, but the ideals which are

1. No missing parts
   - standardized store
   - use of *kanbans*
   - checklist of missing parts
   - due date control table
   - 'just-in-day' production

2. No repairs, defects, or rework
   - teams to eliminate defects
   - clarify standard method (numbers of parts, inventory, etc.)
   - self-check inspection
   - use of jigs, foolproof devices

3. Short setup
   - SUR techniques
   - training

4. No machine breakdown
   - daily routine checks by operators
   - total productive maintenance

5. Standardization
   - standardize operation
   - everyone can do it!

6. Synchronization
   means zero waiting time: all processes must be synchronized!
   - fair job assignment to workers
   - establish proper standards
   - teamwork

7. Multi-function workers
   - break down department barriers
   - education and training

7. Avoid abnormal absenteeism
   - profit share/fair wages
   - investment in people
   - inform foreman in advance
   - introduction of relief worker

Figure 6.11 Facilitating product flow

Low-cost production can be achieved by:
- eliminating waste
- making full use of people's capabilities
- making endless efforts to improve
- asking the question 'why'

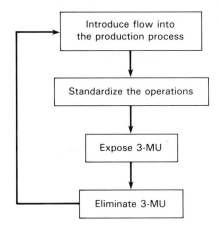

Figure 6.12   Continuous improvement

contained in them (no defects, no breakdowns...). The aim is fully to squeeze 3-MU out of the system, and never to be satisfied. The cyclic process involved can be explained by reference to Figure 6.12. We keep going round the cycle, making improvements and restandardizing as we go. The quest for perfection is endless. The question 'why', repeated as many as five times, is valuable in establishing the key point (see Chapter 6). It is this continuing cycle of improvement which highlights more than anything the difference in emphasis between our views of cellular manufacturing now and 20 years ago.

■ JIT in administration areas

As noted in Chapter 2 and illustrated in Figures 2.5 and 2.6, and noted again at the beginning of Chapter 3, the JIT philosophy for eliminating waste is not restricted to manufacturing alone. Table 6.2 shows how equivalent target areas for the 'war on waste' can be found in administrative areas. Most often, it is manufacturing companies who have progressed a long way with JIT/TQ in manufacture and who have also been most active in spreading the philosophy into other parts of the business. According to Billesbach and Schniedermans, the following techniques have been particularly popular in US companies [20]:

1. **Undercapacity scheduling:** To allow employees the time for improvement

Table 6.2 Corresponding targets for the war on waste

Manufacturing setting	Administration setting
Storing	Batching, filing
Moving	Mailing, transmitting
Expediting	'Rush ordering'
Scheduling	Routing, prioritizing
Inspecting	Proofing

Source: After Billesbach and Schniedermans [20]

activities, the workload should be scheduled for correspondingly less than say 37 hours in a week.

2. **Layout improvements:** Those which improve flow of work, visibility of workload, and speech communication should be attempted before increasing computerization.

3. **Process control:** Educating employees to do the job the right way every time is central to achieving the right disciplines necessary for high-quality work.

4. **Standardization of activities:** This helps to focus resources on only a few tasks which must be done really well. It improves productivity and reduces the cost of cross-training.

5. **Multi-function workforce:** This avoids the paralysis caused by overspecialization of office tasks. Flexible employees who know the whole job are in a superior position to improve operations.

6. **Total quality:** This helps to enforce individual responsibility for the quality aspects of work. Employees must in turn be given the tools to identify and solve problems which affect that work, and the authority to make changes which will improve quality.

7. **Stressing the operation:** This means reducing the resources such as workers, inventory (data or documentation), and backup equipment. The system is monitored until it fails in some way, and problem solving is then used to find better ways of doing things.

Cellular layouts in administration areas appear to be particularly promising. For example, grouping an accountant with finance, customer credit, and customer service personnel may speed up processing and help in the speedy resolution of problems. Focusing routine operations into a 'fast track' handled by designated account administrators helped to cut throughput time by 60% at the maintenance contract group at Wang Computers [21]. In the United Kingdom, the Nationwide Building Society has been using many of the above principles to streamline mortgage processing procedures at its Northampton headquarters. Processes involved in the execution of a given service were developed by a central team, and the results presented to process 'owners' who were invited to add comments and amendments to the team view. Further additions could be made by the owners over the following few weeks. The flowcharts – the processes written on white paper and mounted on wide, brown paper charts – were displayed along the length of complete walls to make them visible so that owners could add their comments using 'Post-it' pads. Natural work teams develop proposals from the suggestions made and present them to management.

■ Conclusion

The vision, embodied in IBM's term for JIT/TQ 'Continuous Flow Manufacturing', is to keep parts and subassemblies flowing throughout the production system as though they were on the final assembly line. Facilitating flow uses many well-established techniques such as process flowcharting and some relatively new concepts like mixed modelling. Some of the techniques like cellular manufacture we have known about for a long time but have not pursued relentlessly enough. JIT manufacture demands continuous and rigorous attention to improvement. Facilitating flow starts from the definition of focused factories. It requires the coordination of many tools and techniques which affect everything from the manufacturing planning and control system to supporting personnel plans and policies. Unnecessary variety is prohibited, and so design for manufacture is essential for maximum effectiveness. The aim is to achieve balanced material flows throughout the supply chain in general, and in the factory in particular. While even continuous process flows can always be improved, the strategy is often to provide the advantages of volume production methods to small-batch manufacture.

■ References

1. *Restoring Our Competitive Edge: Competing through Manufacturing*, R. Hayes and S. Wheelwright, Wiley, New York, 1984.
2. *Manufacturing Strategy*, T. Hill, Macmillan Education, Basingstoke, 1985, p. 100.
3. R. Hayes and S. Wheelwright, *ibid.*
4. 'Manufacturing strategy development at Bibby Sterilin', J. Bodnar and A. Harrison, *International Journal of Operations and Production Management*, **11**, no. 3, 1991, pp. 43–51.
5. T. Hill, *ibid.*, p. 107.
6. *'Flexibility as managers see it'*, New Technology and Manufacturing Management, Wiley, New York, 1990.
7. *Manufacturing Planning & Control Systems*, T. Vollman, W. Berry, and C. Whybark, Irwin, Homewood, IL, 1988.

8. 'Perspectives on experience', Boston Consulting Group, 1972.
9. *A Study of the Toyota Production System from an Industrial Engineering Viewpoint*, S. Shingo, English re-translation 1989, Productivity Press, Cambridge, MA.
10. *Production Flow Analysis for Planning Group Technology*, J. Burbidge, Oxford Science Publications, 1989.
11. *Poka-yoke: Improving Product Quality by Preventing Defects*, Productivity Press, Cambridge, MA.
12. *Attaining Manufacturing Excellence*, R. Hall, Dow Jones Irwin, Homewood, IL, 1987.
13. 'Process design for CFM', in C. Voss (ed.) *JIT's Here to Stay, Proc. 4th International Conference on JIT*, London, October, 1989, IFS, Bedford.
14. J. Burbidge, *ibid*.
15. *Production & Operations Management*, R. Wild, Cassell, London, 4th edn, 1989.
16. 'Why's everyone going back to GT?', A. Harrison, *MBA Review*, December, 1990, Cranfield.
17. *The Introduction of Group Technology*, J. Burbidge, Heinemann, 1975.
18. An excellent description of early problems with GT implementation is given in 'Midland Component Star Line', in *Managing Manufacturing Operations: A Casebook*, T. A. J. Nicolson, Macmillan, London & Basingstoke, 1978.
19. After Professor H. Yamashina.
20. 'Application of just-in-time techniques in administration', T. Billesbach and J. Schniedemans, *Production & Inventory Management Journal*, 3rd Quarter, 1989, pp. 40–5.
21. 'Workflow analysis: Just-in-time techniques simplify administrative process in paperwork operation', J. Feather and K. Cross, *Industrial Engineering*, **20**, no. 1, 1988, pp. 32–40.

7 | The Flexible Facility

The ideal of reducing setup times to zero goes to the heart of making a manufacturing facility more flexible. We are here referring to flexibility in the sense of an organization's capability to react to change, rather than to job flexibility referred to in Chapter 4. Slack [1] has referred to two aspects of flexibility of most concern to manufacturing companies:

1. Variety: of products, processes, and activities with which the system has to cope.
2. Uncertainty: of the system to predict the demand placed upon it.

These are key issues in coping with burgeoning product ranges in markets where it is increasingly difficult to forecast demand accurately. Such issues place strong pressures on manufacturing capability. When a single piece of equipment is used to produce many components of different configurations, the problem of setup time exists: how quickly can equipment be changed from running on one component to running on another? Long setup times cause the following:

- Loss of flexibility, restricting the freedom to react quickly to changes;
- Extended lead times due to large batch sizes, lengthy setup times, and queues due to high levels of 'work not in progress';
- High levels of inventory;
- High cost levels (the setup costs themselves, hidden quality costs, additional overheads needed to expedite and inspect, inventory financing costs, and loss of sales due to inability to respond sufficiently quickly).

If the setup time can be reduced, then smaller batches of components can be produced more frequently without losing overall system capacity. Figure 7.1 illustrates why setup reduction results in lower inventories and lead times.

Setup time is defined as the time taken to change over the equipment from good product to good product [2]. That is, it measures the time from the last part from the preceding batch to the first good part of the succeeding batch.

Case 1: Safety stock   = 1,000 units
        Steady-state usage = 750 units/week
        Suppose that EBQ = 6,000 units
        Then average stock = Safety stock + av. cycle stock
                           = 1,000 + 6,000/2
                           = 4,000

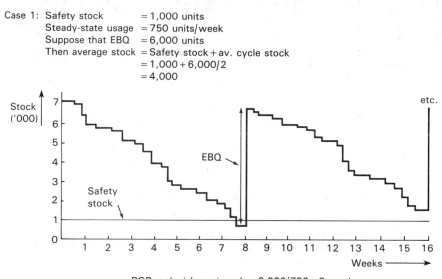

ROP replenishment cycle = 6,000/750 = 8 weeks

Case 2: Safety stock   = 1,000 units
        Steady-state usage = 750 units/week

Assume that EBQ has been cut from 6,000 units to 2,500 units by means of a 75% reduction in setup costs.

Then, average stock = 1,000 + 2,500/2
                    = 2,250

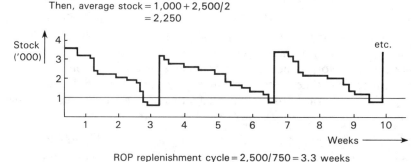

ROP replenishment cycle = 2,500/750 = 3.3 weeks

Figure 7.1 Setup reduction reduces inventory levels

So setup time includes not only dismantling and reassembly but also search time for tools and materials, tryouts, first-piece inspection, and dealing with problems to get the new batch to run well.

To bring home what can be achieved, a good example is provided by the time taken to change the wheel on your car after a puncture. If you are good at it, maybe you can perform all of the operations involved in jacking up the car and removing the old wheel and replacing it in 20 minutes. But a grand prix team of mechanics can change all four wheels in 7 seconds! This results from a combination of excellent design (simple wheel fixings), excellent equipment (hydraulic jacks and air tools) plus maximum pre-preparation and practice. Such principles can be applied on the shop floor too.

In the past, such opportunities have been bypassed through the wide use of the concept of 'economic batch quantities' (EBQs) in an attempt to balance a perceived tradeoff between the carrying cost of inventory and the cost of setups. The traditional illustration of this tradeoff is shown in Figure 7.2. The EBQ calculation for a given part is based on the following assumptions:

- The usage rate for the part is known (based on history) and constant (z).
- Setup costs are known and fixed (C_s).
- The manufactured cost per unit of the part (c) is constant.
- The complete batch of parts is delivered at one instant in time.
- The cost of carrying inventory is known and fixed (C).

A little arithmetic applied to these very dubious assumptions leads to the so-called Wilson formula:

$$EBQ = \sqrt{\frac{2zC_s}{cC}}$$

There are several variations of this formula. Unfortunately, use of EBQs in the past has assumed a high, fixed setup cost, leading to production of different components in different batch quantities and hence to lack of synchronization [3]. The notion that setups and other costs are fixed is particularly dangerous because it implies that once the EBQ has been calculated,

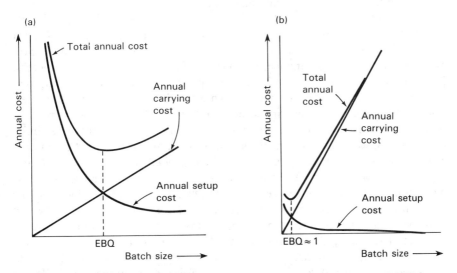

Figure 7.2 Modifying the EBQ concept: (a) classical EBQ graph; (b) EBQ graph modified for small-batch or batchless production (Source: adapted from R. Schonberger and E. Knod, *Operations Management*, Irwin, 1991

it is fixed for good. This undermines the principle of continuous improvement. If the cost of setups is challenged and reduced, then the EBQ also reduces, as also shown in Figure 7.2. As the setup cost approaches zero, so the EBQ tends to one. So even from an EBQ perspective, the setup time should be zero!

Traditionally, setups have been a neglected area of production management. They were carried out as infrequently as possible and put off as long as possible because they were seen as laborious and time consuming. Anyway, you could always buffer yourself from the effects of setups by large batch sizes. Unfamiliarity with what was needed and lack of training meant that setup times remained high. What had to be done was never standardized in the way that direct operations were, so the actual time depended on who carried out the set-up. In consequence, setup times for a given operation varied a great deal in practice. In fact, lack of standardization or of any rigorous attempt to establish setup methods meant that technical problems were not tackled. Operators went from one job to the next, one year to the next, working under the same difficulties and hampered by the same old problems, such as lack of equipment and lack of technical support. The true operating requirements of jigs and tools were not properly understood. There was a concentration on cycle time rather than on 'door to door' time (total manufacturing lead time). As a result of such problems, it is often true that most of the operations associated with the setup are waste. Often, the situation is made worse by poor housekeeping and bad maintenance.

But firms who have broken with tradition and tackled the setup problem have found that they have tapped a rich vein. Not only are there tangible benefits in terms of reduced WIP and lead times, and improvements in machine efficiency and product mix flexibility, but also some unexpected benefits in achieving these. Setup reduction is an excellent vehicle for people involvement, and projects in this area are often very powerful motivators for change. Indeed, the TQ route of multi-disciplinary teams (for example, production operators, maintenance, production engineers) is *the way* to success. In several companies, setup reduction has proved to company members that JIT techniques really do work in their own work situation [4]. It is not a question of throwing big money at the problem, either. Recognizing the need to reduce setup times on the 17 machines on the block line to improve flexibility and reduce WIP, Cummins Engine at Daventry commissioned a conventional engineering study to investigate what would be needed. The study showed that, in order to reduce the total setup time of 9.5 hours for all machines on the block line, £10,000 would be needed to remove 2 hours, after which the law of diminishing returns would apply (Figure 7.3). By ditching this study and instead going for a shop team problem-solving approach, Cummins achieved a reduction of the total setup time for the block line to just 0·5 hours at a cost of a few hundred pounds! Hay [5] describes this as a low-cost or no-cost approach. This early success catalysed other areas to experiment, and allowed the JIT philosophy to gain a firm hold in the culture of the company. The methods which Cummins used will be described later in this chapter.

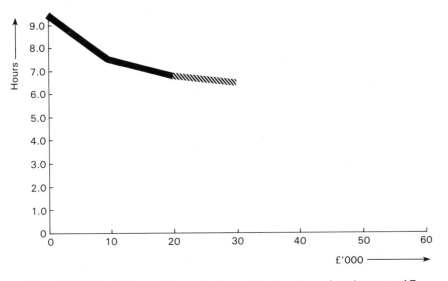

Figure 7.3 Capital requirements to reduce setup duration on 17 machines (Source: courtesy Cummins Engine)

Understanding the business implications of improving setup times becomes a management priority. The key deliverable is better capability of manufacturing to cope with changes in demand, and hence to interface more closely with the external market (Figure 1.5). A number of factors can indicate where to begin finding out about setup times:

- Processes which have the highest existing setup times;
- Major product routes (like the block line referred to above);
- Bottleneck operations.

Increased awareness of the issues and widespread education become the enabling factors for success.

■ Steps for setup reduction

Eight steps are involved in setup reduction projects. They are illustrated in Figure 7.4 and summarized below:

1. **Select:** Selection criteria could include machines with highest setup times, bottleneck operation, most likely to yield savings.

2. **Record:** The current method is recorded as it stands, using time-lapse video, or by recording each activity and its duration using a wrist watch and record forms.

151

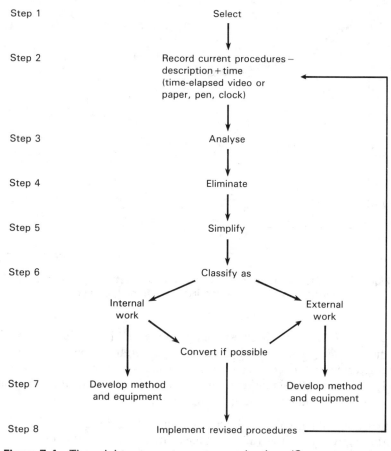

Figure 7.4 The eight steps to setup reduction (Source: courtesy C. Rothwell)

3. **Analyse:** Activities are sorted and analysed (for example, in terms of clamp/unclamp, load/unload tool, transport, adjustment, cleaning, and inspection activities). A Pareto analysis is often useful here.

4. **Eliminate:** Wasteful activities like search and transport are eliminated by means of improvements in the method.

5. **Simplify:** The remaining activities are simplified, for example by use of pre-setting tools and improved material handling devices.

6. **Classify:** The remaining activities are classified as:

   ■ Internal work: work which must be carried out after the machine has stopped;
   ■ External work: work which must be done before the machine has stopped.

The challenge is to convert as much internal work as possible into external work so that the machine is stopped for as short a time as possible.

7. **Develop method and equipment:** These developments will support the new setup activities for both internal and external work.

8. **Implement revised procedures:** The new methods become the standard practice. Setup reduction does not stop here: the new method is re-recorded for training purposes *and* as a further project for improvement.

Ongoing improvements enable further reductions of both external and internal setup times, so it is not a 'one-off' process. Teams may be given the challenge to achieve 'single minute exchange of dies' [6], that is to achieve setup times of less than 10 minutes.

More detail about actions to reduce setup times, focused on the distinction between internal and external setups and illustrated with examples, is now described.

Separate internal from external work

A common mistake is failing to understand the difference between these two categories, and to mix them up. However, a clear distinction between them helps us to recognize the challenge of keeping the machine idle for the minimum amount of time. An example breakdown of these categories is shown in Table 7.1. Avoidable operations, such as searching for tools, should be attacked straight away. Figure 7.5 is a recent photograph of a tool store. It cannot have been easy to get at the one at the bottom of the pile, even after it had been identified! Three rules for eliminating avoidable operations are as follows:

1. Eliminate search time.
2. Use the right tools.
3. Store tools in a setup trolley.

Table 7.1 Breakdown of setup times on the M4 150-ton press at Albion Pressed Metal

Operation	Duration (min)	Classification
Unclamp	7·05	Int
Clean down	2·05	Int
Unload tool	1·47	Int
Load tool	2·20	Int
Fork lift	15·40	Ext
Clamp	24·30	Int
Adjustment	8·04	Adjt
Material procurement	10·12	Ext
Inspection	14·04	Ext
Total	84·67	

Figure 7.5   The dye store in a Midlands manufacturing company

An example of a dedicated setup trolley is shown in Figure 7.6. Setup tools and fixtures should be stored clean and ready for use. Colour coding the tooling and storing it next to the machine helps to eliminate search time. Commonly used small tools can be stored next to point of use, as also shown in Figure 7.6. Simple housekeeping improvements like this can make a big difference, and prove that we are serious about further reductions in setup times. This way, we can work on standardizing the external setup activities. Internal activities need to be analysed and standardized too. A key issue is allocating the correct number of setup operators.

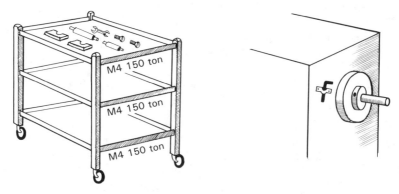

Dedicated tool trolley   Keep small tools near point of use

Figure 7.6   Minimizing search time

Transfer internal work to external

There are three major methods for achieving the transfer of internal setup work to external work [7]:

1. Pre-set tools so that a complete unit is fixed to the machine instead of having to be built up while the machine is stopped. Preferably, all adjustments should be carried out externally, so that the internal setup is an assembly operation only. Pre-heating dyes for injection moulding machines also falls into this category.
2. Attach the different tools or dyes to a standard fixture or jig. Again, this enables the internal setup to consist of a simple and standardized assembly operation.
3. Make the loading and unloading of new tools and dyes easy. Using improved material handling devices such as roller conveyor or ball-bounted surface tables can greatly help. Press tools at Albion Pressed Metal are stored on the inside lane of a two-lane roller conveyor which runs round the light press shop. The new tool is selected, run round the inside lane and mounted into the press by means of a drawbridge, as shown on the photograph in Figure 7.7. The same drawbridge is used to remove the tool when it needs to be changed. The aim is to avoid the 'lash up' shown in the photograph in Figure 7.8!

Figure 7.7 Easy access to dyes at Albion Pressed Metal

Figure 7.8 Avoid 'lash ups' like this one! (Note the specially designed spacers)

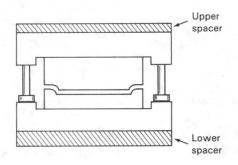

Figure 7.9 Standardizing press shut heights using spacers

1. Pear-shaped holes (Dahma holes) mean fewer turns to release and tighten

2. U-washers also need fewer turns to release and tighten

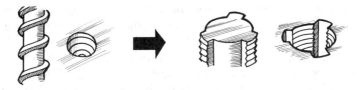

3. Cutaway threads are easier to release and tighten

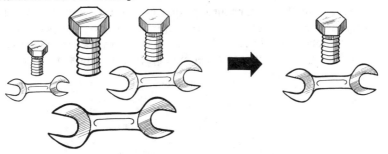

4. Standardize the size of fixings

5. Reduce the number of bolts used

Figure 7.10 Improve fixing methods

Reduce the internal work

There are four major ways in which this can be achieved:

1. Standardize the method and equipment. It would be very expensive to buy
    a new press line in which the shut heights were the same! But maybe we
    can achieve the same result by packing the bolster as shown in Figure 7.9.
    Adjustment to the slide and to the auto-feeder can then be eliminated.
2. Improve fixing methods so that they can be carried out quickly. Nuts and
    bolts which require many turns to remove and replace are the enemy of
    fast setups. Pear-shaped holes, U-washers and cutaway bolts can all help
    to save time here. Better still, air or hydraulic clamping can eliminate the
    need for nuts and bolts altogether. Cutting down on the number of bolts
    used, for example by making flanges with fewer holes, and reducing the
    variety of bolt sizes used (and hence the variety of spanners needed), all
    help. See Figure 7.10.
3. Carry out operations in parallel. By putting a second operator on to a
    setup, it may be possible to improve the method by means of better
    teamwork. A single setup operator was used to change over a bottling line
    in Scotland from one pack size to another. This meant frequent moves
    from one side of the line to the other. Addition of a second operator
    enabled the setup to be completed in considerably less than half the time.
4. Eliminate adjustments. Adjustments and accompanying inspection
    operations are often a major factor in internal setups. Such operations
    require skilled resources which could be better used on value-adding
    work. So methods for cutting out adjustments by making positive
    locations are very worthwhile. Examples are use of stoppers and blocks,
    limit switches and spacers (Figure 7.11). If there are some remaining
    adjustments which cannot be eliminated, then standard procedures and
    training are needed.

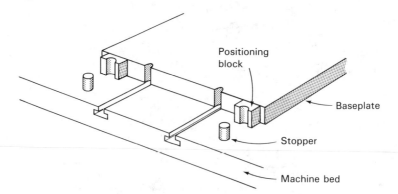

Figure 7.11 Eliminating adjustment by using positioning blocks and
stoppers

Improvements:
- Totally new layout of presses to give improved space utilization
- Creating detailed operation sheets for each piece part operation giving tooling details etc.
- Dedicating each piece part operation to a specific machine, colour coding the tooling and storing it adjacent to the press
- Manufacturing a kit of spacers and air pins for each tool, stamping them with a piece part and op number, and storing adjacent to the press
- Designing and manufacturing tool kits containing standard spanners, nuts, bolts, and so on for each press
- Buying a tool handling trolley
- Fitting rollers into the press bed
- Establishing standard clamping centres and tool shut heights
- Fitting quick-action hydraulic clamps
- Identifying critical dimensions per piece part and providing jigs and fixtures to enable the setter to do the inspection

Figure 7.12 Press shop improvements at KAB Seating

Figure 7.12 gives a list of actions taken by KAB Seating, makers of seats for work vehicles. These actions were taken to make the press shop more flexible and responsive, and show that several of the methods for reducing setup times listed above were applied [8].

■ Taking the total quality route

What we have stated so far is basically about applying good industrial engineering practice to an area which has received little attention in the West until recently. Setups were a 'black hole' – unstudied and unloved. Industrial engineering studies would be an obvious way to correct this omission now that we realize how important quick setups can be in improving competitiveness. However, surely we now know better? Maybe in the short term, such studies would produce some quick results. But if we are prepared to stand back and let the shop experts – the people who actually do the job – carry out the studies after training them, then surely this would provide better and longer lasting results?

Cummins Engine at Daventry decided to use the latter route. Teams would be action teams rather than study teams, and were set targets of 50% reduction in setup times after 6 months, followed by a further 25% reduction after 12 months. Teams were encouraged to use video recording, with a time-lapse feature, of current and improved operations. The deal was that the recording should be taken of the method as it actually was (no rehearsals), that it would not be stopped if anything went wrong (it was important to see real-life problems), and that the video would remain the property of the team. It would not be used on 'mahogany row' (the nickname for management offices) without the team's permission. Although the company already had work measurement on direct operations, setup studies were to be a break with traditional methods. Use of video recording by the shop teams themselves would encourage ownership and trust [9]. Teams consisted of two operators from the subject machine, the industrial engineer as facilitator, process engineer, maintenance operator, and tool control representative. Because of their wide-ranging duties, foremen would only be invited to attend meetings as necessary. But it was also found to be very important that foremen were updated regularly by the team facilitator.

The team was trained together, and a summary of the programme, which was held in 3 × 3.5 hour sessions, is shown in Figure 7.13. A video was then made of the setup on the target machine, and soon afterwards the first team meeting was held. After distinguishing external and internal activities, the

---

The competitive environment and the challenge to the company in terms of:
- cost
- quality
- delivery

The company response and strategy
- business plans

The chosen tool for delivery improvement – JIT
- origins and philosophy

The requirements for reducing setups
- smaller batches providing:
  · increased flexibility
  · shorter lead times
  · improved quality
  · reduced inventory
  · lower costs

Video as an improvement tool
- records what really happens versus what should happen
- no 'rehearsals'
- the sensitivities (video ownership)

Analysis/improvement methods
- use of an analysis form
- brainstorming technique
- root cause analysis
- guidenotes
- protecting quality

Installation and maintenance of improvements
- factor control technique
- construction of factor control documentation
- the 'final' video

Figure 7.13 Training programme for setup reduction at Cummins
(3 sessions × 2 hours)

team broke down the internal activities which had been recorded on the video into the following elements:

- clamp;
- adjustment;
- other (describe);
- unclamp;
- cleandown;
- problems (describe).

Each activity was recorded on a setup analysis sheet, like a simple work study sheet, timed, and classified into the above six categories. These were then analysed by a Pareto chart. The first machine to be attacked was the head face drill, a £500,000 CNC machine tool which drills and reams the cylinder head bolt holes on the engine block. The Pareto chart for this setup is shown in Figure 7.14. Extensive cleaning operations were necessary in order to remove swarf from the machine bed plate, and to clear several Allen key holes around the clamping fixture. This could then be unclamped, and (provided the hydraulic pipes did not become entangled) moved to the new position with the crane (which had to be bagged beforehand!). The clamping fixture then had to be resecured and adjusted, and the machine controls set to the new block size. Ideas for improvement came quickly. Swarf deflectors made the bed plate cleaning unnecessary. Careful analysis of the clamping fixture showed that although the machine tool manufacturers had intended that the workpiece

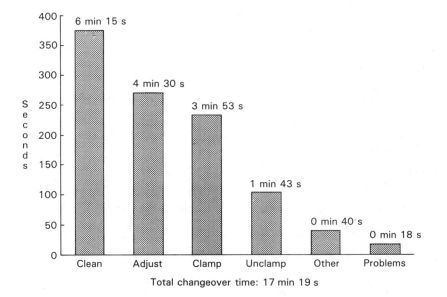

Figure 7.14 Time distribution Pareto: head face drill setup KV16 to KV12

should be rigidly held in place, there was actually a small gap between the clamp and the workpiece in practice. Careful quality studies with and without the clamping fixture showed that there was actually an improvement in conformance quality without it. The fixture was therefore eliminated, and the setup was down to just 8 seconds, the time it took to change the machine controls! The cost was £82 for the swarf deflectors. A minor product change recommended by the team resulted in the elimination of setup times on five further machines.

This early great success prompted volunteers from many other areas, and ensured a high level of enthusiasm for the extension of JIT techniques in the Daventry plant. Further experience on reducing setups prompted Cummins to declare the analysis guides for cleandown and clamping elements shown in Figure 7.15. Where setups were not completely eliminated, the routine was to re-video the improved setup when the team felt that all current ideas had been implemented. This provides a training aid in the new standard method, and helps in the preparation of a 'factor control sheet'. This is again made out by the team, and identifies the critical factors necessary to preserve the integrity

Analysis guide: cleandown
Are we cleaning down the appropriate areas as required to setup? Is it a real setup need or could it be done at shift end?

Can any of the necessary cleandown be performed safely before the machine is stopped for setup?

Can any awkward corners or pockets be eliminated to prevent them harbouring contamination?

Can we better protect areas that need to be kept clear of swarf/dust/oil, etc.?
- simple covers or enclosures
- deflector plates
- 'T' slot covers
- plastic caps

Analysis guide: clamp and unclamp
Are we using the minimum number of clamping points to get the job done safely and produce a quality component?

Are threads (nuts, bolts, screws) very much in evidence and can they be replaced with simple
- slide clamps
- cam clamps
- toggle clamps
- taperlock clamps?

Where threads have to be used, are they of a standard size requiring only one drive tool?

Are we using the best 'driving' tool for clamps?
- speed wrenches
- torque wrenches
- 'T' handles
- sockets/od spanners/ring spanners

Figure 7.15 Analysis guides for cleandown and clamp/unclamp (Source: Cummins Engine, Daventry)

of each activity in the setup. The control sheet identifies the limits (for example, 30–35 psi for a hydraulic clamping system, where system pressure is a critical factor) which must be checked at a specified frequency. It also identifies the corrective actions which must be taken if the specifications cannot be met. The concept of factor control is very much in line with Kondo's views [10] about making clear the *aims* of the job, referred to in Chapter 1.

■ Conclusion

Setup reduction is one of the most fundamental improvements on which many others depend. Much has been written about it, and there are now many documented ideas for achieving it. Shingo's excellent book already referred to [6] is a good source for more detail. The application of numerous small innovations over all processes in the factory add up to a major advance in competitiveness. Many companies have convinced themselves of the power of JIT/TQ as a result of their own experience. But how this was achieved and what happened afterwards are key questions. Setup reduction is part of an ongoing quest for total flexibility: zero setup times are a key step towards achieving that wider goal. How it was achieved is important too, because it is an opportunity to involve shop-floor experts in solving problems which affect the work they do. While industrial engineers can no doubt improve setups themselves, their talents are better used for broader technical issues. The detailed improvements necessary for success can be – and have been proven to be – readily attainable by shop-floor experts themselves, given technical support and encouragement. Once results begin to flow, they must be used to improve competitiveness. A halving of setup time should be matched by a halving of batch sizes. Whereas Cummins used to have batch sizes of 2 weeks' worth of blocks on the production line, it is not unusual to see blocks of different types following one after the other. The improved flexibility can be used to reduce costs or to increase product range at the same cost or both. Such flexibility is becoming mandatory.

■ References

1. 'Flexibility as managers see it', N. Slack, in M. Warner, W. Wobbe, and P. Brodner (eds) *New Technology and Manufacturing Management*, Wiley, Chichester, 1990.
2. *The Just-in-Time Breakthrough*, Ed Hay, Wiley, New York, 1988.
3. *The Principles of Production Control*, J. Burbidge, McDonald & Evans, Plymouth, 1978, p. 175.
4. 'Setup reduction: Making JIT work', D. L. Lee, in C. A. Voss (ed.) *Just-in-Time Manufacture*, IFS, Bedford, 1987.

5. Ed Hay, *ibid.*, p. 56.
6. *A Revolution in Manufacturing: The SMED System*, Shigeo Shingo, Productivity Press: Cambridge, MA, 1985.
7. 'Reducing setup times makes your company flexible and more competitive', H. Yamashina (unpublished).
8. 'The implementation of JIT techniques and its impact on jmh Bostrom Europe', C. Howell and D. Lorraine, *The Challenge of JIT for Small Businesses, IFS Conference, June, 1988.*
9. D. L. Lee, *ibid.*, p. 82.
10. *Human Motivation*, Y. Kondo, 3A Corp., Tokyo, 1989, p. 55.

8 The Crucial Task of Improving Maintenance

It is impossible to present JIT/TQ concepts for maintenance without referring to some of the ideas and practices which we have developed in the past, and which form an essential part of an integrated maintenance strategy. Western experience in this key area has been somewhat chequered. In some industries such as aerospace and nuclear power, maintenance has always been high on the agenda and strongly managed. Many excellent concepts such as preventive maintenance and terotechnology have Western origins. But traditional attitudes across a range of companies are typified by statements like 'it is my job to operate the machine: it is someone else's job to fix it if it goes wrong.' Barriers between production and maintenance personnel shown up by this remark have been matched by barriers between trades themselves. A breakdown is notified to the maintenance department by means of a request to the maintenance pen. First to be allocated to the job is an electrician, who goes over to the machine, and decides that a pipefitter must first disconnect the hydraulics. So it is back to the pen to find a pipefitter, and so on.... The removal of the hydraulics would have been well within the electrician's capability, but restrictive practices between maintenance trades do not allow the electrician to do this work. Such practices are reinforced by different maintenance trades belonging to different trade unions in the United Kingdom. They are also reinforced by the lack of any integrating body at national level like the Japan Institute for Plant Maintenance. One of the sad results has been a traditional lack of further development training for skilled maintenance craftsmen once their apprenticeship has been completed [1]. This often results in undue reliance on maintenance contracts with suppliers of original equipment and an erosion of in-house skills. Loss of in-house experience in maintenance, and of ownership of maintenance problems, has a devastating effect over time. It adds up to subcontracting a core part of the business. Compare two approaches to maintenance management:

1. 'Best in class': maintenance carried out in-house, with an excellent, low-cost, speedy service. High level of training for maintenance and

production personnel carried out. Effective policy for carriage of maintenance spares in place.

2. 'Average' performance: poor level of in-house services. Many external maintenance services purchased, so high external maintenance costs. Blurred responsibilities for who does what. Production operators not involved with maintenance activities. Low level of maintenance training. No coherent policy for carriage of maintenance spares.

Poor maintenance practices have been quoted by multinationals as a major reason for relatively poor manufacturing performance by their UK subsidiaries [2].

A British government report [3] implied that the total loss to UK industry of ineffective and badly organized maintenance was several billion pounds. The coordination of several disciplines was urged in the report, and 'terotechnology' was born. The term was defined as 'a combination of management, financial, engineering and other practices applied to physical assets in pursuit of economic life cycle costs' [4]. It is a multi-disciplinary approach to optimizing the life cycle costs of plant and buildings. Life cycle costs include the specification and design for reliability and maintainability, installation, commissioning, maintenance, and replacement. New ideas like condition-based maintenance [5] were swept up and included in the terotechnology philosophy. In spite of a national terotechnology centre and use in many large organizations, terotechnology was never widely adopted by UK industry. Although a broad-based concept, it did not become a 'total' company philosophy. So although it produced some excellent publications and increased awareness, another Department of Industry (as the DTI then was) campaign did not last.

Faced with such difficulties, it is perhaps not surprising that surveys have shown that maintenance has been an area of weak JIT implementation activity in the United Kingdom [6,7]. Some of the problems which can be experienced are illustrated by an electrical company based near London which embarked on the introduction of JIT 2 years ago. Production personnel were reorganized into manufacturing cells led by 'manufacturing technicians', whose duties were supposed to include machine setting and maintenance. However, maintenance tradesmen were left in a central engineering group, and were expected to look after breakdowns. While the cells were successful in reducing WIP, lead times, and so on, machine downtime became an increasingly serious problem. Several issues came to a head as follows:

■ Machine maintenance was falling between two stools: production and engineering. It was becoming less and less clear as to who was responsible for what.

■ The manufacturing technicians had been selected from production personnel who were inexperienced in maintenance matters in order to avoid confronting the industrial relations difficulties of bringing the maintenance tradesmen into such positions.

■ To compound this, the manufacturing technicians were not given adequate development training, particularly in maintenance matters.

The engineering group sued for peace. A new maintenance strategy was prepared which recommended that maintenance would be decentralized to production, and that a planned preventive maintenance (PPM) programme should be introduced. However, at this late stage, it is going to take even more time and effort to overcome the bad habits which have been made worse by the way in which the cells and engineering were restructured when JIT was introduced. These difficulties will be compounded by trying to introduce PPM when breakdowns are the major barrier to further progress, and unfavourable attitudes persist.

Although maintenance may be one of the most difficult of the JIT1 techniques to implement, it cannot be fudged or put off. New ideas are needed, and new practices sought. There is evidence that the tide is turning, and that companies are being successful in transforming attitudes and in pulling down traditional barriers. But progress comes from excellent management over time.

■ Definitions and maintenance systems

Before addressing some of the human aspects of maintenance, it is appropriate to review some of the major systems for maintenance which have been developed over the years, and to show how they can be fitted together into an overall strategy.

1. **Run to breakdown (RTB):** The equipment is run to breakdown, and maintenance action remedies the problem(s) after the equipment has ceased to function. In a production environment, RTB assumes that spare parts are available, and that maintenance action does not result in unacceptably lengthy interruptions to production flow.

2. **Preventive maintenance (PM):** This aims to maintain machines in satisfactory working condition through preventing breakdowns by means of a system of overhaul, inspection, lubrication, calibration, etc. Planned preventive maintenance (PPM) produces schedules for maintenance elements which must be carried out at predetermined intervals, and is particularly relevant for items which have predictable breakdown characteristics. A company can often get into a vicious cycle because breakdowns are given priority over PPM, so PM work does not get done, so there are more breakdowns'....

3. **Condition-based maintenance (CBM):** Here, maintenance is only carried out when the machine condition requires it. So CBM is valuable when spare parts are expensive, and where production capacity is limited and

costly. Machine condition can be predicted by investigating major characteristics which predict deterioration of the condition of an item. Examples of such monitors are vibration, temperature, and wear debris. Figure 8.1 gives examples of the application of CBM to a variety of problem situations. Statistical process control (SPC) is specially valuable because it can be used as a monitor of the effectiveness of the maintenance process as well as the manufacturing process. Once the characteristics have been identified, an alarm level must be set at which corrective action has to be taken. (SPC is not of course a substitute for the use of statistical methods for monitoring equipment condition through CBM methods.)

Examples of these three approaches to maintenance are shown in Figure 8.2. Car light bulbs are normally only replaced when they fail. A diligent motorist keeps spares handy, and the best-designed cars have an internal warning light to indicate failure has occurred. So it is possible to identify and to repair some types of breakdowns immediately. But it is not a good idea to take such risks with the engine oil, so PM (servicing at set intervals) is used to replace the oil by including it in a regular service schedule. Finally a tyre only needs to be replaced as a result of wear when the tread falls below 1.6 mm, so tyre condition is monitored to avoid unnecessary and expensive replacement. Over time, it should be possible to reduce overall maintenance costs by increasing CBM at the expense of RTB and PM (Figure 8.3).

Both PM and CBM require the support of a suitable computerized database system to keep maintenance records and to plan jobs for each machine [8]. CBM requires the additional facility of analysing recorded data against

1. Vibration of bearings
    - quality and condition of a machine tool can be measured by vibration characteristics
    - vibrations are measured near bearing positions and analysed by a computer program

2. Oil sample analysis
    - instead of replacing oil in presses every 2,000 operating hours, samples are analysed regularly
    - oil is tested chemically, spectrographically, and for particle contamination; an additional benefit is that oil impurities due to impending part failures can be detected

3. Thickness of chain elements
    - assembly conveyors were replaced in sections over time
    - now, thickness of chain elements is monitored and the elements replaced only as necessary

4. Temperature of electric motors
    - constant load and operation leads to constant temperature; regular monitoring of the temperature leads to predictions about condition

5. Machined part quality
    - dimensions of output parts can be an excellent indicator of machine condition
    - SPC linked to CBM is a powerful new maintenance method

Figure 8.1 Examples of CBM applications

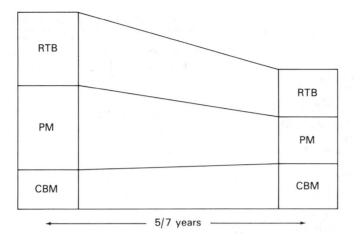

Figure 8.2 Reduction of overall maintenance costs over time

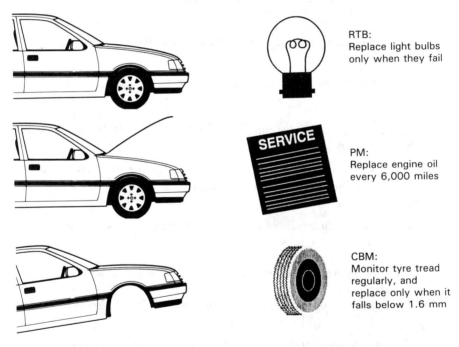

Figure 8.3 Examples of three approaches to maintenance

set alarm levels. Table 8.1 lists the features of some proprietary maintenance software packages.

It is not necessarily the best policy to aim to replace breakdown and preventive maintenance completely by CBM. So *reliability-centred maintenance (RCM)* has been developed as an umbrella philosophy to develop sensitivity

Table 8.1 Comparison of proprietary maintenance software packages

Product: Source: Mainframe/PC:	Teroman SD Scicon M/F	Mainsaver Mercia PC	MCS II CIT PC	Maintenance management Stoltz M/F	ARMS Sulcs M/F
Financial reporting	X	X	X	X	X
Maintenance history	X	X	X	X	X
Preventive maintenance planning	X	X	X	X	X
Predictive maintenance planning	X	X			X
Asset register	X	X	X		
Cost management budgets	X	X	X		
Safety inspections	X				
Material requisitions	X		X	X	
Inventory control	X	X	X	X	
Purchasing	X	X	X		

to the actual maintenance requirements of each item of equipment in its operating context. RCM sets out to integrate:

■ safety, operating economics, and maintenance costs

with

■ selection of the maintenance method (RTB, PM, or CBM) which is most appropriate in a given situation.

The starting point for RCM is the operating context for each item, and the consequence of failure of that item. Failure consequences are classified into four areas:

1. Hidden failure consequences which may increase the risk of subsequent multiple failures.
2. Safety consequences.
3. Operational consequences involving knock-on losses in addition to the direct cost of the repair.
4. Non-operational consequences whose only impact is the direct cost of the repair.

RCM forces a structured evaluation of these consequences in descending order of importance for all failures. When evaluating failure consequences, all of the functions of the item must be considered.

The most likely failure mode is the one taken for evaluation purposes. If the loss of function of the item has no significant consequences, then the usual decision is not to carry out PM or CBM. PM is mandatory for hidden failures and for safety consequences. If the risk of failure cannot be brought down to reasonable levels, then the item must be redesigned. The four steps involved

| ITEM BOERINGER | | | No. BT62L | Compiled by B. McS | Date 24-2-90 | Page 4 |
| COMPONENT BEARING | | | Ref. | Reviewed by | Date | of 28 |

FUNCTION		FUNCTIONAL FAILURE		FAILURE MODE	TASK	INTERVAL	BY
1	TO SUPPORT, CONTAIN & PROVIDE FREE RUNNING FOR CUTTER	A	BEARING NOT FREE RUNNING	1 HEAT BUILD-UP	CONDITION MONITORING		
				2 BEARING DAMAGE	''		
				3 DIRT IN BEARING	''		
				4 WEAR OF BEARING	''		
				5 OVER PACKED WITH GREASE	''		
				6 INCORRECT FITTING	''		
				7 INCORRECT BEARING MANUFACTURE	''		
				8 POOR MAINTENANCE	''		
				9 BROKEN GEAR ON O/D	INSPECT GEAR TEETH	6 MOS	MAINT.
2	DIAMETER SETTING OF THE GENERATED PATH	A	FAILS TO HOLD POSITION	1 LOCK COLLET SLIPS	INSPECT LOCK COLLET	6 MOS	MAINT.
				2 LOCK COLLET BROKEN		6 MOS	''
				3 BROKEN CLAMP SCREW	INSPECT CLAMP SCREWS	TCF	OP.
		B	FAILS TO LOCK	1 LOCK COLLET BROKEN	INSPECT LOCK COLLET	6 MOS	MAINT.
				2 BROKEN CLAMP SCREW	INSPECT CLAMP SCREWS	''	''
				3 PINION SHAFT DAMAGED	INSPECT SHAFT	''	''

Figure 8.4 RCM failure mode analysis and task allocation

171

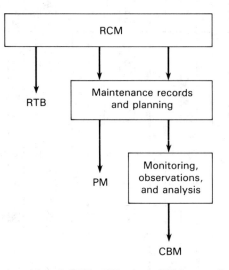

Figure 8.5 Relationship of RTB, PM, and CBM to reliability centred maintenance (RCM)

in applying RCM are the following:

1. Deciding what equipment is significant from the maintenance viewpoint.
2. Analysing and recording the functions, functional failures, failure modes, and failure effects of each significant item.
3. Evaluating the consequences of each functional failure and failure mode.
4. Deciding which preventive tasks are applicable. If none are, what default actions should be taken?

An example is given in Figure 8.4. RCM is essentially an enhancement of maintenance systems in that it provides a logical set of procedures for preparing or reviewing the content of maintenance schedules so that decisions reflect the operating context of each item. Figure 8.5 shows how it is possible for RTB to be an outcome in the same way that, via a maintenance database, PM or CBM could also be outcomes.

■ Breaking down barriers

The preceding section has examined how we can take a new look at the operation of maintenance systems, and come up with an improved overall philosophy. However good the systems are, they will not work without the enthusiasm and drive of the people concerned – especially of maintenance and production personnel. The key point to recognize is that it is production personnel who must take responsibility for their equipment: without their cooperation, maintenance systems cannot work. It is production operators who are first confronted by machine problems, and who can help the maintenance effort in several vital ways as follows:

■ Avoid misoperation of the equipment.

■ Detect machine problems before they become too serious by being alert to abnormal noise, smell, oil leaks, vibration, swarf buildup behind guard plates, and so on. In this way, a number of impending breakdowns can be avoided. With further training, operators can carry out basic repairs (including minor controls on electrical equipment such as replacing solenoid valves).

■ Carry out routine preventive maintenance tasks such as lubrication, cleaning (also a form of inspection), and adjustments.

■ Carry out routine condition-monitoring tasks like data collection.

Such changes do not take place at the expense of maintenance jobs. The challenge is to do things together at a higher standard than was previously possible. Schonberger [9] records that, after they had taken over routine lubrication, operators at Harley Davidson found that some machine lubrication points had never been oiled or greased before! And that is not to say that maintenance personnel had previously been negligent. The role of maintenance personnel is gradually upgraded too by the following:

■ Higher level maintenance, such as long-term maintenance, stripdowns, and refurbishment.

■ Training production operators to carry out more and more routine maintenance.

■ Completing condition-monitoring analysis and acting on results.

■ Closer involvement with purchasing new plant to improve the handover of information from vendors.

■ Developing new machines and processes so that they operate better for the particular company products.

■ Preparing for fast response to breakdowns and process problems.

So maintenance is another area which demands the growth of our people under JIT/TQ. The roles of operator and maintenance personnel must interface in a new and cooperative relationship which is aimed at the common enemy: unplanned disruptions due to equipment failures. Figure 8.6 explains how the new roles should interface with each other. If difficulties with operating a machine are classified as 'maintenance problems', and maintenance personnel regard such problems as caused by lack of care and attention by the operator, there will be little progress. An important management discipline is not to allow complaints either way. Operators are allowed to state problem points and to ask maintenance to improve those points. Progress by maintenance personnel on the other hand should include measuring the number of such problem points raised by operators, so that over time there are fewer points raised [10]. The roles here are similar to a doctor–patient relationship.

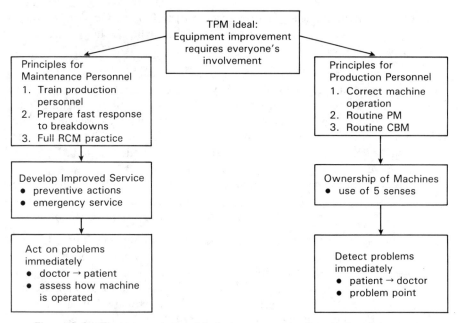

Figure 8.6 The new relationship between production and maintenance

By accepting ownership of the machines they use, operators must use their five senses to identify problems and to report those problems in a clear and accurate way to the maintenance 'doctor'. The doctor must be prepared and capable of dealing with emergencies as well as giving patients instructions for their future well-being. The doctor's instructions must be followed if the patient's health is to improve! So it is with maintenance, where operators must be willing to learn from their maintenance colleagues about improved machine handling. Yuasa Battery in the United Kingdom actually used doctor/patient cards to formalize this relationship [11]. A further example of focusing on the key point is Ohno's concept of asking 'WHY?' five times:

Problem: digital controller on NC machine tool fails.
1. Why? Defective printed circuit board.
   2. Why? It became overheated.
      3. Why? There was an inadequate air supply.
         4. Why? There was a lack of air pressure.
            5. Why? The filter was blocked up.

The key point has been found by persistent questioning, and the solution (cleaning the filter every month) will prevent its recurrence. By attacking the problem, not the person or department, we are more likely to find such a lasting solution.

In order to fulfil their part of the new, integrated relationship, new and enhanced skills are needed by both operators and maintenance personnel. This implies an important training need. Nakajima [12] proposes five skills of particular value in the workplace, to which a sixth (improvement) has been added here:

1. **Attention:** The ability to concentrate and to discover deviations.

2. **Judgement:** The ability to think logically and to make sound decisions.

3. **Corrective action/restoration:** The ability to restore normal conditions in the minimum time with minimum losses.

4. **Prevention:** The ability to prevent problems from arising through knowledge of correct operation.

5. **Prediction:** The ability to predict that problems are about to happen by spotting deviations.

6. **Improvement:** The ability to propose ideas to eliminate the problem point so that problems do not recur.

Skill levels are improved by training and practice in the right way. Constant repetition leads to error-free and consistent performance. Auditing skills periodically helps to ensure that standards do not slip, so operator requalification is not demeaning but simply good practice. As referred to in Chapter 2, Murata and Harrison [13] propose three levels of quality of work:

1. **Repair level:** People carry out instructions, but cannot foresee the future. They simply react to problems.

2. **Prevention level:** People can foresee the future by predicting problems, and take corrective action.

3. **Improvement level:** People can foresee the future by predicting problems. They not only take corrective action but also propose improvements to prevent recurrence.

As an example, the screws on a jig become loose. Each week it jams up and is passed to maintenance to be fixed. The 'repair level' maintenance engineer simply repairs it and hands it back to production. The 'prevention level' maintenance engineer spots the weekly pattern to the problem, and tightens the screws in advance of their loosening. The 'improvement level' maintenance engineer recognizes that there is a design problem here, and redesigns the jig so that the problem cannot recur. Any company has people at all three levels, and the challenge is to create more and more improvement level personnel through encouragement, training, and practice.

■ Total productive maintenance (TPM)

So far, we have focused on the systems and people involvement necessary to develop a reliability-centred maintenance programme with increasingly close integration of production and maintenance personnel. This is the essential foundation for TPM. Unless the basic PM disciplines and operator/maintenance cooperation are in place, it would be fruitless to attempt to introduce a full TPM programme. TPM is an evolutionary approach to excellence in maintenance, and feeds off many basic people preparation processes such as the housekeeping and safety disciplines discussed in Chapter 5. There is also a strong link, and many analogies, between TPM and TQ. As a result, TPM is incapable of independent existence!

So TPM is rooted in the good maintenance and other practices discussed so far. There is accordingly some repetition of what we have already said about the way in which TPM models are presented. But two key additions are as follows:

1. Minimizing the total life-cycle cost of ownership, including purchase cost, maintenance cost, and the cost of deterioration. In this sense, TPM has some similarities to terotechnology, although the scope is narrower because TPM is practised only by the equipment user. One report [14] indicates that Japanese companies spent more on improvement than their Western counterparts, who allocated most of their capital to new capacity and replacement machines.
2. As a result, TPM brings the maintenance issue on to the total company agenda, and demands the involvement of everyone in one role or another. This could, for example, make the reduction of overall maintenance costs over time, shown in Figure 8.2, a formal company objective.

TPM was defined by the Japan Institute for Plant Maintenance in 1971 in terms of five goals:

1. Maximize equipment effectiveness.
2. Develop a system of productive maintenance for the life of the equipment.
3. Involve all departments that plan, design, use, or maintain equipment in implementing TPM.
4. Actively involve all employees – from top management to shop-floor workers.
5. Promote TPM through motivation management: autonomous small-group improvement activities.

Willmott [15] refers to the fundamental changes in attitude that must take place:

■ If a process is not working well, we will not only fix it, we will determine why it was not working well in the first place and correct those fundamental causes.
■ If the process is working, can it be improved?

The starting point for changes in attitude must be within the top team. By recognizing the key role of total life-cycle cost of ownership in the company, several important decisions flow [16]. If everyone can be brought to recognize this key role, and their individual contribution, then we are well on the way to realizing the need to plan for achieving TPM and for the education which is needed to support it.

■ The five goals of TPM development

The Japan Institute of Plant Maintenance lists five interdependent goals which represent the minimum for TPM development as follows.

1. Improve equipment effectiveness

Equipment effectiveness is limited by six major sources of loss:

1. **Stop losses – breakdown losses:** These are caused by a combination of sporadic and chronic losses, a reference to the Juran Trilogy [17]. It is the sporadic losses, for example facility breakdowns, which are the obvious deviations and which receive immediate attention by restoring normal performance. However, it is the chronic losses (caused for example by machine deterioration) which typically go unchallenged and which are more difficult to identify. Correcting them requires innovation.

2. **Stop losses – setup and adjustment losses:** These result from equipment downtime between the last good piece from the preceding batch and the first good piece from the succeeding batch, as discussed in Chapter 7.

3. **Speed losses – idling and minor stoppage losses:** These are caused by many small incidents which may not in themselves seem important, such as temporary conveyor jams, or a sensor activates and shuts down machinery. They are usually easily cleared, and so have not been regarded as serious before. But their eradication is mandatory before automation can proceed.

4. **Speed losses – reduced speed losses:** These are the difference between the actual and designed running speed. A machine may have been deliberately derated because of the need for synchronization. But increasing the speed of bottleneck operations may reveal new defects which can be remedied and so lead to faster operation.

5. **Defect losses – quality defects and rework:** Losses which have been caused by machine problems can again be analysed as sporadic and chronic losses. Again, it is the sporadic losses which are most obvious and which

can be attributed to specific process problems. Chronic losses are more difficult, and require detailed studies over time to be identified and dealt with.

6. **Defect losses – start up losses:** These occur during the period from start-up to stable production. Again, such losses are often dismissed as normal, so no effort is made to eradicate them.

Pilot projects can be targeted at selected types of equipment loss on known problem machines. Small-group improvement activities should focus on the improvements needed to eliminate chronic losses as well as the more obvious causes of sporadic losses.

2. Autonomous maintenance

This goal aims to build on operator responsibility for maintenance. Seven steps are defined in order for it to be achieved:

1. Initial cleaning: the routines discussed in Chapter 5 as cleaning and cleanliness (*seiso* and *seiketsu*).
2. Take measures against sources of dirt and make cleaning easier to perform: for example, fitting swarf guards which prevent inaccessible machine areas from becoming contaminated again after step 1 has been completed.
3. Formulate cleanup and maintenance standards: autonomous standards (set by the operators themselves) promote commitment. Frequencies for cleanup, lubrication, checking bolt tightness, and so on should be set, for example per shift, per week, and per month.
4. Inspection training: requires that operators are trained in the various aspects of their equipment (hydraulics, pneumatics, electrical systems, etc.). This is a detailed and extensive investment over time, and lies at the heart of the development of autonomous maintenance.
5. Autonomous inspection: the implementation of general inspection check sheets so that specific signs of equipment deterioration are checked on a set-frequency basis.
6. Workplace standards: implementation of standards for tidiness which we discussed in Chapter 5 (*seiri* and *seiton*). This extends to everything in the operator's control, including WIP, jigs and tools, gauges, and maintenance equipment.
7. Improvement: setting out continuously to improve equipment operation and performance.

The seven steps form a sequence: thus, step 1 must be mastered before going on to step 2. But the aim over time is for more and more operators to achieve step 7.

3. Planned maintenance

In parallel with the development of autonomous maintenance by the operator, PM and CBM must be developed from the perspective of the maintenance specialists. The role of the maintenance specialists must be integrated with the autonomous maintenance role of the production operators. This includes the preparation of equipment and maintenance standards and their implementation. It also comprises PM planning and execution, including major maintenance. Other tasks of the maintenance specialists are PM record keeping, and the control of spare parts.

4. Maintenance skills training

This goal reinforces step 4 (inspection training) under autonomous maintenance above. Skills training is aimed at developing technical skills by means of a formal programme of in-house theoretical and practical training for both operators and maintenance personnel.

5. Early equipment management

This goal is directed at avoiding maintenance altogether by 'maintenance prevention' (MP) during the equipment design, manufacture, installation, and commissioning stages. MP is well known in the aerospace industry, where life-cycle cost is an important purchasing consideration. But there is still plenty of scope for improvement in its application to machine tools. MP applies to existing equipment, too. Changes can be made which are aimed at eliminating the need for maintenance.

These five goals of TPM are described in detail in the publication *TPM Development Programme* by the Japan Institute of Plant Maintenance [18].

■ Performance measures

Monitoring maintenance costs against budget has never been a sufficient way to measure maintenance effectiveness, and yet has been the only management information traditionally available. In order to bring maintenance into the total company arena, we will be interested in measures of performance which tell us about such aspects as the following:

■   how quickly breakdowns are being fixed;
■   whether PM is being carried out to plan;

1. Service factor $\quad = \dfrac{\text{time up}}{\text{total time}}$

2. (i) Availability $\quad = \dfrac{\text{operating time}}{\text{scheduled running time}}$

   (ii) Performance efficiency $= \dfrac{\text{operating time} - \text{speed loss}}{\text{operating time}}$
   (speed losses) = yield

   $\qquad\qquad\qquad\quad = \dfrac{\text{actual production/hour}}{\text{cyclic capacity}}$

   (iii) Quality rate $\quad = \dfrac{\text{no. processed} - \text{no. defective}}{\text{no. processed}}$
   (defect losses)
   SPC: use of

   Overall equipment
   effectiveness $\qquad = $ (i) × (ii) × (iii) [17]

3. Breakdowns
   - response time: average time from notification to start of job
   - MTTR (mean time to repair): average time taken to fix breakdowns

4. MTBF (mean time between failure)
   Set for a group of machines,

   $$\text{MTBF} = \dfrac{\text{no. of machines}}{\text{failures}} \times \text{period}$$

   e.g. for a group of ten compressors, two failures occurred in a 4-week period: MTBF = 20 weeks

   The result can be used to determine PM frequency (say 16 weeks) and to highlight machines requiring improvement action (those with low MTBFs)

Figure 8.7 Maintenance performance measures

- trends in equipment reliability;
- total life-cycle costs of ownership.

Software packages provide much useful information, such as the following:

- backlog jobs (jobs not yet planned);
- overdue jobs (jobs behind schedule);
- equipment reliability reports;
- history reports by machine or by job.

History reports can also be produced by interrogating NC machine tool control systems. Figure 8.7 shows a summary of possible TPM performance measures. Figure 8.8 relates the measures of performance for equipment effectiveness (grouped together in section 2 of Figure 8.7) to the six major sources of loss.

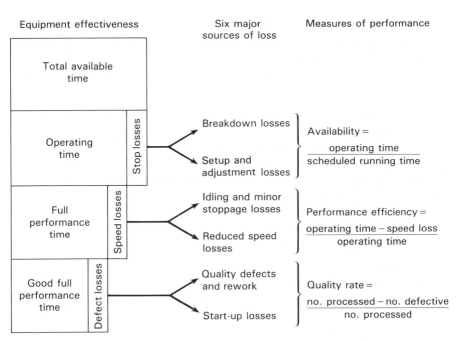

Figure 8.8 Measures of performance related to equipment effectiveness

■ Conclusion

TPM is one of the most difficult of the JIT/TQ techniques to understand and to implement. The starting point is often in such poor shape that there are severe demarcation problems, very low PM achievement (for example, 85% of PM jobs behind schedule), and as a result poor up time (for example, 55% up time related to total time). Such difficulties are typically underpinned by management's incomprehension of the damage caused by traditional pressures for high labour and machine utilization. This leads to poor sensitivity to the need to balance running time and maintenance time. So maintenance windows are compromised, organization for maintenance is poor, and there is lack of a maintenance strategy. Poor equipment reliability is often a major cause of variability for the entire production system. Some of the key questions to be answered are the following:

■ Should we aim to undercapacity-schedule, so that there is normally 1 hour per shift available to maintenance personnel for PM? (Production operators can be carrying out improvement activities during this time.)

■ What sort of shift patterns should we work? For example, two shifts by production personnel and three shifts by maintenance means that PM can be carried out on the nightshift.

■ Should maintenance personnel be decentralized to manufacturing teams under an area foreman (responsible for both production and maintenance)? Decentralized maintenance has the attractions of improving coordination with production, and bringing priority setting under one person.

Following the principles of total quality leads us inevitably to the conclusion that machine maintenance should be owned by production personnel, and that maintenance personnel have an integrated responsibility for equipment effectiveness. In the past, equipment was the domain of plant engineering, processes the domain of manufacturing engineering, the product that of product engineering, and quality that of inspection. We can no longer afford the luxuries such specialization brings!

In this chapter, we have looked at developing excellence in maintenance as a two-stage process:

1. Developing good maintenance practice by breaking down barriers and by implementing integrated maintenance systems.
2. Building on this foundation to develop total productive maintenance.

Developing such excellence is a long-term programme of reform. It must not be fudged or put off. It must form part of the basic plans for introducing JIT/TQ.

■ References

1. 'JIT and its implications for maintenance', C. Spratling, in J. Mortimer (ed.) *JIT Manufacturing – An Executive Briefing*, IFS, Bedford, 1987.
2. For example, a joint management/trade union comparison of productivity at Ford's Halewood and Genk plants in 1977, widely reported in the press at the time.
3. *Report on Maintenance Engineering*, Dept of Industry, HMSO: London, 1970.
4. *Terotechnology: An Introduction to the Management of Physical Resources*, Department of Industry Committee for Technology, HMSO: London, 1975.
5. *A Guide to the Condition Monitoring of Machinery*, Dept of Industry, HMSO: London, 1979.
6. 'The application of just-in-time in the UK', C. A. Voss and S. Robinson, *International Journal of Operations & Production Management*, 7, no. 4, 1987, pp. 46–52.
7. 'Implementing just-in-time: A US/UK comparison', T. Billesbach, A. Harrison, and S. Croom-Morgan, *International Journal of Operations & Production Management*, 11, no. 10, 1991.
8. See for example *Production/Operations Management*, R. Wild, Cassell, London, 1990, p. 682.
9. *World Class Manufacture*, R. Schonberger, Free Press, New York, 1986, p. 68.
10. *How to Make Japanese Management Methods Work in the West*, K. Murata and A. Harrison, Gower, Aldershot, 1991, p. 42.
11. K. Murata and A. Harrison, *ibid.*, p. 45.

12. *TPM Development Programme*, H. Nakajima, Productivity Press: Cambridge, MA, 1989, p. 74.
13. K. Murata and A. Harrison, *ibid.*, p. 47.
14. *Competing through Manufacturing*, R. Hayes and S. Wheelwright, Wiley, New York, 1984, p. 357.
15. *Total Productive Maintenance*, P. Willmott, Dept of Trade & Industry, (in press).
16. 'Do it right the first time: Getting started on TPM', E. Turcotte and M. Stickler, *Actionline (AIAG)*, October, 1990.
17. *Juran on Planning for Quality*, J. M. Juran, Free Press, New York, 1988, p. 12.
18. H. Nakajima, *ibid.*, p. 20ff.
19. *TPM in Japan*, Y. Monden, Japan Management Association.

9 | Produce Only as Needed

One of the popular misconceptions about JIT is that it is synonymous with *kanban* [1]. Many articles comparing the relative advantages of JIT, MRP, and OPT loosely refer to 'JIT' when they really refer only to the pull scheduling and/or *kanban* techniques of JIT. Another popular misconception is that pull scheduling creates the benefits in JIT [2]. In reality, true pull scheduling is possible as a result of putting many other JIT techniques into place. Figure 9.1 shows some of the more important influences on pull scheduling, and serves to emphasize some of the factors which will render pull scheduling inoperable unless satisfactory progress has been made on their introduction. While it is possible to see applications of pull scheduling working in some sections of a factory where there is a high level of repeatability and schedule stability, it is more common to see applications which are not working very well. Such disruptions as loss of *kanban* boxes and breakdowns are countered by continued management interference in rescheduling work. While some reductions in work-in-progress may have been made, delivery reliability is still poor. Such difficulties with pull scheduling are typically caused by trying to introduce the technique too early, before supporting techniques have been allowed to progress sufficiently. Voss and Okazaki-Ward [3] reported that *kanban* was not used by a selection of Japanese companies in the United Kingdom because 'it is one of the most difficult of tools to implement', and so was very low down on the implementation list.

Nevertheless, the logic of pull scheduling cannot be dismissed so easily. The ideal of producing at the same rate that customers are using products, extended throughout all factory operations, is an attractive one. It should be possible to replace batch control by rate control. A key point to recognize is that progress must be made in stages, and that we must resist the temptation to rush fences. Edwards [4] proposes a process of 'migration' towards integrated material flow by means of stages. The first is to install pull scheduling links between subassembly and final assembly, followed by pull scheduling links between subassembly and component manufacture supported by MRP

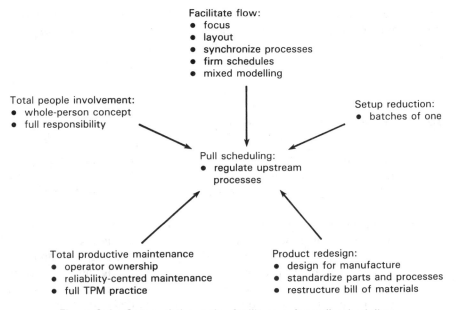

Facilitate flow:
- focus
- layout
- synchronize processes
- firm schedules
- mixed modelling

Total people involvement:
- whole-person concept
- full responsibility

Setup reduction:
- batches of one

Pull scheduling:
- regulate upstream processes

Total productive maintenance
- operator ownership
- reliability-centred maintenance
- full TPM practice

Product redesign:
- design for manufacture
- standardize parts and processes
- restructure bill of materials

Figure 9.1 Some of the major facilitators for pull scheduling

(Material Requirements Planning) raw material scheduling and kitting. Finally, complete integration of MRP with JIT forms a new and superior planning and control system. Toyota envisage a production system where the goal is to connect all external and internal processes with 'invisible conveyor lines', the role performed by *kanban* [5].

Another attractive aspect of the pull scheduling ideal is the concept of the paperless factory. Miller and Vollman [6] refer to a second 'factory' supporting product manufacture. The second factory makes paperwork and processes computer data. Its costs have been going up over time relative to the costs of the manufactured products. Its work is non-value added, and includes the transactions necessary to plan, purchase, expedite, receive, inspect, and ship parts and products. The opportunity under JIT is to challenge hidden factory costs and eliminate the transactions which make them necessary. For example, *kanban* offers a paperless method for material control, and bar coding greatly simplifies notification of material movements.

So pull scheduling goes to the heart of the manufacturing planning and control system. It offers the potential to simplify what we already have. And it offers the potential to meet customer demand with minimum inventories and maximum responsiveness. Yet to begin with, purveyors of MRP systems saw this potential as a threat, and claimed that MRP was fundamentally more important than JIT. This was countered by consultants who claimed that JIT is new and that you do not need a computer any more, or that JIT is the key to your survival! As Karmarkar [7] pointed out, this debate needs clarity, and then it needs to end. What is important is to develop sensitivity to which tools and techniques help to make the business more competitive and customer oriented. This is a learning process for the business in which there is today a greater variety of choices. The trick is to make the right ones!

■ Push v. pull scheduling

Poor inventory timing (parts arrive too early or too late) causes waste in operations management – higher costs, longer lead times, and poor customer service [8]. Inventory timing is governed by two principal schools of thought:

1. **Push systems:** Parts are completed as scheduled, and sent to the next work station. The supplier pushes out parts without considering whether the customer can actually use them yet. Coupling between supplier and customer is provided by the production control system. Usage and production rates are different anyway – subject to numerous sources and causes of variability. Supplier and customer are often separated and do not talk to each other. Idle inventory often characterizes push scheduling. But push scheduling is often the only way to schedule, for example bottleneck operations.

2. **Pull system:** Parts are drawn or sent for by customers as needed. If the customer has problems, then the supplier must respond to those problems. So the system becomes sensitive to variability. If the supplier has problems, then the customer is forced to stop work, so the sources and causes of variability become visible and must be controlled. Material movements become tuned to the actual usage rate, not the scheduled usage rate. Variability is catered for up to a point by holding a limited amount of pipeline inventory. As this pipeline inventory reduces, so every usage by the customer becomes a signal for action by the supplier to produce more [9]. A characteristic of pull scheduling systems is that inventory is live, and not kept in pallets or stores.

Kanban is the Japanese for card or signal. It is the 'invisible conveyor' referred to above, and is the means by which a customer (succeeding operation) instructs a supplier (preceding operation) to send more parts. There are numerous variants of *kanban*, and some of the more popular are as follows:

■ *Kanban* **cards:** Cards or tokens are exchanged between user and maker sections to indicate that more parts are needed. Cards or tokens are marked with the part number, user and maker locations, and quantity per container. The tokens can be colour coded to indicate relative priority – red for top, amber for moderate, and green for normal. A given part number is used in the sequence green–amber–red, and made in the sequence red–amber–green. The system is referred to as a 'traffic light system', and the loading board from the making section is illustrated in Figure 9.2.

- **Toyota two-card system:** This variant is a little more complicated, but provides tight control – not only over production, but also over movement of parts. The move card allows the movement of a standard container of parts from one work centre to another. The production card allows the production of a standard container of parts to replace those removed [10].

- **Container-as-*kanban*:** A simpler method is to return the empty container back to the supplying operation as a signal for more to be made. The container must be clearly marked with the relevant number, or be uniquely shaped or colour coded in some way. The production *kanban* from the Toyota two-card system is eliminated in this variant.

- **Verbal and 'golf ball':** The user signals that more is needed by telling the maker by telephone, by electronic message, or simply by shouting 'send me some more!' A variant is to roll colour-coded balls (colour refers to part number) down a tube.

- **Coloured squares:** Larger subassemblies are controlled by means of areas marked out by coloured tape (most often yellow) on the floor. In this way, work-in-progress is controlled: once all the squares are full, the making section stops work.

- **Packaging:** Often, a supplier's packaging can be used as the *kanban*. The close relationship between *kanban* and the two-bin system of stock control becomes apparent in this variant. Parts are stored in two boxes by part number. As one part number is used up, the empty box is placed at the back of the rack (nearest the gangway), so that it can be replaced with a

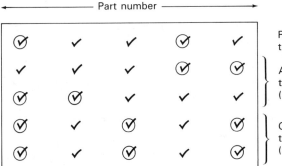

Scheduling rule: clear red tokens first

Figure 9.2 *Kanban* 'traffic light' system loading board

full one on the next 'milk round'. This variant works very well for class C and D items (fixings, etc.), and helps to avoid very large numbers of transactions on the MPC system. The supplier has an overall contract for a group of part numbers and is charged with the responsibility of ensuring that they do not run out.

Kanban is a simple-to-operate, visible control system which offers the opportunity to delegate routine material control transactions to the shop floor. Further, it offers the mechanism for linking all operations together in a synchronized way throughout the factory and ultimately to suppliers as well. The rules by which *kanban* is used are simple but strict. They are listed in Figure 9.3. Pull scheduling is locked into the manufacturing planning and control (MPC) system by starting off with the final assembly schedule (the short-term, day-by-day build sequence). This schedule has been frozen (apart perhaps from a few minor changes) for the next short-term planning period (say, 1 week). Final assembly pulls subassemblies from feeder operations, which in turn pull parts from component manufacture.

This sequence is illustrated in simplified form for a Midlands automotive components manufacturer in Figure 9.4. The kit marshaller selected subassemblies from gravity-feed racks of *kanban* boxes arranged in front of him or her by part number, and passed them on to the final assembly cells on a roller conveyor. As the kit marshaller created empty boxes, so these were used to signal to subassembly lines that more parts were needed. A standard number (40) of parts were used in each *kanban* box wherever possible. (A number divisible by eight facilitates hourly quantities for synchronization purposes.) In turn, boxes were exchanged between subassembly and component manufacture, and thence to suppliers. While the concept of the system was excellent, it was in fact run in a disorganized way as follows:

- It was claimed that the system was very responsive to change, and that the factory assembly schedule could be changed at 1·5 hours' notice with a similar rapid response from the feeder sections. This advantage was used frequently to alter plans at short notice so that the latest round of material shortages could be accommodated. This became self-perpetuating, because

1. Each container must have a *kanban* card, indicating part number and description, user and maker locations, and quantity
2. The parts are always pulled by the succeeding process (the customer or user)
3. No parts are started without a *kanban* card
4. All containers contain exactly their stated number of parts
5. No defective parts may be sent to the succeeding process
6. The maker (supplier section) can only produce enough parts to make up what has been withdrawn
7. The number of *kanbans* should be reduced

Figure 9.3 *Kanban* operation rules

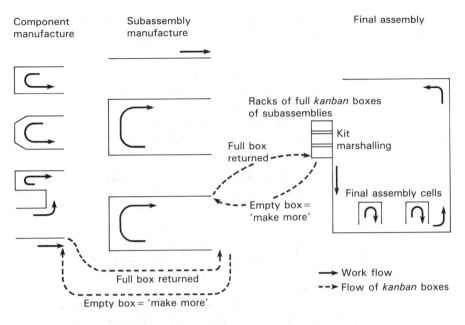

Component manufacture   Subassembly manufacture   Final assembly

Racks of full *kanban* boxes of subassemblies

Full box returned

Kit marshalling

Empty box = 'make more'

Final assembly cells

Full box returned

Empty box = 'make more'

→ Work flow
--→ Flow of *kanban* boxes

Figure 9.4 Flow of parts between stages of manufacture

constant schedule changes meant that material control was haphazard, particularly in respect of bought-out items.

- Weak material control was compounded, and to a large extent caused, by weak master scheduling. In spite of the 'modern' approach to pull scheduling in the factory, master scheduling was still carried out manually in the offices. Inflexibility was made worse by attempts to impose a lengthy 'fixed' scheduling period (8 weeks) on customers.

- Instead of operating sequences of *kanban* boxes on a strict 'first in, first out' (FIFO) scheduling rule, sequences were in fact being constantly changed, again to work round material shortage problems.

So although the company claimed that it was operating *kanban* and pull scheduling, bad habits were perpetuated. Success depends on excellence across a broad front: weakness in any one link reduces the performance of the whole system.

The number of parts in each *kanban* loop is governed by the extent to which the linked processes can cope with variability in the system. If the linked processes are robust and have a large band width (ability to cope with volume and mix changes), then a relatively small number of parts should be possible. Disruptions like breakdowns and absenteeism will poison the system and render it inoperable. The ultimate objective is *kanban* = 0, that is no stock in the system. This ideal is often referred to as the 'bucket brigade'. To begin with, we may be a long way from such a state, and it is necessary to keep buffer stocks relatively high. Buffer stocks will be influenced by:

- the lead time needed to make and deliver a part;
- the setup time needed to change over from one part to another;
- the time needed for quality checks or testing;
- specific delays like heat treatment or anodizing;
- the risk of disruptions like breakdowns and absenteeism.

A formula for determining the number of *kanbans* which play the most important part in a given system is shown in Figure 9.5. But over time the pressure to improve should be relentless. So in reality, calculations of the number of *kanbans* are only a starting point. What matters is improving the process towards *kanban* = 0. This can be addressed by removing *kanban* cards from the system until it fails, and then finding out what was the key point of failure. The key point is then fixed, and the system restabilized. Then, more *kanban* cards are removed... and so on.

One mistake is to go too far too fast. Cummins Engine at Daventry decided to squeeze work-in-progress hard by strictly limiting the number of in-house components – to two parts only. One part would be at the side of the assembly track waiting to be fitted, the other would be in the machining cell being processed. The next part for machining would not be loaded into the cell until the lineside part had been fitted. This gave the foreman ulcers! The slightest problem (notably, the familiar one of facility breakdowns) led to the need urgently to subcontract the part machining. It was decided to back off, and to recognize that some additional buffer stocks were needed until such time that facility problems were under better control. PM was introduced for at least 1 hour per shift. A greater buffer stock was allowed between machining and assembly. Contingency stock was also held in a lockable store, the key of which was held by the most awkward person in the company! Gradually, these stocks have been reduced. But this has been achieved by getting rid of the 'rocks', not by risking the sinking of the ship!

Let y = number of *kanbans*

  D = planned usage rate per day, from the factory assembly schedule
  T_w = movement cycle time (total waiting time)
  T_p = processing time through the supplier work centre
  α = risk/inefficiency factor
  a = number of units per standard container (not more than 10% of D)

Then $y = \dfrac{D(T_w + T_p)(1 + \alpha)}{a}$

Figure 9.5 Formula for calculating number of *kanbans* playing most important part in system (Source: Sugimori *et al.* [11])

■ The role of transportation

As batch sizes reduce, pull scheduling replaces push, so the role of transportation between operations increases. Smaller quantities are delivered more frequently. Surely this is increasing the waste of transport? Well, the materials have to be moved anyway, so whether that is in small or large quantities does not affect the issue. Costs, however, are increased because someone has to move them, so there is a potential increase in the waste of operator movement and thus an incentive to cut down flow distances. Because such routes have to be traversed many more times under *kanban* rules, simple and flexible transportation methods become attractive. Better to use supermarket trolleys than fork lift trucks – *and* the paint on the floor is likely to last a lot longer! Transportation methods which do not involve operators are even more attractive. Gravity-feed methods are often the simplest and cheapest. The principle is to aim for an ideal of use-one/make-one; hence there should be no storage between operations, close coordination on quality issues and priorities, and transportation should be governed by the customer process (hence the Toyota 'move' *kanban*). The processes concerned should work together to reduce the waste of transportation over time.

A traditional means of moving parts between linked operations is power conveyors. But the speed of these can be adjusted to reflect actual demand and manning requirements, and therefore should reflect the required cycle time referred to in Chapter 4. So power conveyors should only transport what is needed by the next process. Operators should be able to stop the line if there are problems. Japanese factories usually have *andon* (meaning 'lantern') boards above assembly lines to indicate running status as follows:

- A green light on the board indicates a normal condition.
- A yellow light alerts the supervisor to a problem (for example, with material shortages or quality).
- A red light is turned on if the problem has not been solved, and the line stops for problem-solving work to fix it.

Andon boards help to broadcast line status and to alert supervisors to problems, thus helping to strengthen the link with operators and to expose problems for action.

Another change from traditional conveyors is to make the work itself independent of line speed. Operators of the 'K' series engine assembly line at Longbridge stop the work plattens at their work station, and return them to the conveyor only when they are satisfied that the work has been correctly completed. The potential weakness of such a system is the erosion of the cycle time concept, and hence that problems may become hidden. The same argument applies to roller conveyor assembly, where the work is performed in a stationary position and passed on to the next work station only when it has been finished.

■ MRP v. JIT

The introduction to this chapter observed how the features of pull scheduling/*kanban* and material requirements planning (MRP) were frequently the source of a contest between vested interests. Papers such as 'MRP, JIT, and OPT: What's best?' [12] appeared, often with dubious conclusions. This section sets out to compare pull scheduling and MRP, and to identify the strengths of each approach in MPC systems. The next section goes on to identify how the approaches can work together, and where other approaches are needed.

MRP is a materials management system which is aimed at minimizing inventories. It converts the master production schedule (the major input to the MPC system, detailing expected volumes by planning period) into detailed, time-phased material plans for all subassemblies and component parts. This is achieved by exploding the MPS by means of the bill of materials (BOM). A simplified version of an MPC system is shown in Figure 9.6. Some of the

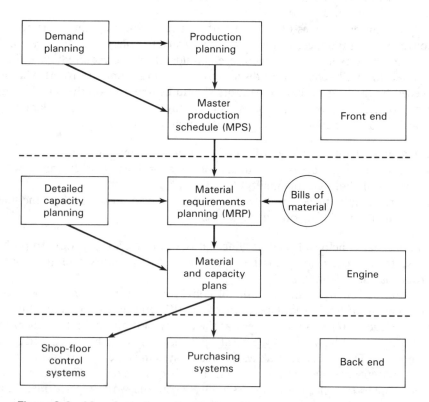

Figure 9.6 Manufacturing planning and control system (simplified)
Source: adapted from Vollman *et al.* [13])

features of MRP are as follows:

- It is driven by the MPS. It aims to ensure that sufficient inventory is available for the factory assembly schedule (the day-by-day short-term, final schedule).
- Although MRP is designed as a pull system (the MPS drives the system), the way we use it is actually as a push system. Inventory is driven through the factory in response to detailed, time-phased plans by part number.
- MRP uses production orders, derived from the MPS, as the unit of control. So scheduled production achievement is a key control monitor.
- MRP is normally operated as a computer-based system, requiring substantial investment in hardware and software and systems support. It has a complex, centralized structure. This can make it difficult to understand final customer requirements when you are one or two levels down the structure. It is highly dependent on data accuracy across a broad front, from BOMs to stock records. Implementation training is just as important as the system itself.
- MRP models a fixed production environment. In order for material to arrive in time at the next operation, a fixed lead time is used, and start dates for production orders for each part number are offset by the lead time for that part number. In reality, lead times can vary according to actual shop loading conditions (and several other factors) which MRP finds very difficult to model accurately. (Capacity requirements planning and routing are the most detailed and difficult of MPC modules to get right.)
- Because of the length of time necessary to update MRP records, MRP batch runs are typically only run weekly (often, monthly!). While some MRP packages permit net change runs on a daily basis, there is a limited number of changes which can be accommodated. So MRP is only responsive to daily or weekly changes.

While MRP is good at materials planning and coordination, it is weak on timing. Material shortages often dominate the MPC system, and expediting and hot lists weaken MRP authority [14].

Pull scheduling/*kanban* is a system of manufacture aimed at producing the number of parts which have been withdrawn by final assembly. The same principle is worked back through subassembly and component manufacture, and hence to suppliers. By means of close links between supplier/customer operations, *kanban* sets out to achieve the same coordination that MRP achieves by working through the BOM structure. Some of the key features of pull scheduling are the following:

- It is driven by the factory assembly schedule, so it is closer to actual day-by-day customer requirements.
- By definition, it is a pull system, and is driven by the process nearest to the market (usually, final assembly). Material requirements for preceding operations are derived from this demand.

- In a pure pull system, there is no need for production schedules and production orders for each stage of manufacture. Orders are, however, still necessary for make-to-order production situations, as will be explained later.

- Pull scheduling is normally operated as a means of cutting down on data and paperwork transactions. However, it may still be necessary to retain inventory 'count points' for material control purposes. Such count points may be used to accumulate batch tracking information where it is needed, for example in the defence and pharmaceutical industries. By itself, pull scheduling is usually operated as a manual system, but several software packages are available to support JIT, like the Hewlett-Packard JIT system [15]. (Use of such systems is best left until the manual system is well understood.)

- Because production operators 'own' inventory, the benefits of reducing lead times are clearly visible. Reduced lead times enable closer coordination and better customer service. Normally, the supplier should be able to satisfy a customer demand immediately.

- Pull scheduling should be capable of rapid response to changed customer requirements, within defined band widths. The aim is to be in a position to produce any part in any sequence.

Pull scheduling is particularly strong on shop-floor control. Routine material control transactions are delegated to production personnel, who 'own' the system itself. However, pull scheduling makes little contribution to planning material requirements, and assumes that sufficient parts are available in the system to be called off 'just-in-time'. It works best in a balanced and levelled production environment within a defined band width: it is a reactive system. Table 9.1 summarizes the above points for MRP v. JIT.

Table 9.1 Comparison between MRP and pull scheduling

	Material requirements planning (MRP)	Pull scheduling/ *kanban*
Description	A material management system aimed at minimum inventories	A system of manufacture aimed at producing number of parts which have been withdrawn or sold
Difference in philosophy	Driven by the master production schedule	Driven by factory assembly schedule
Difference in method	Operated as a push system by scheduled orders	Operated as a pull system from the process nearest to the market
Unit of control	Weekly scheduled orders	Achievement of daily factory assembly schedule
Pre-condition	Data accuracy, discipline, training	Balanced levelled schedules, flow, TPM, etc. (see Figure 9.1)

■ MRP and JIT together

To a large extent, MRP and pull scheduling have complementary strengths. The planning strengths of MRP combined with the shop-floor control strengths of pull scheduling seem attractive. Similarly, the simplicity of *kanban*-style transactions and other JIT improvements offer the prospect of 'downsizing' MRP, that is greatly reducing its complexity. Further, JIT can be used to attack some of the wasteful assumptions built into many MRP applications, such as fixed reorder rules and quantities, and lead times. Many MRP applications have scrap allowances: scrap is anathema to JIT!

The best-known pull scheduling cases are those which have been documented in the automotive industry, where high-volume, repetitive manufacturing methods apply. But an increasing number of applications have been outside this industry, and illustrate further innovative features of MPC system design. Some of the principles on which design can be based include the following:

■ Pull scheduling using *kanban* for runners and repeaters (the same product or key features manufactured frequently or periodically). The advantages of this system to increase responsiveness and inventories make it worth while actively to seek out such parts, and also to increase their number by design simplification. Class C and D parts should be removed from MRP ordering and expediting as far as possible.

■ MRP planning of supplier materials to ensure that sufficient parts are in the pipeline to enable them to be called off 'just-in-time'. Figure 9.7 illustrates a simplified version of what may be achieved by use of pull scheduling in manufacture supported by MRP material procurement. The MPS is broken down by means of MRP for supplier schedules (forecast future demand). Actual material requirements for suppliers are increasingly signalled by means of *kanban* to facilitate JIT delivery. Within the factory, all material movements are governed by *kanban* loops between operations. The 'drumbeat' for the factory is set by the factory assembly schedule. Figure 9.8 summarizes the advantages of such a system over attempting to model complex factory systems with complex computer systems using MRP II (manufacturing resource planning).

■ MRP control for strangers (the same product or key features manufactured at irregular intervals), in which works orders are issued to explain what must be done at each stage and then the work itself is monitored to push materials through manufacturing stages [16].

■ Use of OPT for improved capacity planning and scheduling, and for improved bottleneck identification and control (see next section).

■ Continued use of networking techniques for jobshop planning and control, but combined with the use of pull scheduling to control the buildup of work-in-progress on the shop floor. Processes are instructed what to do next by means of works orders which are generated by MRP, but work

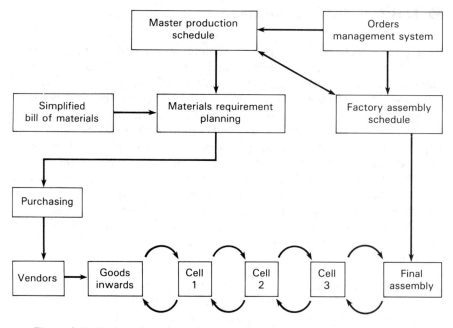

Figure 9.7 Pull scheduling in manufacture: material procurement supported by MRP

1. No interstage Works Orders
2. WIP only needs to be monitored between cells (not for each operation)
3. Much simplified bill of materials (fewer levels)
4. Single, visible process route information
5. Cell planning and control greatly simplified
6. Reduced lead times and WIP

Figure 9.8 Advantages of pull scheduling/MRP shown in Figure 9.8 v. manufacturing resource planning (MRP II) (Source: after Parnaby [16])

cannot move to the next operation unless a *kanban* square is free [17]. The MPS completion dates are determined by loading bottleneck work centres on a first-come, first-served basis, while work is pulled from non-bottleneck work centres while using slack time to even the plant load.

As an example of the application of the first three points, Berry [18] describes product structure analysis as providing a key understanding of MPC system redesign in the case of a fork lift truck manufacturer. The firm had always looked on itself as a jobshop, with 240,000 possible end product options of which 20,000 were currently offered for sale, and 8,000 were master scheduled. The product range was divided up into five families, and detailed analysis of the bill of materials for each member of the product range in each family showed that, in the worst case, 50% of the part numbers were common. In the best case, 76% of the part numbers were common. (Strict rules were applied – in order to be classified as 'common', a part number had to be used in all family members.) The opportunity arose of using pull scheduling for the common parts without using time-phased MRP records. So common parts (runners and repeaters), both made in and bought out, could be controlled by rate-based weekly requirements. Irregularly made parts (strangers), on the other hand, would continue to be governed by time-phased, weekly MRP. Figure 9.9 shows how the bill of materials could be redrawn in two parts: a common parts planned bill, and an options record for strangers. Further opportunities are then opened up to downsize the MRP system and to run it more frequently and more accurately, to control options more closely, and to rethink product designs to increase common parts.

Figure 9.10 illustrates how relative complexity of product structures, and corresponding relative routing complexity, can be used to judge selection of the MPC system. With simple structures and routings, simple systems are all that is needed. As the complexity increases, so the power of the computer is needed to make the calculations necessary to break down forecast demand into supplier schedules using MRP. But internal scheduling and control can largely be catered for by means of pull scheduling. As structures and routings increase in complexity, so the possibilities of using pull scheduling reduce. Finally, with

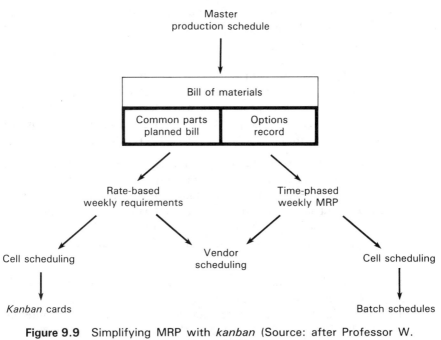

Figure 9.9 Simplifying MRP with *kanban* (Source: after Professor W. Berry [18])

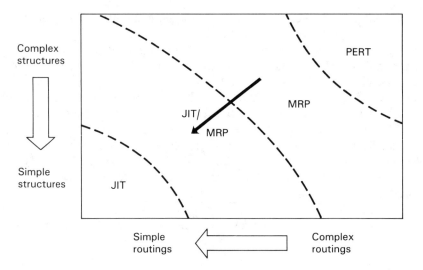

Figure 9.10 JIT/MRP applications [19]

very complex structures and routings, network-based systems such as **PERT** (Program Evaluation and Review Technique) are needed. But the direction of the arrows in Figure 9.10 is important, too. They indicate that pressure for simpler structures and routings is rewarded by simpler MPC system design.

Within each band in Figure 9.10, there may be several possibilities. For example, Karmarkar [20] identifies four of the many possible hybrids between MRP and pull scheduling:

1. **JIT/MRP:** The shop floor operates as a JIT flow system, while MRP is used only for planning, coordination, and purchasing of materials. This system is applicable where production is at a levelled rate, and lead times are constant. Usage of actual parts can be notified to MRP by means of backflushing MRP on-hand stocks by actual production figures [21].

2. **Tandem push–pull:** Where build requirements are not levelled, and where volume and mix vary within limits, push and pull systems can be made to work together. MRP is used for scheduling bought-out items and run only as necessary. Subassembly and assembly are flexible short-cycle processes which can be run on a pull basis. This version is well suited to situations where manufacturing lead times are much shorter than component lead times.

3. **Requirement-driven *kanban*:** Where volume does not vary much, but mix does, then MRP could take a closer interest in determining the number of cards allowed in each component manufacturing cell. So although internal cell control is still managed by *kanban*, the number of permitted cards is calculated by MRP from forecast schedules.

Part grouping / Control technique	'Can build' assemblies/units	Pareto class A (60% spend)	Pareto class B (30% spend)	Pareto class C (7% spend)	Pareto class D (3% spend)	Non-standard specials not coded	Needs
Sequence control	5% parts						Rapid communication and feedback / Make within trigger time
Just-in-time pull scheduling		15% parts					Stable quality demand / Communications / Employee support
MRP batch			30% parts				Good data / System updates / Planning parameters
MRP or two-bin min./max.					49% parts		Stores controls / Bin quantities / People based
Special purchase						1% parts	Adequate specification / Lead time to procedure

Figure 9.11 Material control framework (Source: David Higham Associates)

4. **Dynamic *kanban*:** Where volumes alter considerably, for example as a result of planned promotions or seasonality, the forecast can be used to calculate the number of cards necessary to support the changed level of demand.

Such hybrids are aimed at preserving or improving orderlines, and avoiding resurgence of informal manual systems like hot lists that weaken the MRP vision.

A further way of rationalizing material control strategies is due to Higham [22], and illustrated in Figure 9.11. Parts are grouped into four Pareto categories (A, B, C, and D), and also into the following:

■ Major subassemblies or units which are called for by means of sequence control. Such items are produced to specific sequence instructions from the factory assembly schedule. This requires sophisticated communications systems, for example assembly line broadcasting, to be deployed. Such items must be capable of being assembled within a given 'trigger time', and require a sequence number, not a part number, to simplify 'can build' scanning.

■ Non-standard specials which are made to specific customer specification, and which are not coded. Such items require PERT-type planning to allow for design, specification, and manufacturing activities to be completed within a given lead time.

The key issue is often the control of the large number of parts in the four Pareto categories, which are used to build the major subassemblies referred to above. Initially, most parts may be 'controlled' by MRP time-phased batches. The logistics drive in any business should be to move away from control of batches by means of MRP and towards control by means of sequence, JIT pull scheduling, and two-bin stock control. In this way, the number of parts on traditional MRP batch control may end up at only 10% or even less. This effectively argues for the direction of the arrows shown in Figure 9.10 towards simpler MPC systems design.

■ A few more words about OPT

The goal of optimized production technology (OPT) is to make money now and in the future by increasing throughput while at the same time reducing inventory and operating expense. These categories are defined as follows:

■ Throughput is the rate at which the company generates money through sales.

■ Inventory is all the money the company has invested in things it intends to sell.

■ Operating expense is all the money the company spends in order to turn inventory into throughput.

OPT philosophy says that the best decisions are the ones which achieve an increase in throughput while reducing inventory and operating expense simultaneously. The nine principles of OPT are listed in Figure 9.12. The basic scheduling philosophy of OPT was described in Chapter 2 (page 64). A description of OPT methodology is given by Vollman *et al.* [23], and – in more picturesque form – in Goldratt and Cox's famous book *The Goal* [24]. OPT has attracted a great deal of attention in recent years, and there is an increasing number of users in the United Kingdom.

One of the strengths of the OPT system is greatly improved scheduling and finite capacity planning. The focus for this improvement is the identification of bottleneck operations, and the need to keep these operations totally utilized. As a result, OPT was initially seen as impacting mainly on the 'engine' and 'back end' of the MPC system (see Figure 9.6). But OPT impacts on the front end of the MPC system too by reworking the MPS until an achievable schedule is arrived at. OPT principles can be of value even without installing the software [25]. At York International, makers of industrial refrigeration equipment, OPT principles were used for the following [26]:

■ identification of bottlenecks;
■ as a focus for capital investment;
■ rescheduling the factory to increase throughput;
■ deterring the harmful effects of traditional cost accounting.

York used OPT principles in combination with JIT pull scheduling and MRP. At the pulley manufacturing unit of Fenner's power transmission division in Hull, data about stock (WIP, finished goods, and raw materials) is fed from MRP II into the OPT scheduling system. OPT is used to cover for the weaknesses of MRP in terms of fixed batch sizes, fixed lead times, and infinite capacity [27].

1. Balance flow not capacity
2. The level of utilization of a non-bottleneck is not determined by its own potential but by some other constraint in the system
3. Utilization and activation of a resource are not synonymous
4. An hour lost at a bottleneck is an hour lost for the total system
5. An hour saved at a non-bottleneck is just a mirage
6. Bottlenecks govern both throughput and inventories
7. The transfer batch may not and many times should not be equal to the process batch
8. The process batch should be variable not fixed
9. Schedules should be established by looking at all of the constraints simultaneously; lead times are the result of a schedule and cannot be predetermined

Figure 9.12 The rules of OPT (Source: Scheduling Technology Ltd)

There is no question that, in spite of a chequered history of ownership and delays in publishing details of the scheduling algorithm, OPT has left some excellent concepts and principles for us to work with. Often these can be built into MPC system design with advantage. Some of the best MPC systems are OPT principles in combination with pull scheduling and MRP.

■ Conclusion

The number of tools and techniques which we now have available to assist in the development of excellent MPC systems has been greatly enriched in recent years. The opportunities which have opened up as a result should use that richness to the full. There is no reason why elements of pull scheduling, MRP, and OPT should not be used in the same application. They are *not* mutually exclusive. However, many companies still fall into the trap of thinking that a systems solution like MRP II will solve all of their MPC problems at a stroke. Such companies fail to appreciate the massive investment in management time and effort and the substantial cost and time involved in training user personnel. It can be 3 years before substantial benefits begin to accrue. More often than not, large systems solutions do not work very well. MRP logic is still flawed for control purposes: it simply is not responsive enough for dynamic situations, and suffers from the major handicaps of fixed lead times and batch quantities. Companies who take the large systems route exclusively ignore the tremendous opportunities for JIT/TQ philosophy to cut down on the number of transactions and to simplify greatly the whole system. At the same time, JIT/TQ offers the implementation process the importance of doing the simple things right first – of getting the basic disciplines into place. It is these basic disciplines which so often prove to be the Achilles' heel of systems implementations, in spite of large training budgets. In just the same way, pull scheduling itself is no easy option, and is the end result of achieving progress in many facilitating areas, as shown in Figure 9.1. Excellence in MPC systems depends on progress across a broad front: there are no easy answers. But there is an increasing opportunity for innovation.

■ References

1. *Just-in-Time: A Global Status Report*, C. A. Voss and D. Clutterbuck, IFS, Bedford, 1990.
2. *Manufacturing Planning and Control Systems*, T. Vollman, W. Berry, and C. Whybark, Irwin, Homewood, IL, 1989.
3. *The Transfer and Adaptation of JIT Manufacturing Practices by Japanese Companies in the UK*, C. Voss and L. Okazaki-Ward, 1988.

4. 'Integrating MRP II with JIT', J. N. Edwards, *BPICS Control*, October/ November, 1988, pp. 45–53.

5. *Toyota Production System and Kanban Production System: Materialisation of Just-in-Time and Respect-for-Human Systems*, Y. Sugimori *et al.*, *International Journal of Production Research*, **15**, no. 6, 1977, pp. 553–64.

6. 'The hidden factory', J. G. Miller and T. Vollman, *Harvard Business Review*, September/October, 1985, pp. 141–50.

7. 'Getting control of JIT', V. Karmarkar, *Harvard Business Review*, September/October, 1989.

8. *Operations Management: Improving Customer Service*, R. Schonberger and E. Knod, Irwin, Homewood, IL, 1991.

9. *Zero Inventories*, R. Hall, Dow Jones Irwin, Homewood, IL, 1983, p. 40.

10. R. Hall, *ibid.*, p. 41.

11. Y. Sugimori *et al.*, *ibid.*

12. 'MRP, JIT and OPT: What's best?', G. Plenert and T. Best, *Production and Inventory Management*, 2nd Quarter, 1986.

13. T. Vollman *et al.*, *ibid.*, p. 16.

14. 'MRP or JIT: What's best?', J. Hartland-Swan, *Proc. Second International Conference on Just-in-Time*, IFS, Bedford, 1987.

15. The HP software is described in T. Vollman *et al.*, *ibid.*, p. 281.

16. 'A systems approach to the implementation of just-in-time methodologies in Lucas Industries', *International Journal of Production Research*, **26**, no. 3, 1988, pp. 483–92.

17. See for example 'Integration of MRP and JIT', *Proc. Second International Conference on Just-in-Time*, IFS, Bedford, 1987.

18. 'Product Structure Analysis for the Master Scheduling of Assemble to Order Products', W. L. Berry, W. J. Talon and W. J. Boe, Working Paper at Center for Manufacturing Excellence, Kenan Flagar School of Business, University of North Carolina.

19. 'Strategies for implementing JIT', C. Voss and A. Harrison, in C. Voss (ed.) *Just-in-Time Manufacture*, IFS, 1987, Bedford, p. 209.

20. V. Karmarkar, *ibid.*, p. 209.

21. See for example 'JIT: The first steps', *BPICS Control*, **16**, no. 1, December 1989/January 1990, pp. 43–6.

22. Source: David Higham Associates.

23. T. Vollman *et al.*, *ibid.*, pp. 844–56.

24. *The Goal*, E. Goldratt and E. Cox, Scheduling Technology Group, 1986.

25. 'OPT uncovered: Many production and scheduling concepts can be applied with or without the software', R. Jacobs, *Industrial Engineering*, October, 1984.

26. 'Leaving traditions behind: The case of York International', J. Booth, *The Challenge of JIT for Small Businesses*, IFS, June, 1988.

27. 'MRP/OPT', J. Dwyer, *Works Management*, December, 1990.

10 | Invest in Suppliers

The objective of JIT supply is to have parts delivered just-in-time (neither too early nor too late) for assembly or processing. So inventory timing – now related to the delivery of external parts – is again the crucial factor here. If the customer uses products one at a time, and the manufacturer makes them one at a time, and suppliers make components one at a time, why stack up parts and products into large transport or storage inventories? This only serves to interrupt flow and to create the waste of inventory within the supply chain. JIT supply contracts mean replacing adversarial relationships with cooperation between customer and supplier, and also mean maximum simplicity of transactions by minimizing paperwork. Or so the theory goes.

Consider the position of a component supplier to the automotive industry. A few very powerful original equipment manufacturers (OEMs) – perhaps 20 world-wide – can buy anywhere in the world. They understand the supplier's business, and indeed can choose to make the components in-house. Faced with overcapacity in Europe and the USA, and pressure from Japanese manufacturers, the OEMs are all looking at costs and quality. The supply base constitutes 70% of their costs, and so is fundamental to their improvement plans. Increasingly, they will use their supply base leverage to attack those costs. The opportunities for component suppliers to pass on those pressures unaided to their own suppliers (manufacturers of castings, forgings, rubber, and so on) is limited. If too much pressure is exerted by the component manufacturer, the casting supplier tells the company to 'take your tools and go away'. The component manufacturer is in a delicate position. And so it is perhaps surprising in retrospect that some of the initial interpretations of 'Japanese Inspired Terror' by the OEMs included the following examples:

■ Tough contractual terms which required component suppliers to maintain stocks of parts in a concentration warehouse at their expense. The OEM would call off those stocks on a JIT basis, and pay only after they had been withdrawn. So if the OEM's schedules changed, which they often did, the supplier could be left with the unwanted stock. The prime beneficiary of such moves was the OEM, whose component stocks were greatly reduced and yet who could rest assured that there was still a satisfactory buffer stock available. (To add insult to injury, the supplier had to pay rent for use of the warehouse.)

■ Single sourcing manoeuvres which led to the disappearance of competitors, such as the closure of the Rubery Owen wheels plant in 1982. The objective was to place larger volumes with a single source, and hence to extract large price reductions. The effect was to reduce competition.

■ The appointment of 'preferred suppliers' for 3-year contracts, but accompanied by demands from the OEM for immediate and substantial price reductions. Many component suppliers figured that it was better to retain existing relationships!

OEMs were frequently able to benefit from lower material stocks and costs in the short term, but the policies which achieved this improvement left many suppliers feeling that they were doing all the work and getting none of the benefits. Southern Components, quoted by Oliver and Wilkinson [1], stated that 'JIT has been used as a myth on which to hang the transfer of responsibility for stockholding to another point in the supply chain – anywhere so long as it does not cost the assemblers money.'

Some OEMs were imposing new, tougher terms of business, and yet were still guilty of the same old problems themselves, notably an inability to provide stable schedules. Table 10.1 summarizes the characteristics of two types of OEM, which we have labelled class A and class B [2]. Class A OEMs are characterized by genuine attempts to improve commercial and logistical arrangements with their suppliers. For example, firm schedule periods are defined and agreed, and the OEM agrees to accept and pay for suppliers' production made to such schedules. Class B OEMs on the other hand have no such arrangements with their suppliers. For example, schedules are forever

Table 10.1 Two types of original equipment manufacturer

Class A	Class B
Schedules regularly transmitted through a single mechanism	Schedules – and changes – transmitted by different sources in the company
Firm schedule period defined and agreed with supplier; further improvements under way	No firm schedules; no sign of improvement
Data transmission policy defined and in place	Data transmission policy not yet defined; probably will not be compatible with other customers
Payment system much simplified, fast	Invoices, etc., still used; payment slow and bureaucratic
Deliveries regulated (time spot) or customer collects; further improvements under way	Deliveries chaotic: lengthy queues at site; no sign of improvement

being changed and the supplier has no recompense for parts made against forward schedules from the OEM and subsequently cancelled. One of the difficulties for a supplier is to be in the position of having to service a mixture of both classes of customer: class B customers can have a disproportionately damaging effect on operations at the supplier.

But suppliers could and should support the OEM to compete in the market at large. The destinies of the companies concerned depend on each other. Add in the companies involved in distributing the final products to end customers and you have a supply chain. Supply chain management is defined here [3] as the management of the flows of goods and services valued by end customers, from raw material source to ultimate customer. JIT supply is one of several reasons why supply chain management is increasing in importance. Others include increasing internationalization so that parts are made in a single low-cost location, and improved transport, computing, and communications technologies. The transport specialist is becoming the cement which binds the supply chain together, and which can act as a principal facilitator for JIT supply to take place. Electronic data interchange (EDI) is also fast becoming a major facilitator of rapid and flexible response up and down the supply chain. EDI is the transfer of structured data (for example, production schedules and invoices) from computer to computer by means of agreed message standards.

JIT supply depends on assuring a variety of factors which influences the relationship between buyers and suppliers. If either the OEM or the supplier is neither capable nor committed, then JIT supply will not work. Table 10.2 lists some of the principal concerns which the supplier has when the OEM starts to become excited about 'going JIT'. JIT supply depends on convincing the primary suppliers to join the OEM's 'club'. The aim is to convert these suppliers into 'comakers', who share in the benefits of the new relationship and with whom the OEM can develop a long-term supply strategy. JIT supply works because comakers are capable of delivering mutual benefits to each other and because all parties want it to work. The needs of secondary suppliers need to be attended to as well.

Table 10.2 Why JIT does not work

Supplier is asked for	Supplier sees
Smaller batch sizes delivered more frequently	Higher costs
Preferred supplier	Lower prices now
Reduced fixed schedule, more changes	Shorter runs
Rapid model introduction	Weekend working, greater scrap rates
Greater variety, more materials	Greater stocks

Note: if either the OEM or the supplier is neither capable nor committed, then JIT will not work

■ The new activities of JIT supply

The principles which we discussed in Chapter 4 and in Chapter 7 apply equally to the supply chain as to internal material control. Although the customer cannot control the supplier in the same way as an internal department, the supply itself can be controlled. The onus is on the customer to facilitate flow and inventory timing with suppliers by first removing 3-MV from his or her own plants and tightening up on his or her own manufacturing planning and control system. There is little point in introducing 'just-in-time' supply when no one is quite sure what 'time' is actually meant! But while internal JIT is progressing, there are several activities which can be started off in parallel on the lengthy road to JIT supply. The starting point is a supply strategy, which will address questions like the following:

- What are the key objectives we are trying to achieve over the next x years, and how can our suppliers help us? How can we measure progress?
- What will our supply base be like in x years' time? Will we have focused factories by country, supplied by local manufacturers, or will we have preferred suppliers for Europe (and which need not necessarily be European) as a whole who supply all factories? What are the implications for our existing supply base?
- What changes do we need to make in the way information is passed through the supply chain? What are the opportunities for EDI, and how should they be implemented?
- How will we involve suppliers in future new products? Will we devolve all or part of the responsibility for component design to our suppliers? Are they equipped to respond?
- What transport policy should we adopt? Should suppliers continue to deliver parts to us, or do we need to have an integrated transport system under the control of a limited number of carriers?

Once such questions have been answered, the preparatory work can be put in hand. Some of the key activities will be as follows:

1. Supplier selection

Most OEMs have been examining their supplier base in recent years to move away from the multi-sourcing policies of traditional purchasing. Some of the reductions have been substantial: Ford UK have reduced the supplier base from about 2,500 to 850 over the last 10 years, and plan for a further modest reduction over the next 5 years. Most companies have been wary about going for single sourcing as a short-term policy. While Dr Deming counsels that single sourcing is essential to reduce variability [4] there are several practical difficulties in progressing this policy. Table 10.3 compares the advantages and disadvantages of single sourcing. Chemicals buyers argue that, for most

Table 10.3 Single sourcing

Advantages	Disadvantages
Better price break	Competitor's prices may be lower
Reduced overheads	Complacency on quality or innovation
Focused SQA	Vulnerability to disputes or delays
Predictability of schedules and response	Bargaining chip removed
Continuous improvement	Losers (non-preferred suppliers) may be lost for ever
Tooling one-off, and long-term view on investment	Cannot handle large schedule variances (up or down)
Consistent specifications and quality	Tooking breakdowns increase risk
Smaller supplier base means more focused purchasing admin.	

purchases, it is worth while leaving the buyer free to shop around Europe for the best deal: many specifications are international, so the quality risk is not great, and you will always find someone with stocks on their hands who is desperate to sell! Deals for 6 months and even 3 months are still normal in the chemicals industry, with longer-term deals being the exception for supply security. Hewlett-Packard UK went for a single-sourcing policy, but with a version that many buyers have found attractive. That is, to single-source by part number, but multi-source by commodity [5]. For example, there might be five sheet metal assembly suppliers, but each part number is single sourced to one of them. This overcomes some of the disadvantages in Table 10.3; for example, complacency on quality or innovation is easily spotted when there are several other suppliers being dealt with in the same area of technology. Further protection for the buyer in single-source contracts can be provided by contractual clauses which build price comparisons and continuous improvement into the supply contract.

A further consideration in supplier selection is location relative to the buyer's factory. Obvious advantages are protection against fluctuating exchange rates, the avoidance of freight and duty costs, and much faster shipping times. But less obvious advantages are that improved communications, close coordination, and true 'just-in-time' delivery are most likely achievable when the supplier is next to the buyer. So Japanese OEMs often set up a trading estate of suppliers, each focused on the OEM factory. Because this means that a supplier may end up with as many factories as the OEM, the supplier factories are often referred to as 'clones'. Thus Nissan Manufacturing UK has helped many of its preferred suppliers to set up on the trading estate at Washington, all focused on to Nissan's needs. Figure 10.1 shows the setup for the JIT supply of front seats from NHK Spring to Fuji (a comparatively

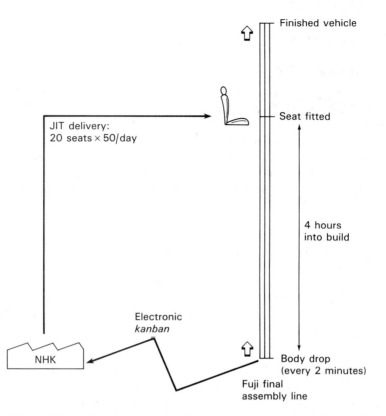

Figure 10.1 Clone plant operation: seat supply from NHK to Fuji

low-volume auto producer selling under the name Subaru in the West) in Japan. As the car body is dropped on to the trim and final assembly line at Fuji, an electronic *kanban* is sent to NHK, who then have 4 hours to make and deliver the seats for that model specification. NHK delivers loads of 20 seats 50 times per day, and its production control computers are run by Fuji's. NHK's factory is 10–15 minutes' delivery time away from Fuji, and NHK's 60 major suppliers are in turn mostly situated within 1 hour's delivery time. NHK is in effect run by Fuji and the factory produces for no other customer. Such a system has clear advantages over a policy where a preferred supplier is situated in Spain, and there is a 10-day transport time (and hence pipeline inventory) to a UK factory. But it is not all plain sailing: NHK is under intense pressure from Fuji for two price reductions each year.

However attractive local sourcing may seem, a local supplier will not be preferred if it cannot measure up to the OEM's basic requirements. Black and Decker UK [6] look for suppliers who can provide:

- product and component design;
- quality (a series of objective measurements are used to judge capability);

- flexible supply;
- cost reduction;
- management support;
- efficient administration.

Suppliers are regularly rated by a multi-disciplinary team which assesses the above factors on a 0–10 scale. The 'good' ones are retained, the 'bad' ones disposed of, and the 'ugly' ones further evaluated for development into good, or for disposal. Hewlett-Packard UK's supplier selection criteria are shown in Figure 10.2, and show some additional interesting points. For example, HP wants parts to be delivered directly to its manufacturing process without goods-inward inspection, and therefore specifies good internal process control as a selection criterion.

2. Supplier quality assurance (SQA)

The OEM wants to be assured that the supplier is capable of delivering parts which work totally in the buyer's process. Suppliers should be fully responsible for the quality of their products, and operate a quality system which aims to control and to improve product quality. The Nissan quality policy statement to its suppliers [7] is as follows:

> Nissan expects suppliers to adopt its quality philosophy, and will encourage any joint efforts to achieve quality improvements. Suppliers are totally responsible for their products used by Nissan and will establish quality systems accordingly. These will include continual review and development of product design, material specifications and manufacturing processes to bring about quality and productivity improvements to the shared benefit of the suppliers and Nissan. Suppliers must ensure through self-management, that each product meets all the specification requirements. Suppliers are expected to

Criteria:
- lowest total cost of ownership (not just lowest quote)
- parts that work 100% in our process (no goods in inspection)
- on-time delivery (up to 3 days early, 0 days late)
- low, consistent lead times
- weekly/daily shipments
- good internal process control
- cost reductions passed on to HP
- good communication
- good control of internal planning activities (purchasing, production planning, despatch, etc.)
- financially sound
- HP business between 10% and 25% of turnover (substantial but no monopoly)

Figure 10.2   Hewlett-Packard supplier selection criteria

operate quality control systems which meet all the requirements prepared by Nissan.

Quality assurance is the foundation of the buyer/supplier relationship. The buyer can do much to help the supplier to set up an effective quality system, and requalifying the supplier periodically helps to ensure that standards are maintained and improved. More about quality later.

3. Performance measurement and feedback

The buyer's expectations of the supplier need to be clearly spelt out. The three basic issues are quality, delivery, and price. Intel Corporation added to these technical support, service, and responsiveness, as show in Table 10.4. These and other expectations can be communicated by supplier seminars which explain why we want it this way, and which help suppliers to understand us and how we operate. The seminars can be backed up by further presentations at the supplier site, and by exchanges of shop-floor personnel. The supplier is then monitored against the stated performance measures, and feedback is given through defined channels regularly (say, quarterly). The buyer can give

Table 10.4 Intel Corporation: supplier selection criteria

Performance criteria	Expectations
1. Quality	100% incoming SPC Source inspection/compliance Supplier performs first article inspection: we teach them how
2. Delivery	100% on time 3 days early, 0 days late JIT on class A items Penalty: fly it!

3. Price	Landed cost (includes transport,
	    duty, etc.)
	'Should be' analysis
	Cost reductions (experience
	    curve) built into contract

4. Technical support	Process improvement Technology exchanges Quality programmes Technology leader
5. Service	In-process communications 'Open plant' audits Account status available Client factory contact
6. Lead time (responsiveness)	'Quick turn' capability Response to changes Lead time reductions

supplier comparisons by commodity group which help the supplier to understand the need for improvement. A striking example of this is shown in Figure 10.3, where Toshiba UK compared part count accuracy of Far Eastern suppliers of electronic components with their UK counterparts. Not only were the Far Eastern suppliers overall more accurate (78% of deliveries correct), but errors were skewed to overdelivery. Such comparisons had a very beneficial effect on the UK suppliers, who responded with considerable improvements in part count accuracy [8].

4. Delivery schedules

While delivery flexibility may be a sought-after performance objective, suppliers cannot be expected to perform better than their existing capability. Developing such capability takes time and the encouragement and support of the OEM. Figure 10.4 shows how Cummins Engine saw the dilemma:

- The supplier wants the firm portion of the forecast requirements to be as long as possible, so that detailed and firm plans may be made.
- The OEM wants the adjustment period to be as long as possible so that schedule changes may be made up to the last minute.

Class A OEMs are the ones which recognize this dilemma, and produce schedules which are firm for a defined period of time. Again, the principle is the

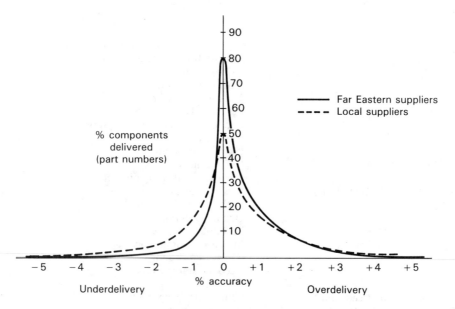

Figure 10.3 Comparison of part count accuracy for Far Eastern and UK suppliers (Source: Winn [5])

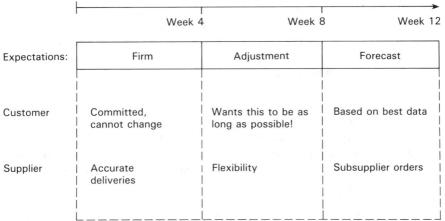

Figure 10.4 Material planning at Cummins Engine

same as for internal material control, where we noted that a defined firm period is necessary. Tinkering with schedules and priorities is self-perpetuating. Once a supplier has mastered quality assurance, then delivery reliability is the next major challenge. To achieve this, the supplier needs to be shown that the OEM has its own material control system in good shape. Over time, it will then be a much more achievable task for the supplier to demonstrate improved on-time performance against defined delivery windows. Once satisfactory progress has been made, then we can start to think about further improvements, such as how the firm period might be reduced. But start off by achieving basic control! Zero inventories (just-in-time supply) are *not* the immediate goal. We start by introducing basic controls, and go on to improve system capability, which will be reflected in improved 'band width'. As with quality, responsibility for expediting passes to the supplier, thus eliminating another non-value-added activity. The story goes that Nissan was initially forced to set up expediting systems in the United Kingdom because suppliers defaulted on deliveries and did not tell Nissan, a problem not encountered in Japan!

5. Transport

Some of the most substantial savings in operating costs come from improved transport mechanisms. Visibility of total transport costs is a good starting point. CIF-type contracts (supplier delivers) hide transport costs in material prices. Ford UK began its ex-works (buyer collects) programme about 10 years ago, and has been able to make savings by running 'milk rounds' to collect parts shipments from suppliers associated with five regional collection centres.

Further savings accrue from being able to process class A parts more quickly through the system. The key measure of performance is delivery accuracy against increasingly tight delivery windows at the buyer. Improved performance gives the customer the confidence to operate with low stocks. Often, the haulier can facilitate major improvements, and form a key component of Schonberger's 'partners in profit' concept (suppliers, carriers, and customers) [9]. The task is to take costs out of the system *and* improve reliability and service quality. Figure 10.5 shows how BRS acted as the facilitator in coordinating Mothercare (a retailer of baby clothes and accessories) with its 150 supply sources and 235 retail outlets. Again, 'milk round' collections from suppliers were coordinated via a central warehouse (situated in Wellingborough, near the centre of England). Bulk deliveries to retail stores were made overnight by fixed unit and drawbar via five regional BRS branches which acted as outbases. The same fixed units were used (hence minimizing capital costs) to make morning deliveries to the High Street stores. But the penalty clauses for the haulier can be very high in the event of failure. Bunzl

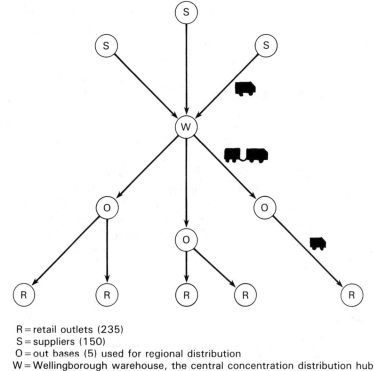

R = retail outlets (235)
S = suppliers (150)
O = out bases (5) used for regional distribution
W = Wellingborough warehouse, the central concentration distribution hub
    Fixed unit
    Fixed unit and drawbar

Figure 10.5 Transport coordination at Mothercare (courtesy of BRS)

(a haulier) was on a £1 million penalty clause if deliveries to the IBM plant at Greenock in Scotland were missed! 'Time spot' deliveries, requiring the haulier to deliver within 0·5 hour windows or join the queue, are an increasingly favoured way of regulating deliveries to a busy site. Although 'many gate' delivery of parts to specific stations of the OEM production line may be a difficult concept to introduce in old factories, three holes have been knocked into the wall at East Works at Longbridge to allow deliveries direct to point of use on the K series engine assembly line.

6. Communications

Closer relationships with the reduced supplier base are reflected by improving communications. Specific personnel are tasked with the broadening technical, commercial, and operational relationship. It becomes advantageous to establish formal data transmission links for production schedules, test data, exchange of technical information, and so on. Inclusion into the customer's networking system (such as Fordnet and Massey Ferguson's FAME) brings further opportunities for exchanging data in real time. The supplier can be brought more closely into the OEM's future product plans, and be involved in developing those plans. Figure 10.6 lists some of the opportunities for speeding up and improving communications.

The new activities of JIT supply are listed in Table 10.5. These new activities should be developed in a planned and orderly way over time. Again, it is important not to rush fences, or to try to grab advantages at the expense of other links in the supply chain. JIT supply works by breaking down traditional barriers between buyer and supplier, and by working together to mutual advantage. Electrolux UK have been implementing JIT supply with selected comakers as new models are introduced. Eventually, all major supplies will be on this basis. There have been few examples of clone plants apart from Japanese transplants in the United Kingdom. One example of a focused supplier plant is Venture Pressings at Telford, which is jointly owned (50/50) by Jaguar Cars and GKN. The company presses body panels for Jaguar's Castle Bromwich plant, and in its original concept, this would have been its only

How well are we communicating?
- order processing speeded up and directed to correct supplier/customer personnel;
- notification to suppliers of schedule changes as they happen;
- bar coding of products to speed up correct identification and notification;
- self-billing invoices and electronic funds transfer to cut down paperwork and to reduce errors and delays;
- early warning systems in the supplier's process to notify customers of problems as they happen;
- EDI of supplier test and inspection data.

Figure 10.6 How well are we communicating?

Table 10.5 The new activities of JIT supply

Supplier selection	Supplier reduction
	Location
	Close plants
SQA	Quality systems
	Help in implementing
	FMEA, SPC, etc.
Performance	Quality–delivery–price
measurement and	Supplier seminars
feedback	Action plans
Delivery schedules	Levelled schedules
	Firm/adjustment periods
	Delivery accuracy
Transport	Ex-works v. CIF
	Combine and coordinate
	Smaller order quantities,
	more frequent deliveries
	Time-spot deliveries
	Many-gate access
Communications	Defines contacts
	Data interchange

customer. VP has already been able to give a much enhanced service from that previously available when Jaguar's panels were outsourced to a volume manufacturer. Surviving the current very depressed market in its existing form will be a major challenge for VP.

■ The expanding role of quality [10]

The traditional role of quality in the supply system has been based on conformance to the customer's quality system specification. The major specifications were set by large national organizations like the electricity generators (formerly the CEGB), British Rail, and the Ministry of Defence. Such specifications have spread rapidly to other industries over the last 10–15 years, and key activities include the following:

■ The formulation and introduction of a supplier quality system by the major end user.
■ The audit of suppliers by the end user against the quality system.
■ The requirement for the supplier to correct deviations.
■ The requirement for witnessed stage inspection and test (of capital goods, etc.).
■ The duplicated inspection and test by the major end user of goods delivered by the suppliers.

■ The rejection of non-conforming goods by the major end user's goods-inward inspection, and a requirement for replacement by conforming goods.

Suppliers also had to perform by introducing more detailed documentation and procedures to demonstrate to the major end user's auditors that they were carrying out required operations like assuring the quality of incoming material, operating stage inspections and recording results, and arranging and recording the results of witnessed tests. Traditionally, quality systems were used by the major end users in a directive rather than an educative way.

The major change brought about in recent years has been the recognition by major end users of the need to perform a facilitating role on supplier quality. A supplier quality system such as Ford's Q101 describes fundamentals which must be in place. The supplier is 'responsible for building on those fundamentals to produce an effective quality system'. Often the OEM will help in the introduction of key techniques such as SPC and FMEA. But conformance to the major end user's quality system is only part of the comakership quality issue. The principal issues at stake are as follows:

■ Delivered goods are fit for purpose.
■ Deliveries are on time.
■ Part counts are accurate.

On-time deliveries are included because of the potentially adverse effects on quality of rescheduling or retrofitting. Techniques in addition to quality systems are needed in order to achieve these objectives. Such techniques, aimed at continuous quality improvement, require that a foundation of cooperation exists for comakership to flourish.

Garvin points out [11] that the interpretation of 'quality' is increasingly about external perceptions. Quality is a function of perception by customers and comparison with competitors. From the OEM's point of view, this impacts on the timing of defect discovery. Two examples serve to illustrate what is at stake:

1. The cost of failures escalates up the supply chain, and is at its greatest when the product is in service. This point was well made in a study at General Electric of the USA, and is illustrated in Figure 10.7. An error of $0 \cdot 003$ at the supplier is magnified to $300 if it has to be corrected when the product is in service. The results of this study [12] support the view that the earlier an error is detected, the less waste is created. Quality needs to be built in at each stage in the supply chain.
2. Final assembly is an integrative process, and this implies that all errors in components are also integrated. Consider an automotive product, which typically comprises 3,000–5,000 components, and compare an acceptable quality level (AQL) of 1% for each component with an equivalent defect level of 1 ppm. Table 10.6 shows this comparison. Defects of 30 to 50 per

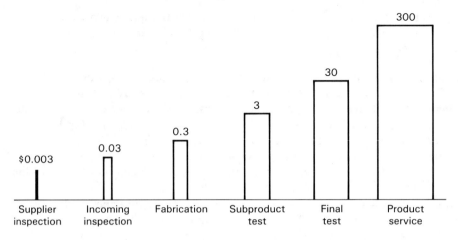

Figure 10.7 Escalation in cost of errors up the supply chain

Table 10.6 Comparison of defects from AQL and ppm quality levels

Quality level	Potential defects	
	Per unit of FP	Per 1,000 FPs
AQL = 1%	30–50	30,000–50,000
1 ppm	0·003–0·005	3–5

unit of finished product mean not only that the product is uncompetitive, but also that there are severe implications to material control and to product costs.

The key principle from the OEM's point of view is that defects are discovered and eliminated in the supplier's or subsupplier's process, and that they are not transmitted up the supply chain to cause greater disruption as they go. As the comakership relationship develops and confidence grows in the supplier's quality system, responsibility for part quality can be increasingly delegated to the supplier. This is logical because it becomes less and less practical to inspect quality into a product as the defect levels approach parts per million. New opportunities arise to:

■ reduce or eliminate goods-in inspection;
■ receive in quantities which meet only the shift's requirements;
■ deliver parts to point of use, not via the delays and double handling of goods-in stores and inspection.

Gradually, the customer's role becomes one of audit and review, and of problem solving. The role of the buyers in the customer firm changes from order placers/expeditors to inventory/availability management [13]. The steps involved in progressing to the ideal state for the supply contract are listed in Table 10.7:

Step 1: Since no inspection is carried out at either the supplier or the customer, the customer's production section must inspect parts before they are built into the product.

Step 2: It becomes too costly to continue to operate step 1, so an inspection department is set up at the customer. The buyer still has no clear responsibility to improve quality, however.

Step 3: The supplier establishes its own inspection department. But the customer does not trust this, and continues his or her own inspection process.

Step 4: Performance improves at the supplier, so the customer scales down his or her inspection to sampling only.

Step 5: Responsibility for QA is taken on by the supplier's production section. Inspection at the supplier is also scaled down to sample inspection only.

Step 6: Process control at the supplier leads to the gradual elimination of defects. Customer's inspection continues to be on a sample basis, but supplier's inspection is reduced to random checks.

Step 7: Once confidence in process control at the supplier has been achieved, the customer's inspection is also scaled down to a random check.

Step 8: The quality of products from the supplier's production section is completely trusted, and there is no need for further quality checks, either at the supplier or the customer.

Table 10.7 Stages in development of quality between supplier and customer

	Supplier		Customer	
	Production dept	Inspection dept	Inspection dept	Production dept
Step 1				Total inspection
Step 2			Total inspection	
Step 3		Total inspection	Total inspection	
Step 4		Total inspection	Sample inspection or check inspection	
Step 5	Total inspection	Sample inspection	Sample inspection or check inspection	
Step 6	Process control	Sample inspection	Check inspection or no inspection	
Step 7	Process control	Check inspection	Check inspection or no inspection	
Step 8	Process control	No inspection	No inspection	

Source: After Professor H. Yamashina

Note that 'process control' here refers not just to the individual manufacturing processes (like machining) at the supplier. It relates to the total process of manufacture, handling, and error-free delivery to the customer's process. This ideal is achieved in stages, making progress continuously by working together. At each stage, the parties need to define the role of quality and understand the process limitations they are working under. The prizes become greater the closer they approach the ideal. Progress is marked by an evolution in the role of quality from narrow (conformance to customer specification) to wide (total quality management of the supply chain).

■ Supply chain management

Supply chain management is about taking an overview of the processes involved in moving parts, subassemblies, and final assemblies through the various stages of manufacture and supply to the end customer. A simplistic model of the 'chain' is shown in Figure 10.8(a). It is easy to visualize the various flows by means of this model:

- **upstream:** orders, forecasts, schedules, quality specifications;

- **downstream:** materials, advice notes, delivery promises, test results.

One can also visualize how logistics management can be applied to integrate the flow of materials between suppliers within the supply chain. EDI can also be used to speed up the flow of data. The benefits of providing such supply chain management are as follows:

- **Improved end customer service:** Working towards end customer requirements can provide a focus which did not previously exist. For example, orders may be won with end customers as a result of delivery speed (time from placement of order to time of receipt of goods). Wherever the supplier is placed in the chain, helping to meet such an order-winning criterion [14] helps to improve the competitiveness of the whole chain.

- **Synergy:** Traditionally, individual companies in a supply chain have set out to maximize their own profitability. Recognition that working together improves the competitiveness of the service to the end user brings improved benefits for the whole group of companies.

- **Reaction speed:** True end customer demand needs to be correctly transmitted upstream so that the chain reacts quickly and accurately to changes in those needs. But there is often a big difference between end customer demand and upstream activity because of the methods used by downstream companies to time their own inventory requirements. For example, MRP lead time offsets and batching rules lead to lumpiness in demand for components at lower levels in the bill of materials. (Amplification of the effects of demand changes upstream is called the Forrester effect [15].)

In reality, companies work in more complex supply networks than that shown in Figure 10.8(a). The true environment includes interconnections and knock-on effects from other networks. Figure 10.8(b) shows the simple expansion of the chain of an automotive component supplier to include the after-market as well as OEM supply. The main requirements of after-market customers is delivery speed because most demand is based on distress purchases. Price is not so important. However, OEMs buy much more on the basis of quality and

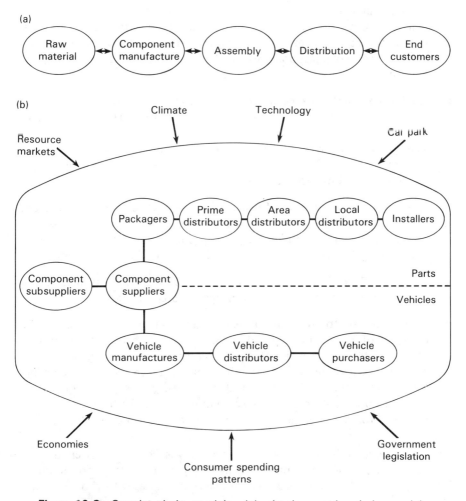

Figure 10.8 Supply chain models: (a) simple supply chain model; (b) supply chain management generic network model

221

price, with delivery reliability to production schedules also important. The same component manufacturer is required to meet both sets of criteria.

In order to test the above concepts, the supply of remanufactured starters and alternators and ancillary services was investigated [16]. The following chain links exist:

component supplier → remanufacturer → prime distributor →

local distributor → installer

The following points of interest were found:

- **Lack of harmonization of strategy:** The repair installers at the end of the chain required a 1-hour replacement service from the local distributor. So delivery speed and reliability were the most important criteria. These criteria were also recognized as being crucial in all chain links except the last – the component supplier whose stated market strategy was being low-cost supplier!

- **Conflicts in performance measures:** Although the remanufacturer had stated that delivery speed and reliability were its key performance criteria, the performance of its purchasing department was measured on cost savings! So it was hardly surprising that the component supplier thought that low cost was the key issue, and was unaware of the importance of delivery to its downstream links.

- **Ignorance of the activities of other links:** Both the prime distributor and the installer, members of the same group of companies, commissioned market surveys for a similar range of products and services. Both were unaware of the activities and results obtained by their sister company.

- **Forrester effect:** Stock replenishment policies caused increasing deviation from true end customer demand in upstream companies.

- **Fixed channels for information exchange:** There was a fixed route for exchange of information up and down the chain. This was the well-worn commercial route for materials – the commercial/purchasing links. However, the fixed route becomes cumbersome in the case of other demands for information, such as technical enquiries. JIT supply requires the opening up of new, more direct communication links between all chain members for the exchange of information across a broader front.

The above research is beginning to throw up key issues of supply chain management. Opportunities for improving harmony of interests, coordination of information, and synchronization of material flow will provide many challenges and hold out the prospect of many rewards. Within supply chain management, JIT supply increases the pressure for such reforms.

■ Electronic data interchange (EDI)

EDI, the exchange of data from computer to computer by means of agreed message standards, has revolutionized business communications. In particular, the speed and cost of transactions between companies, both nationally and internationally, has collapsed. Within the JIT supply context, EDI offers many potential benefits, which are listed in Figure 10.9. EDI can be used as an important technique in the campaign to improve quality (by providing faster, more accurate information) and to reduce stocks and costs at all points in the supply chain. The development of EDI in Europe was pioneered in the United Kingdom. Indeed, by 1987, 60–70% of all European EDI was attributable to UK activities [17]. While this was a high-water mark, UK work has shaped both European and world developments.

The simple way to start data interchange is to hook a group of suppliers into an OEM's electronic mail network. (The purists would argue that this is not strictly EDI.) Such an application is described in the case study in Appendix B, and resulted in considerable benefits in terms of earlier notification of more accurate schedules to the supplier. But the challenge of EDI is to link all supply chain members using agreed message standards, and so the need to think bigger soon presents itself. So major retailers like BhS use a private viewdata system to link all suppliers, and Ford use a networking system of their own to link supply chain members. This can leave individual suppliers with the need for several systems in order to be able to talk to different major customers, all with their own systems. So there is a need to think bigger again, and trading groups form with their own message standards. Examples of trading groups which have formed for various industries include:

- retailing (TRADANET);
- chemical (CEFIC);
- electronics (EDIFICE);
- motor manufacturing (ODETTE);
- shipping (DISH, SHIPNET).

EDI objectives:
Order cycle times ↓
Inventory ↓
Service levels ↑
Purchase costs ↓
Errors ↓
Administration costs ↓

EDI helps to provide:
- improved links with suppliers
- improved control over suppliers
- improved control over payments
- more competitive prices
- competitive advantage

Figure 10.9 Electronic data interchange (EDI)

Other EDI associations were formed to cover banking, ports and airports, and transport. Two types of communication have developed:

1. **Indirect:** Data is received, stored, and forwarded by a clearing centre to allow for time-window differences or non-standard protocols. The 'clearing house' is more correctly referred to as a value-added data service (VADS). An example of such a system based on TRADANET and ISTEL's EDICT is shown in Figure 10.10.
2. **Direct:** Data is transmitted directly to the addressee. This leads to an increasing number of leased line connections.

This still leaves the problem for suppliers who service two or more customers based in different industries, or who need to communicate with companies in different continents. So the need is to think bigger still. EDIFACT (EDI For Administration, Commerce and Transport) standards have been developed by the United Nations Economic Commission for Europe to produce a universal international standard. Movement towards EDIFACT through the 1990s can be expected.

Initially, EDI was slow to take off, especially for international trade. The reasons for the failure of EDI initiatives, or the failure to achieve maximum benefits, include [18] the following:

- Closed user groups, formed around a major OEM or retailer.
- Lack of standards (especially for protocols).
- Lack of motivation to grasp the opportunities.

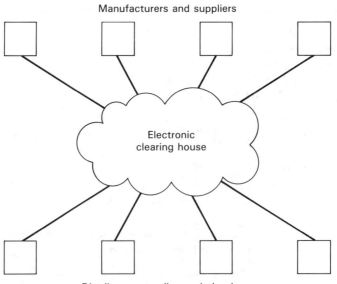

Figure 10.10   Electronic clearing house (value-added data service)

- The service provides for the self-interest of the OEM, which is not shared with other supply chain partners.
- A bias towards scheduling material movements, at the expense of other opportunities for EDI such as technical information exchange.

EDI initiatives fail because they lack drive and are on too small a scale. Successful introduction considers the supply chain, industry, and international contexts of product needs. It builds on a strong commercial relationship between the parties concerned, and seeks to provide advantage for all of those parties.

■ Conclusion

Just-in-time supply offers the most glittering prizes for cost savings. Directed into the very area of greatest cost to the OEM – material costs – supply chain management in general and JIT supply in particular promise to become major activities in all manufacturing industries during the 1990s. There is a strong parallel with issues raised in Chapter 4: social responsibility, treating suppliers as equals, and joint improvement programmes are relevant, parallel values.

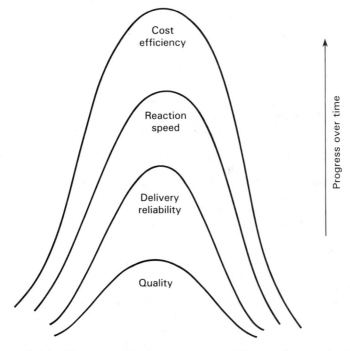

Figure 10.11 The pyramid of progress... applies to the supply chain too? (Source: after de Meyer and Ferdowes [19])

The benefits of JIT supply grow over time, and each improvement opens up the possibility of further savings. Gone are the days when suppliers put in a demand for an annual price increase based on the year's wages settlement! Determined exploitation of the experience curve, greater involvement by co-makers in the design and development of new products, and joint improvement activities are rapidly becoming the currency of the new supply relationships.

JIT supply follows the implementation of superior material planning and control systems by the dominant supply chain member (whether that is the OEM or the retailer). Material movements must be orchestrated by people who know what they are doing, and who have earned respect by first demonstrating their capability by putting their own house in order! While this is going on, some of the strategy issues can be started, such as supplier selection, transport policy, and supplier QA systems. But progress in comakership should be in stages, as suggested in Figure 10.11. Begin with a foundation of quality, the basis for selecting the comakers in the first place. Build on to this a capability for delivery reliability. Then comes reaction speed – the capability to change volume and mix more quickly. As a result, the crowning achievement is cost efficiency. In the past, this prize has been sought while the foundations on which it is based have been neglected.

■ References

1. *The Japanisation of British Industry*, N. Oliver and B. Wilkinson, Blackwell: Oxford, 1988.
2. 'The role of JIT in supply chain management', A. Harrison and C. Jones, *Manufacturing Technology International*, pp. 283–5, 1990.
3. 'Strategic supply chain management', C. Jones, *5th International Conference of the OMA, Warwick, 1990*.
4. *Out of the Crisis*, W. E. Deming, MIT Center for Advanced Engineering Study, Cambridge, MA, 1982, p. 36.
5. 'JIT purchasing in the UK', V. Winn, in C. Voss (ed.) *Just-in-Time Manufacture*, IFS, Bedford, 1988.
6. 'Establishing vendor rating based on quality performance and other criteria', N. Parker, *International Journal of Quality & Reliability Management*, 7, no. 2, 1990, pp. 23–8.
7. 'Nissan quality standard', Anon., Nissan Motor Manufacturing UK, 1985.
8. P. Baylis, in C. Voss (ed.) *Just-in-Time Manufacturing, Proc. 2nd International Conference, 1987*, IFS, Bedford, p. 225.
9. *World Class Manufacturing*, R. Schonberger, Free Press, New York, 1986, p. 155.
10. Based on 'Comakership as an extension of quality care', A. Harrison, *International Journal of Quality & Reliability Management*, 7, no. 2, 1990, pp. 15–22.
11. *Managing Quality*, D. Garvin, Free Press, New York, 1988.
12. 'How to gain the competitive edge: Productivity through continuous feedback', R. E. Cole, *Management Review*, October 1983, p. 10.
13. V. Winn, *ibid.*

14. *Manufacturing Strategy*, T. Hill, Macmillan, Basingstoke, 1985.
15. *Industrial Dynamics*, J. Forrester, MIT Press: Cambridge, MA, 1961.
16. 'Effectiveness framework for supply chain management', C. Jones and J. Clark, *Computer Integrated Systems*, **3**, no. 4, 1990.
17. 'A review of the development of EDI in the UK', Euromatica SA, Brussels, September, 1987.
18. 'EDI in JIT purchasing', A. Harrison and P. Friend, in C. Voss (ed.) *Just-in-Time Manufacturing*, 1987, *ibid*.
19. 'Lasting improvement in manfuacturing performance', K. Ferdowes and A. de Meyer, *Journal of Operations Management*, **9**, no. 2 (1990).

Implementing Just-in-Time

One of the most striking responses from our survey of experience in implementing JIT in over 130 US and UK companies [1] (described in Chapter 1, page 25) was the strong feeling that the implementation could have been better handled. Part of this response could be attributed to the 'normal' dissatisfaction felt by a JIT/TQ company which knows that there is always a better way. Many US companies which we visited told us that theirs was a company 'in a state of transition', and that we should not be put off by some of the things we saw! But we attributed the response more to a strong feeling that, if things had been better handled, the company would have progressed further than it had. The most common negative was lack of top management commitment and support – poor leadership showing through. This was followed by poor communications in every sense, between functions and throughout the organization – especially as it impacted on the shop floor. Lack of training was especially criticized by UK companies. Here, the emphasis was more towards training supervisory and middle management, while shop-floor personnel – the very people whose growth most drives the progress of a JIT company – were neglected. Further, the resources and teaching methods adopted in the United Kingdom were predominantly of the short-course type, with little evidence of workshops, videos, plant tours, literature, or shared experience being used other than in isolated examples. (The DTI campaign 'Inside UK Enterprise' is aimed at overcoming at least the plant tours deficiency by listing many UK companies which are prepared to host visits focused on specific topics.) On the positive front, many respondents to our survey identified cross-functional implementation teams as being invaluable to the success of JIT.

Our findings led us to propose two types of JIT implementation. The first is 'strategic JIT', where the company takes a long-term view of JIT implementation and acknowledges the impact on the total business. The second approach we called 'transitory JIT', where the company sees JIT as another short-term, temporary management technique which can yield some inventory or labour cost savings. Actually, there are several views which can lead company management to one form or other of transitory JIT:

JIT is an inventory reduction programme. It is basically about running the factory on lower stocks.

JIT stands for just-in-time, and is about getting your suppliers to deliver that way. This helps us to reduce our stocks of bought-out parts dramatically.

JIT refers to single sourcing. This means that we give all the volume to a single supplier, and of course demand a 15% price reduction for giving him all the extra volume *and* a long-term contract.

JIT is limited to the high volumes and repetitive manufacturing environment of the automotive industry. Therefore, it has no place in our company.

While some improvements can be, and often are, made by transitory JIT, this is not the route to becoming a world-class manufacturer. The key problem seems to come back to short-term thinking, and a lack of management consistency. In fact, it is often better to drop the name 'just-in-time' altogether, because there are too many false views that are prevalent. Use of a company-specific name like 'Jaguar Production System' helps to emphasize that the JIT/TQ philosophy has been adapted to meet specific company needs, and that we are not simply trying to implement techniques which have worked in Japan.

In order to establish a virtuous cycle of improvement, it is essential to view JIT in the context of the overall business strategy, as we discussed in Chapter 1, page 25. JIT/TQ becomes the manufacturing strategy, with major implications to other business strategies. Voss and Clutterbuck [2] state that:

JIT cannot be introduced in a hurry. It must be a strategic exercise, with detailed preparation and planning. The major problems need to be foreseen, tested and overcome before implementation, because the little ones will require more than enough management attention on their own.

The consequence of not paying sufficient attention to the pre-planning process is that major obstacles become apparent when we are too far down the line, like the company described in Chapter 6 which had fudged the maintenance issue. A radical change is needed in the way we do things. While this may seem comparatively easy in a greenfield situation, it frequently has to be addressed in an existing plant with its attendant 'traditions' and bad habits. Both situations require a clear vision of the future: what needs to be achieved and how that might be accomplished. The real danger of transitory JIT is that we kid ourselves that we are doing the right things, when in reality progress is not sufficiently far reaching. In their survey of UK Logistics, Ingersoll Engineers concluded that 'targets are not aggressive, resources are inadequate and progress far too slow' [3]. As noted in the Introduction, 'no matter how hard you try, there is no victory if your competitors work harder'.

■ Getting started

The busy executive today is bombarded by many 'catchy tune' programmes, each claiming to put his or her world to rights. Whether it is MRP II, simultaneous engineering, intelligent systems, total quality, world-class manufacturing, or JIT for that matter, someone has to understand the conflicting claims and put them together into some form of sense for the specific company. This 'sense' becomes the vision. Somehow, the vision must be prepared and shared with colleagues. Aspects of the vision may include the need to alter radically the way that business is done. An example of the changes envisaged is shown in the table below:

Year	1990	2000
Rejects	5%	0.05%
MTBF	15,000 hours	50,000 hours
Customer lead time	9 months	2 months
Customized features	5%	30%
Delivery accuracy	1 month	1 day
Cost (1990 base)	35,000	15,000

The vision impacts on company strategy, and eventually we are in a position to start planning the transformation process. Parnaby [4] refers to this process as a 'total systems approach', because many aspects of the business have to be changed simultaneously across a broad front, as indicated in Table 11.1. The techniques of JIT1 (see Figure 1.28) – such as simplicity, flow, fast setups,

Table 11.1 Analysis areas for JIT implementation

 1. Performance measures
 2. New organization structure based on interdisciplinary teams
 3. Simpler, more flexible job structures
 4. Training programmes
 5. Process flow routes and process capabilities
 6. Setup reduction
 7. Communication systems
 8. New systems for interfacing with customers and suppliers
 9. TQ improvement mechanisms (involvement, targets, projects)
10. New systems for capital authorization
11. New QA systems
12. New disciplines for material control
13. Improvements to factory scheduling and computer-aided planning systems
14. New customer/supplier relationships within the organization

Source: After Parnaby [4]

and total quality – are the key ones to focus on first. In the absence of Japanese 'advisers', the task of planning for JIT/TQ falls to a multi-disciplinary project team, identified above as a key success factor for JIT implementation. Parnaby [5] refers to the need to put in place a professionally staffed team who can lead and train in the environment of traditional British companies where the managers are not conversant with modern manufacturing systems. Planning and managing the process of change is described in more detail in the last section of this chapter.

■ Five key questions

Voss [6] proposes that the top team asks itself five key questions before starting on the JIT journey. The questions are really aimed at forging the link betwen JIT/TQ deliverables (see Figure 1.8) and the company strategy. If no such link can be found, then transitory JIT may have some appeal: this book is not aimed at such companies because it emphasizes the holistic nature of JIT/TQ. The five key questions are as follows.

1. Will JIT improve our business performance?

Hill [7] emphasizes the need to link a firm's manufacturing strategy with product performance in the market place and hence to the overall company strategy. If a Western company is competing against the Japanese, then it is competing against JIT. If it is not competing against the Japanese yet, then it will be, either directly or against Western versions of Japanese methods. Industries which have been relatively unscathed by Japanese competition so far, such as process industries and banking and insurance, will not be exempt in the longer run. If a firm decides not to use the JIT route, then it must convince itself that its chosen route is better in the full knowledge of what it will be up against. If it does decide to adopt the JIT route, then JIT deliverables need to be considered in terms of their impact in the market place. For example, design and manufacturing lead time reductions can make the company much more responsive to changing market needs. The company can elect to use the advantages so obtained to proliferate product offerings, or to improve profitability, or both.

2. How suitable is JIT for our manufacturing environment?

It is a potentially fatal mistake to view JIT as being effective only in high-volume, stable manufacturing situations. The Lucas terms 'runners–repeaters

–strangers' can be applied to most environments. Runners and repeaters are prime candidates for applying JIT concepts of flow, such as cellular manufacture and JIT/MRP. Flow concepts can be applied to a much wider range of manufacturing situations than traditionally used: this has been part of the 'JIT revolution' [8]. Further, as shown in Figure 7.10 the challenge is to move more parts and subassemblies out of the grip of more complex control systems into the pull scheduling arena by product and process simplification. In companies where there is already a high degree of flow in manufacturing, such as process industries, the power of selected JIT techniques like setup reduction and TPM cannot be ignored.

3. Should we invest in JIT, new process technology (for example, CIM), or both?

Developing competence and simplification in the way we do things is an essential step on the route to implementation of advanced manufacturing technologies. Table 1.1 proposes a sequence of strategy–competence–automate–integrate. JIT is directed primarily at the second step. This helps to create the basic orderliness and waste elimination which prepare the ground for further advances in automation and integration. For example, GT enables us to group processes together and prove the new methods without major capital spending. Once we have learned how to manage the new opportunities, then automation will comprise a more clearcut set of decisions which are less likely to involve automating waste. Further, the focus of JIT/TQ on people building helps to prepare better trained operators of new technology who know how to apply continuous process improvement. You cannot buy the people who are going to operate the machine in the same way as you can buy the machine itself [9]. Finally, Schonberger [10] encourages us not to automate unless process variability cannot otherwise be reduced. Often the most cost-effective alternative to automation is to let improvements keep coming from the lessons of tightening up on waste.

4. How should we implement JIT?

Once it has been decided to implement JIT, then the next question is how to do it. Figure 11.1 shows three key features of the formal implementation organization. A steering committee with cross-functional representation meets regularly to coordinate and monitor the implementation process. Members should have enough clout to be able to fix people and financial resources for JIT projects. Regular meetings which are well attended are a sign of health: irregular meetings which are not well attended are a sign that things are not being taken seriously. The steering committee identifies where and how to kick off, selects the tasks and composition of the early project teams, and handles

Steering committee:
design, purchasing, quality, manufacturing,
finance, marketing, personnel

Project manager:
the product champion
preferably full-time

Project teams:
layout, setup, TPM, design, scheduling, product, etc.
part-time, cross-functional, regular reports

Figure 11.1 Implementation organization

the necessary communications to all company members. It ensures continuing company support and sets up a budget to ensure speedy allocation of funds for projects. It also steers the overall development of JIT in the company – a task which requires meticulous planning. This task is handled on a day-to-day basis by a project manager, or JIT champion. The person selected should ideally be someone with great energy and enthusiasm who is well known and who has sound process and product knowledge. The JIT champion should work full time on JIT implementation in all but the smallest companies – this is likely to be a long-term appointment. Finally, the implementation project team is set up to plan and execute technique-specific projects (such as layout and flow, setup reduction and design) and area-specific projects (applying JIT techniques to specific sections), as explained further in the next section. The JIT champion helps to facilitate these projects by helping to select and plan projects (in collaboration with the steering committee), and by helping to fix terms of reference. Teams should have the necessary support to implement improvement decisions immediately: this is the spirit of JIT! The implementation team forms the powerhouse of progress, and members work long hours, particularly in the early stages. There is so much to be done!

5. What fundamental changes do we have to make to become a JIT company?

Strategic JIT is not an easy option, and its implementation requires great determination over many years. The transformation process requires leadership, not supervision of existing methods. It requires improvement so that problems do not recur. It requires continuous investment in company members so that they too become improvement oriented. Figure 11.2 lists some of the fundamental management values that are needed to achieve a TQ culture. The changes need to be 'institutionalized' [11] by changing the way success is defined in manufacturing. This means changing the way that performance is measured by empahsizing the new goals.

Discipline: the critical essence of a manufacturing company; key quality and safety standards must be followed

Drive out fear: so that company members are not afraid to participate in improvement activities

Plan and replan: continuous improvement is a journey of discovery where new opportunities keep appearing; keep asking 'what can we now do as a result of this improvement?'

Do it now: push hard for improvement proposals to be implemented straight away

Never be satisfied: there is always a better way! Keep asking why, and maintain the relentless war on waste

Excellent people: make an excellent company, so keep people development at the forefront and aim to hire the whole person

Be honest: recognize the shortcomings and do not try to move faster than company members currently are capable. Learn to tolerate mistakes

Promote flexibility: throughout the company, and provide a strong example yourself

Buy yourself time: to push through the transformation; 2 years is rarely sufficient

Figure 11.2 Becoming a JIT company: some key management values

Satisfactory answers need to be developed to these questions before embarking on the JIT journey. There is no point in superficial answers being given, or transitory JIT will be the result. Begin the way you intend to continue by starting off the planning process in TQ fashion!

■ JIT implementation projects

The sequence of implementing JIT projects requires careful planning and thought. As indicated in Chapter 1, implementing JIT/TQ is not like collecting goodies at random in a supermarket. The sequence in which things are done is important. Stages in the development of JIT/TQ, shown in Figure 1.1, indicate the need for early preparation stages to be technique specific. Stages 2 (introduce basic disciplines) and 3 (process control) require the implementation of specific techniques like housekeeping, safety, and quality standards. Just as important is preparation of the accompanying attitudes which ensure that the new disciplines stick, and that they become the norm for everyone. While 'JIT' and 'TQ' are shown in separate columns in the JIT/TQ development diagram, in reality they take place in a parallel and intertwined manner. But 'JIT' development activities should not run ahead of 'TQ' development. The new standards of tidiness and cleanliness become a source of pride when showing visitors round. New attitudes to safety- and quality-critical processes also help to prepare the foundations for the war on waste. Training in problem-solving techniques prepares company members to take over greater responsibility for the work they do. Once a satisfactory start has been made on basic disciplines and process control, a pilot project which is area specific can be launched. This can be done early in the implementation programme, and is key to learning about how JIT works (and does not work) in your environment. Selection of

Features:
- product has stable characteristics in terms of volume and design
- there is scope for considerable improvement, and a high chance of a successful outcome
- area is self-contained (and so is not critically dependent on the performance of other areas)
- receptive attitude from supervisor and operators
- representative of product and process problems found elsewhere

Figure 11.3 Useful features for the area selected for the pilot project

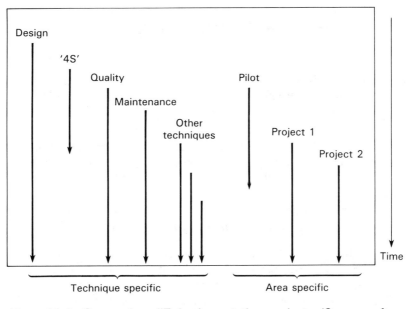

Figure 11.4 Sequencing JIT implementation projects (Source: after Bicheno [10])

the area for the pilot project again benefits from careful thought, and useful features are listed in Figure 11.3. Lessons from the pilot project need to be carefully evaluated before going on to set up more project teams in other areas. In this way, major problems can be foreseen and acted upon before full-scale implementation starts. The pilot project may well show up the need to give high priority to other technique-specific projects like design or maintenance. It will certainly be the centre of much natural curiosity and perhaps concern from other company members. Therefore it plays a vital role in communication. This factor can be used to considerable effect, for example by making a video of the pilot area in action, and by taking photographs of the state of the area before and after improvement activities. The video and photographs can then be used as training aids for subsequent projects, and have a value which is enhanced because applications of JIT/TQ is shown in a 'home' company setting. A typical sequence for implementing JIT projects is shown in Figure 11.4, illustrating a possible relationship over time between technique- and area-specific projects. Planning and coordinating the triggering and management of projects requires careful and meticulous planning by the JIT champion and steering committee, bearing in mind the resources available and the capability of the organization to cope with change. The actual timing and nature of the technique-specific projects is particularly important.

■ New measures of performance

What gets measured is what gets done. Therefore, it is necessary to ensure that company members are given the right messages about what is important. Some examples of performance measures which can be appropriate in a JIT environment are as follows:

- **Flow factor:** This is the ratio between manufacturing lead time and the sum of manufacturing process times. Ideally, the flow factor should be unity, but it will actually be much greater than this because of non-value-added activities like waiting time, transport, setups, and material shortages. These activities should be analysed by means of process flow charting so that we can focus on the major causes of waste.

- **Lead time:** This records the reduction in manufacturing lead time itself. But the $P:D$ ratio (product lead time to customer expected lead time) needs to be watched as well. One company was so successful in reducing the manufacturing lead time for electric motors that it was flooded out with work and was forced to quote 6-week delivery lead times. Lack of capacity can suddenly make things much worse!

- **Flow distance:** This records the total distance travelled by a product or subassembly during the course of manufacture. Again, the aim is to reduce this over time.

- **Quality costs:** These are often categorized into prevention (such as training), detection (such as inspection, measurement, and calibration), and failure (such as warranty, scrap, and defects). The aim over time is to reduce total quality costs by investing more in prevention and so reducing detection and failure [12].

- **Maintenance measures:** For example, mean time between failures, service factor, and others referred to in Chapter 8.

- **WIP reduction:** Although WIP is classified as a part of current 'assets', its reduction is often a useful reflection of progress in JIT implementation.

Many of the above measrues of performance do not have a cost basis. The assumption is that if such measures greatly improve over time, then this will be reflected in the bottom line because competitiveness (cost, quality, and delivery performance) will undoubtedly have improved.

■ New costing systems

Accounting periodicals have been featuring regular articles about new financial systems for the last few years. Professional institutions have been running seminars supporting the revolution. What is going on? Under attack from authors such as H. T. Johnson and R. S. Kaplan [13], traditional management accounting has been exposed as incapable of coping with modern management systems. Some of the weaknesses which have been been brought out into the open are as follows:

- Direct labour is no longer the main cost driver in manufacturing. So variance accounting based on analysis of direct labour off-standards, and flexing variable costs by standard hours produced, no longer give the right signals. Under traditional costing systems, direct labour assumes an importance out of all proportion to its relative size, a point made in Figure 6.1.
- Apportioning overheads on the basis of direct labour is as bad as justifying capital spending solely on the basis of headcount reduction. For one thing, the impression is given that savings in direct labour will also save the overheads allocated.
- Indirect costs have been growing more rapidly than direct costs. The sources and causes of these costs are not well understood. One reason is the rise of the 'second factory' referred to in Chapter 9: the factory which makes paperwork and processes data and does lots of non-value-adding activities.
- Performance measures based on historical performance (what happened last month) are too late to be useful.
- When there has been a considerable reduction in manufacturing lead time, it is often no longer appropriate to track the buildup in costs of WIP through many stages of manufacture.
- In-company financial reporting has been constrained by the overriding need to reconcile what is said with external reports.
- Material costs, the greatest contributor to manufacturing spending, do not form part of the management information pack.
- The benefits of improvements in delivery and quality performance, and in the reduction of waste, are not reflected in improved figures from the costing system.

- The costing system has been the domain of the professionally qualified accountant, and has received little input from other business functions.

Once such drawbacks have been recognized, the inevitable conclusion is that profitability does not depend on cost control alone. The opportunity presents itself to make cost accounting reflect how a business is trying to compete, rather than vice versa! There is a need to change. But what should replace the old systems? One of the most popular alternatives is activity-based costing (ABC), and we will go on to explain the way in which ABC thinking has developed.

A proposal for changing the focus of the cost management system is shown in Table 11.2. New demands for the system are listed under the JIT heading. The demands are a simple shopping list, stating for example the need to focus on material costs, to control overheads at source, and to improve

Table 11.2 The changing focus of cost management systems

Cost management area	Traditional	JIT
1. Control of direct production resources	Focused on the control of direct labour	Focused on all production resources, especially materials
2. Product cost buildup	Summation of numerous labour and overhead rates applied to each operation performed	Based on costing at a cell level which can be as simple as a cell throughput time multiplied by a cell rate
3. Control of production overheads	The method of allocating, apportioning, and recovering overheads does not attempt to establish relationship between costs and their causes; it is an accounting exercise	Overheads are controlled at their source using such methods as the 'cost driver' approach which relates cost behaviour to causal factors identifiable in products and processes
4. Accuracy of product costs	Refined during the manufacturing process	Refined at the design stage — before the product is produced
5. Recording of scrap and rework	Complex systems are utilized to record, value, and report scrap and rework	As quality improves, the need for system to report scrap and rework diminishes
6. Performance measures	Primarily based on financial variance analysis	Visibility and non-financial measures are used
7. Important performance measures	Labour efficiency, material usage, overhead recovery, cost centre control, etc.	Quality measurement, machine/cell utilization, cell contribution/ profitability, etc.

Source: Williams and Taylor [13]

visibility – including use of non-financial measures. The CAM-I studies [15] have shown that product costs can be related to only a small number of activities, and that these activities can therefore be used as a basis for apportioning costs. Such considerations have led to the following simple principles for ABC:

- Products require activities (such as processing sales orders, procuring materials, and delivery activities).
- Activities consume resources (such as materials, manpower, and energy).
- Resources cost money.

Management does not control costs, only the activities which cause that cost. The aim of ABC is to recognize all of the various activities undertaken by a company, and to allocate a cost to each one. Activities are grouped into 'cost pools' by major reason for their performance – called a cost driver. Cost drivers identify the manufacturing view of the degree of difficulty in making the product. This view could be influenced by such factors as size, special facility requirements, particular build difficulties, number of stops in manufacturing process, and manufacturing lead time. A relative weighting is allocated to these factors using input from manufacturing personnel, and the overall weighted score by product used to allocate the costs. The reworking of traditional costing structures into ABC cost pools/cost drivers and direct costs (materials) for a plstics injection moulding company is shown in Figure 11.5. (This is not a general method for collecting ABC cost pools, and there is scope for initiative in how ABC is applied in a given company.) As an example to show how ABC works from here, the pallet movement cost driver will be used. Activity analysis had shown that the activities which had been identified against the pallet movement cost driver were as shown in the table below.

Activity	Person
Stretchwrapping	Operator
Move pallets to warehouse	Operator
Stack pallets	Fork lift driver
Load vehicles	Fork lift driver
Stock control	Chargehand
Pallet control	Operator
Pallet repair	Operator

The number of pallet movements were measured, and the sum of the costs of all activities which have pallet movements as a cost driver found. This pool of costs was divided by the number of pallet movements to give a cost per pallet movement. The same methods were then applied to the other cost pools. Direct costs and pool rates are then applied to products using information gathered from many sources – not just production and finance. For example, sales have a major input in terms of number of orders, calloffs, and production run length. This input is a key issue now that setup costs have been identified through the toolchange cost driver. Product costing is completed

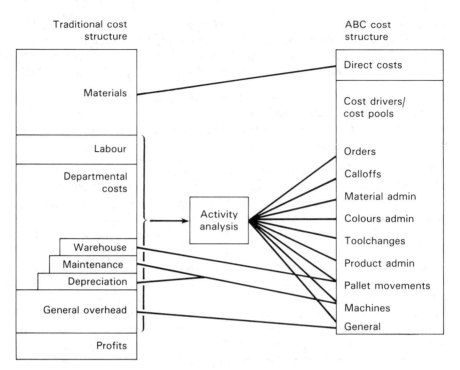

Figure 11.5   Reworking of traditional cost structure into ABC cost pools for a UK plastics manufacturer

regularly (say every 3 months), and is carried out on a personal computer using a suitable software package.

The above example showed up a number of problems with the ABC concept:

- It is assumed that all pallets spend an equal amount of time in storage. This is not true in practice. Analysis of stock holding in weeks for each product would be a major undertaking.
- The effect of cost increases is difficult because of the complex route by which cost pools are formed.
- Allocation of activities by cost driver is difficult, and requires input from many functions to be objective.
- Some activities are complex, but simplistic solutions are necessary to get the job done.

But these difficulties were offset by the better understanding of the sources and causes of costs and above all the focus on activities (processes). A further development once ABC is in place will be to attain greater visibility of non-value-added activities.

Another new approach to cost accounting is called throughput accounting. It is based on OPT-style concepts, and has four assumptions:

1. Profit varies inversely with lead time. So total factory cost reduces as the lead time reduces.
2. Manufacturing costs other than material costs are fixed in the short term.
3. The rate at which the business makes money is determined by the ratio of the throughput (defined as sales revenue less direct material cost) to the total factory cost (also excluding direct material).
4. The profitability of a manufacturing business is determined by the overall rate at which money is generated by the factory, not by individual product margins.

Throughput accounting has some attractive concepts, such as the focus on manufacturing lead times. It appears less sophisticated than ABC, and has fewer applications in the United Kingdom. But it does have some 'enthusiastic users' [16].

Modern systems perhaps sacrifice accuracy for realism and timeliness, and detail for simplicity and visibility. They call in particular for closer involvement of accounting professionals in knowing and understanding the manufacturing processes they are dealing with, and for working much more closely with production and other line functions.

■ Managing change

This section aims to pull together several of the themes raised in this chapter by relating them to the 'Map of the change management process' proposed by Beckhard and Harris [17] and shown in Figure 11.6. There are four key aspects to consider, as follows.

1. Why change?

Major drivers for change in British companies over the next 5 years compared with the last 5 have been analysed in a survey by Ingersoll Engineers [18]. The results of this aspect of the survey are shown in Figure 11.7. Financial performance continues to dominate the thinking of the senior managers of the 150 responding companies surveyed. This prompted the authors of the survey to coin the term 'tuners' for the most popular view of changes planned (66%): small-scale improvements. The 'shakers' – leaders who believe that their companies needed to undergo fundamental change – were in the minority (33%). In my experience, the 'tuners' are typically the MDs heading up companies which are currently financially successful, and who are convinced that their mission is to hold a steady course. Often, they cannot see the tidal wave of

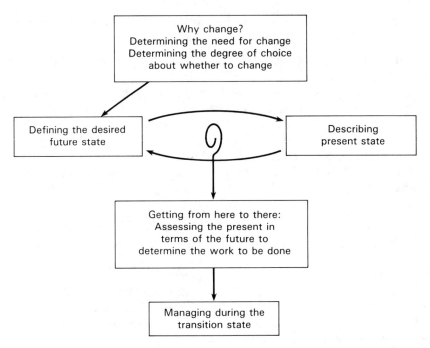

Figure 11.6 Map of the change management process (Source: R. Beck-hard, R. Harris, *Organisational Transitions* © Addison-Wesley Publishing Co. Inc. reprinted with permission of the publisher)

new, leaner competition approaching! The 'shakers' recognize the need for change, brought about by such factors as the following:

- **Crisis:** The market for the company's products collapses, or the company degenerates into a period of low profitability or loss. HQ puts in a new management team with a remit to turn things round. Toyo Kogyo introduced the Toyota Production System as part of its reaction to the collapse of company sales in the USA following the first oil shock.
- **Competitors:** It is recognized that competitors have superior products, manufacturing methods, or other key competitive features of their operations. Such awareness can come from benchmarking studies or from a visit to Japanese or other companies who are 'best in class'. Albion Pressed Metal embarked on their improvement programme following a visit to Japan by the Chairman and MD, who recognized the huge gap between Japanese and UK performance.
- **Customer pressure:** A major customer demands that changes are put into effect to start the journey towards world-class manufacture. This is how Sumitomo Tyres commenced the JIT journey – as a result of pressure from Toyota, as mentioned in Chapter 1.

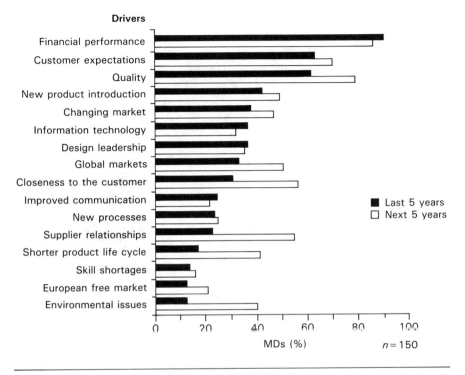

Drivers

Question: What have been the main drivers for change in your organization in the last 5 years, and what do you see as the key ones in the next 5 years?

Figure 11.7 The main drivers for change (based on a survey of UK companies by Ingersoll Engineers)

Understanding the sources and causes of the need to change is the starting point for managing the change process.

2. Vision of an excellent company

Defining the vision of the future is the next logical step in the process. Here, JIT ideals – such as perfect quality and no waste – may be helpful, although some more realistic intermediate goals would be decided on in practice. A detailed description of the goals must be prepared and shared by the top team. Beliefs and company values have a key role to play here: unless you believe in what you are doing, it is unlikely that you are going to get very far – and progress will be short-lived as in transitory JIT. Goals could include specific objectives such as those set at Yuasa Battery in the United Kingdom [19].

■ Achieve quality levels equal to or better than Japanese quality levels.

■ Attain Japanese productivity levels.

Here, Yuasa was helped by having a Japanese parent with whom it was possible to make direct comparisons. It is often simpler to focus on similar industries rather than competitors. A competitor is rarely prepared to disclose useful information. But companies in similar industries are prepared to share non-confidential performance data, particularly on things they do well. The DTI 'Inside UK Enterprise' initiative can provide many useful contacts here.

A strategy to achieve the goals is produced next, and needs to be spelt out explicitly to company members so that they too can share the vision. Yuasa saw two fundamental factors here:

1. Increasing the output of individual company members.
2. Ensuring that the company advances in the correct direction for the future.

Both of these factors need to be elaborated and quantified, but explaining them is very important. The second factor is responsibility of the top team, and this must be spelt out clearly to all company members. The first gives most difficulty to Western managers. Increasing output is achieved first and foremost by company members themselves. In Japanese-managed companies, this is typically achieved through involvement methods like quality control circles. SP Tyres view this area as part of a core philosophy which believes in the individual and in the need to help individuals reach their full potential. Another belief which is fundamental to Japanese companies is that of teamwork. The philosophy of strategy development or decision-making is called *nemawashi*, or watering of the roots. Ideas are canvassed and ideas sought so that a consensus gradually develops. Although the planning phase takes longer, it is carried out more thoroughly and commitment is achieved by a wider group of company members.

3. Analyse the present

A thorough 'stocktake' of company status is the next step. One of the key issues here is an understanding of the core mission of the business. For example, Albion Pressed Metal stated their mission in terms of being a volume presswork manufacturer, and consequently weeded out low-volume customers (see Figure 2.17). The aim is to build up an accurate picture of the present state of the business. This picture is then compared with the vision, and decisions made as to what needs to be changed and what does not need to be changed. From this comparison, an action plan emerges.

4. Transition state management

The transition state is a temporary situation which is designed to facilitate change. A road map is first identified which selects the initial areas for intervention, and which also identifies the change methods. These could include the following:

■ Experiments to try out new ideas in a controlled environment. This could include simulation such as the computer modelling of new material flows.
■ Pilot projects to advance such ideas into normal operating conditions.
■ Education. SP Tyres do most of the training in house using line managers and supervisors, who often study a subject and build up a course to a surprisingly high standard. Advantages are relevance to local needs, trainers learn a lot in the process, and training is clearly management led.
■ Seeing is believing. A visit to an excellent company which has gone some way further down the JIT road can help sway people in the same way as the visit to Japan convinced the Chairman and MD of Albion Pressed Metal.

A facilitator or JIT champion can be a major agent of change. Key requirements are that the person appointed should have sufficient authority to get things done, sufficient respect from all quarters, and strong interpersonal skills.

But the most effective agent of change is consistent, supportive management action over the period of change. Here, one of the most worrying aspects of the Ingersoll survey referred to above shows up. Nearly three-quarters of the MDs had changed jobs in the last 5 years. One-third of the companies surveyed had changed ownership over the last 5 years. I am reminded of the story of a recent takeover:

> The first we knew of it was when these black BMWs arrived on the drive. These guys were from the HQ of the company which had taken us over. They were financial analysts, and had come to run the rule over our company. If they thought that a ratio was wrong, they put yellow stickers on the desks of a selection of people. We had to fire those people.

It is impossible to think in the long term under such circumstances. Also, it is impossible to manage change effectively, because there is no planning, only 'action'. Companies are commodities. Beckhard and Harris [20] put it this way:

> Although the pressures for immediate results often arise ... it has been our experience that ... change efforts fail due to a lack of understanding on the part of the organisational leadership of what the process of intervention and change involves.

Short-term thinking, inadequate planning, and ignorance of the processes involved are major inhibitors of change.

■ Conclusion

Implementing JIT/TQ does not follow any fixed pattern. There are no quick-fixes, and no 'golden routes to success' as some people would have you believe! Setting tough targets, such as Hewlett-Packard's tenfold reduction in defects, seems often to have the desired effect if encouraged by a helping and dedicated management leadership. The current business environment often creates the need for urgent change. It is also important not to push harder than the company can cope with, or before enabling attitudes have been developed. Another useful principle is not to try to do the difficult things too early, for example to introduce pull scheduling or quality circles at an early stage in JIT development. Instead, go for the simple techniques first, so that people learn, get into good habits, and have an early taste of success. Most JIT implementations go through a 'JIT plateau', where progress levels out. Here, the danger is that performance will drift back towards the starting position unless the trend can be quickly reversed. This is a task for the JIT champion: the implementation must be re-energized by the input of some fresh ideas for improvement. There are always plenty to chose from! Finally, JIT is about applying techniques for getting rid of waste. Theory without action is deadly. So are false starts and major changes of direction which owe more to the personality of the MD than to the needs of the company. JIT/TQ becomes the company culture.

■ References

1. 'Just-in-time; A US–UK comparison', T. Billesbach, A. Harrison, and S. Croom-Morgan, *International Journal of Operations & Production Management*, **11**, no. 10, 1991, pp. 44–57.
2. *Just-in-Time: A Global Status Report*, C. Voss and D. Clutterbuck, IFS, Bedford 1989.
3. 'Procurement, materials management and distribution: A survey of logistics in British industry', Ingersoll Engineers, November, 1987.
4. 'A systems approach to the implementation of JIT methodologies in Lucas Industries', J. Parnaby, *International Journal of Production Research*, **26**, no. 3, pp. 483–92.
5. J. Parnaby, *ibid.*, p. 491.
6. C. Voss and D. Clutterbuck, *ibid.*, p. 118.
7. *Manufacturing Strategy*, T. Hill, Macmillan, Basingstoke, 1985.
8. *JIT Factory Revolution*, H. Hirano, Productivity Press: Cambridge, MA, 1988.

9. *How to Make Japanese Management Methods Work in the West*, K. Murata and A. Harrison, Gower, Aldershot, 1991, p. 50.
10. *Operations Management: Improving Customer Service*, R. Schonberger, Irwin, Homewood, IL, 1991.
11. *Implementing JIT*, J. Bicheno, IFS, Bedford, 1991.
12. See for example *Quality is Free*, P. Crosby, McGraw-Hill, 1979.
13. *Relevance Lost: The Rise and Fall of Management Accounting*, H. T. Johnson and R. S. Kaplan, HBS Press, Cambridge, MA, 1987.
14. 'The impact of JIT on financial management', K. Williams and P. Taylor, *Proc. 3rd International Conference on JIT Manufacturing*, IFS, Bedford, 1988.
15. *Cost Management for Today's Advanced Manufacturing: The CAM-I Conceptual Design*, HBS Press, Cambridge, MA, 1988.
16. 'Measuring the cost', *Industrial Computing*, December, 1989.
17. *Organisational Transitions: Managing Complex Change*, R. Beckhard and R. Harris, Addison-Wesley, Reading, MA, 1987.
18. 'Change: The good, the bad and the visionary', Ingersoll Engineers, 1991.
19. K. Murata and A. Harrison, *ibid.*, p. 2.
20. R. Beckhard and R. Harris, *ibid.*, p. 116.

Appendix A
Early Days at
Mitsubishi Aluminium

Mitsubishi Aluminium was started in 1962 by Mitsubishi of Japan and Reynolds International of the USA. The Fuji plant near Tokyo was completed in June 1965 and comprises three main divisions:

1. Sheet rolling: up to $2 \cdot 7$ m wide on a 4-Hi reversible hot mill, various cold mills, a roughing mill, and a finishing mill.
2. Extrusion: equipped with several hydraulic extrusion presses ranging from 1500 to 3500 tons capacity.
3. Foil and packaging: foil stock processed through hot and cold mills is fed through foil mills and rolled down to 6μ thickness.

This description of the early days of JIT implementation is based on a visit which I made to the plant in 1988, when there were 850 employees. Dr H. Nakamura had arrived at the plant in July 1986 as senior managing director and general manager of the Fuji plant. He immediately launched a new initiative for improving competitiveness, which he called the 'MAF Production System' (MAF stands for 'Mitsubishi Aluminium Fuji'). Experiences with MAF were chronicled for the first year in a series of six booklets, the second of which forms the basis of this description.

The MAF production system is aimed at reducing the effects of three defects (3-MU) which affect production: *muda* (waste); *mura* (irregularity); and *muri* (excessiveness) (see Chapter 6). A steering committee, called the Improvement Project Team, was set up with 23 representatives from the three divisions of the Fuji plant. Its task was to plan and to coordinate MAF. Each division set up its own project team, and other project teams were set up in staff areas like technical control and the cafeteria. It was seen as very important that all company members knew what the Improvement Project Team was thinking, what it was trying to do, and the results which had been obtained as a result of improvement activities. The chosen start date was 1 September. The first team meeting was attended by two directors of Mitsubishi Aluminium, and 'ideas and opinions were enthusiastically exchanged to ensure an efficient start-up.'

■ First 40 days

Dr Nakamura saw the initial task as one of 'broad slimming.' The attack on 3-MU was focused by the project team on four areas:

1. **Offices:** Streamlining office paperwork was seen as the first choice, because it would be a good example to production. The following instructions were given:

   ■ No documents must be left on a desk when leaving the office. If it is impossible to place all documents in desk drawers then the remaining ones should be placed on the chair.

   ■ All filed documents must be examined. All unnecessary documents must be weighed and destroyed. All necessary documents must be checked for duplication.

   ■ Brochures and catalogues which are more than 1 year old must be destroyed.

   Japan Industrial Standards required that all documents must be retained for 5 years, a requirement that was overruled. 'Why should it be necessary to keep waste paper for five years in case JIS inspectors want to look at it when production activities must be planned efficiently to ensure good quality with fast delivery?' it was argued. 'We believe that the true objective of the JIS system is to establish an efficient production system rather than excessive completeness of paperwork,' said Dr Nakamura.

2. **Simplified reports:** An instruction required reports to be summarized on one page. All documents were to be marked up with a 'destroy by' date. In this way, a fresh buildup of documents would be avoided. An aim was to create an effective filing system which made it easy to access the required document, easy to use the document, and easy to replace it in the correct place afterwards.

3. **Putting life into spare parts:** Dr Nakamura commented on the many spare parts which lay around the hot mill. 'I found that they were covered with dust and placed in a disorderly fashion. Some of them were in broken boxes, some were damaged. It seemed impossible for us to expect that they could be used readily to replace broken parts. They are lifeless: they cannot be relied on to play their part when needed.' A team of seven maintenance personnel was given the task of cleaning and ordering spare parts within the next 6 weeks. (The techniques which were used are illustrated in Figure 5.5.)

4. *Kanban*: After all tools and parts have been put into order, and the obsolete ones scrapped, a *kanban* (sign) should be made. This will indicate the number of tools needed per month, reorder levels, and actual consumption of tools by date. The control of tools can then be carried out more

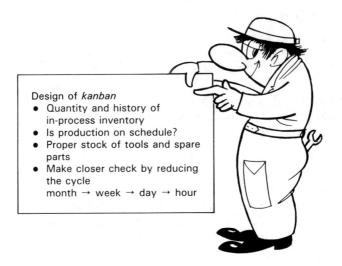

Design of *kanban*
- Quantity and history of in-process inventory
- Is production on schedule?
- Proper stock of tools and spare parts
- Make closer check by reducing the cycle
month → week → day → hour

Figure A.1 MAF rules for *kanban* design

economically. *Kanbans* can also be used to find out at a glance how many slabs or coils are being worked on at a given process. Also, *kanbans* are very effective when used for scheduling the rolling sequence of coils with the hot mill, and for planning daily production volumes. The time span on each *kanban* would depend on the process. For example, a *kanban* by month would suit the cast house, but foil or reroll stock needs only 3 days' cover. The important thing is that the time period should be shortened by improvement activities. Figure A.1 shows MAF rules for *kanban* design.

All improvements were to be achieved as early as possible, measured, and reported to company members. *Kanban* introduction required careful planning over the 40-day period, but several projects were in place within the target timescale.

■ Early results

With typical Japanese drive and energy, the project teams set about their task. Some examples of early progress were as follows:

1. **Cast House:** Bricks, tools, and spare parts were checked. Some 2,400 nuts and bolts were discarded along with 17 tons of bricks. Discarded documents weighed 1·2 tons, and were in addition to improvements made

previously by QCC activities. Many workers complained: 'Don't throw that away – we may need it in future.' But once only the needed tools and spare parts had been neatly arranged into labelled cabinets, the complaints reduced. Because the cast house is dusty, polycarbonate doors were fitted to the cabinets.

Kanban cards were written for each slab which was held in stock. The cards were colour coded for age. Red meant that the slab was more than 2 months old, yellow that it was 1–2 months old, and green that it was under 1 month old. The cards were then displayed on a bulletin board in the workers' rest room. At the beginning, there were over 1,200 cards, and the bulletin board was not big enough to hold them all. But by 10 October, the number had been reduced to 995, a saving of 1,230 tons.

2. **Coil Rolling:** Some 3·4 tons of paper was discarded, along with 9 tons of steel material. Storage of parts and tools became a structured task, aided by shadow boards on tool panels for orderly arrangement.

   Over 1,500 coils were kept in storage, and scheduling was driven by a computer program. However, use of *kanban* methods showed that it would be possible to exert tighter control by this means. For example, 50 coils had been eliminated by checking stocks more frequently than the twice per month which had previously been the case. Displayed on an inventory status board, cards again helped workers to know the state of coils in progress and to identify surplus and coverage coils.

   Hot coils took 2 days to cool off. Cutting this time down by 1 day would save 500 tons of inventory. Early attempts at water cooling resulted in corrosion damage. The answer was eventually found to be fan-assisted air cooling.

3. **Foil Rolling:** Progress reported by the division manager again related the advantages of sorting and classifying tools into cabinets with the front doors removed. *Kanban* cards were again assigned to individual coils, but, here, green meant that a coil had been in process for less than 3 days, yellow for 4–6 days, and red for more than 7 days. Within 6 weeks, the number of 'red' in-process coils had been reduced from 68 to 27, and the number of 'red' finished coils had been reduced from 263 to 105. The reduction was due to a greater awareness of the need to avoid wasteful ways of processing coils. A spin-off from the reduced in-process times was that scratches and other surface defects caused by crowded storage conditions were considerably decreased.

Following this initial phase of 'broad slimming', the shop floor and walls were painted in ice blue, with dark-blue gangways. This helped to promote cleanliness and tidiness further. Set off by mercury-vapour lamps and the bright, shiny product, the workplace was already showing the benefits of the MAF system.

Dr Nakamura had demonstrated how it was possible to apply the concepts of 3-MU to Mitsubishi Aluminium. In a short time, company members were coming to accept that operating with a smaller stock was better than what they had been doing. Only four simple areas had so far been attacked. Now, he was ready to lead his people further up the mountain.

Appendix B
Supplier Relationships
at Massey Ferguson

This case study summarizes aspects of a research project undertaken in 1986–7 by the author and Professor Chris Voss. The purpose of the project was to identify issues in setting up JIT supply at the customer (the Massey Ferguson (MF) tractor plant in Coventry, England) and at a supplier company (referred to in this case as Car Products, CP) based near by. A particular issue for investigation was the effect of demand variability on the supply of parts from CP to MF. A major conclusion of the project was that both parties could work together to mitigate the effects of demand variability, but that traditional buyer/supplier systems and attitudes tend to obscure the opportunities for doing so. Flexibility of supply could and should be a major goal towards which both parties work.

MF exports tractors from its Coventry plant to markets around the world. Because of the volatility of some of these markets, schedule variability tends to be relatively high. For example, delays in clearing letters of credit can lead to last-minute schedule changes. Sales forecasts are collated from major market areas, and an overall forecast developed for the next 6 months. This forecast is broken down into material delivery schedules for MF suppliers, and the method by which this was done at the time is shown in the central column in Figure B.1. The forecast was converted into a master production schedule (MPS) by major product groupings, and the groupings broken down into derivatives based on historical records. After ensuring that orders had not been double-counted by interfacing with the orders management system, the actionable forecast was broken down by means of material requirements planning (MRP) into material delivery schedules by supplier. These schedules were then collated and posted. Because of various management reviews and relatively slow interfacing of the computer programs concerned, the whole process from production of a new forecast to receipt of the new delivery schedule by the supplier was 6 weeks. Like the forecast on which it was based, the schedule was also in 6 monthly time buckets. Such supplier schedules tended to be very variable, as illustrated by the examples shown in Figure B.2.

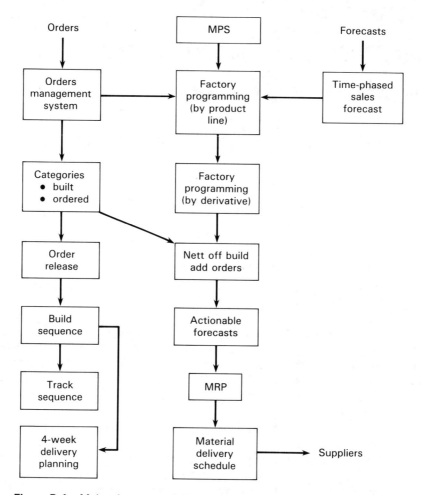

Figure B.1 Main elements of MF manufacturing planning and control system

MF's actual order bank extended at the time only for about 3–4 weeks into the future. In order to make the detailed material delivery calculations necessary, MF processed orders by a different but parallel route to the forecasts referred to above. This route is shown in the left-hand column in Figure B.1, and resulted in a factory assembly schedule – the short-term version of the MPS. This planned build sequence was broken down by means of a mini-MRP programme into 4-week delivery planning reports for each principal part number. These reports, which were refreshed weekly, were used by MF's expeditors to keep parts availability within target inventory levels. At the time, the reports were not revealed to suppliers. In the case of the parts supplied by CP, these target levels were 10 days at MF and a further 10 days at CP. Because

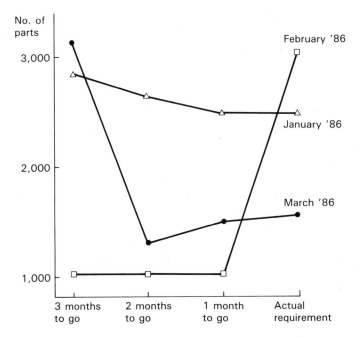

Figure B.2 Variability of monthly delivery schedules (Part number: 1868285 M3)

of the many short-term changes which often occurred in MF's order board, the expeditors often asked suppliers like CP to amend schedules which had been previously called for on the monthly material delivery schedules. However, variability of the delivery planning reports was not as marked as the variability of the monthly schedules. Table B.1 illustrates the changes in the weekly planning requirements for the same part number as that illustrated in Figure B.2 over an 8-week period. Changes in scheduled demand from one report to the next can be seen from the figures in the column under the appropriate week-ending date for requirements. Variability is generally much

Table B.1 Variability of weekly delivery planning reports

Report date	8/8	15/8	22/8	29/8	5/9	12/9	19/9	26/9
28/7	266	233	294	306				
4/8	291	319	270	179				
11/8		357	367	218	307			
18/8			379	160	315	310		
25/8				404	283	266	184	
1/9					509	275	128	238
8/9						514	187	249

less than that for forecast demand. Increases which sometimes occur in the last figure in a column were usually caused by stock which had already been supplied not being netted off the figures in time before the report was issued.

■ The supplier's MPC system

From what has been stated so far, it is apparent that the supplier was being scheduled on long-term, forecast data, and expedited on data from a different source (actual orders) which was only being used internally by the customer. The situation was made worse from the supplier's point of view because schedules for the part numbers in the study were shared with a Japanese supplier on a roughly 70/30 basis. It was made worse because the calloff for the Japanese second source was fixed at 432 per month. The effect of withdrawing a fixed element from a variable demand is to increase the variability of the remaining schedules! So CP often found itself being called on to make changes in delivery schedules. Withdrawing a fixed element from MF's schedules further slowed down the provision of delivery scheduled to CP: MF's MRP system was incapable of extracting a fixed number of parts for the Japanese supplier, so this had to be carried out manually. A further week of delay was the result.

How did CP react to this difficult situation? CP had spent a lot of effort in making its manufacturing facilities more flexible. The company had improved layout and flow with extensive use of cellular manufacture. It had introduced *kanban* boxes to facilitate pull scheduling between cells and with final assembly. Internal schedules could be altered at $1 \cdot 5$ hours' notice. However, such flexibility was not used to improve service to customers such as MF. It was used to make up for deficiencies in CP's own MPC system. Factory targets at CP were set by means of a rolling, 5-month schedule. This was based on a '2 + 1' system: 2 months firm and 1 month variable. In effect, this meant that CP resisted changes to schedules in the next 2 months. In the case of MF, it was argued, the monthly delivery schedules had already stated MF's requirements and these could not be changed at less than 8 weeks' notice! While CP claimed that they 'bent over backwards' to accommodate MF schedule changes, the reality was that this was done in spite of CP's own very unresponsive scheduling system.

■ Interaction of the two MPC systems

From the above, it is apparent that the supplier's and the customer's MPC systems were relatively incompatible. While MF needed a high level of flexibility from suppliers like CP to respond to sudden market changes and to make up for the slowness of its own MPC system, CP responded by resisting short-term changes. One obvious result of this incompatibility was that stock levels were either too high or non-existent at both MF and CP. CP claimed that it was holding over £100,000 worth of parts for MF for which schedules had been cancelled. There was a mutual feeling of dissatisfaction between customer and supplier.

■ Improvements made to the supply system

Once the two parties had agreed jointly to work on the problems outlined above, some relatively straightforward changes were made. Changes to the MPC system at MF meant that it was possible to extract forecast data at an earlier stage. Refinements included allowances for lead times, batch quantities (supplier's pallet sizes), and last receipts. A saving of about 2 weeks was made in processing forecasts into material delivery schedules. Dual sourcing was continued, but only for individual part numbers. This reduced the effects of variability on the UK supplier, and also eliminated the need to extract the fixed content from the delivery schedules, thus saving a further week of processing time.

A further major reform was to use the weekly delivery planning reports in conjunction with receipts to provide a new, 5-week delivery schedule for CP. Because a buffer stock of 5 days was built in, the high variations evident in Figure B.1 would no longer have to be passed on to the supplier. The new schedule evaluated the last supplier schedule against the new delivery planning report, and provided an opportunity to reconcile demand versus supply imbalances. The whole process was speeded up by using MF's electronic mail facility.

In turn, CP had to deliver 1 week in advance of MF's weekly requirement. CP fed back delivery information, and took over responsibility for expediting: there were 5 days for problems to be overcome. Monthly delivery schedules were used to provide CP's own suppliers with forecast demand to ensure that there was sufficient material in the pipeline to be called off 'just-in-time'. No doubt, further work could have provided CP's suppliers with more up-to-date demand information from OEMs like MF − a supply chain management issue.

■ Conclusions

By dismantling barriers between the customer's and supplier's MPC systems, and by a close working relationship developing between the parties concerned, many of the problems previously attributed to 'variability' of demand can be overcome. While the actual variability of demand in the market place remained, it was conceivable that the supplier would be able to meet the customer's needs fairly well given the following improvements:

- MPC systems at both customer and supplier must be mutually understood and made to be compatible.

  - Customer long-term forecasts repay accuracy and speedy presentation to the supplier.
  - Customer short-term requirements must be available to the supplier immediately they are produced, and should become calloff quantities under JIT purchasing.
  - The supplier must use this data to action deliveries. Eventually, expediting becomes the supplier's responsibility alone.
  - Telecommunication links (EDI) between users become essential to ensure fast, accurate transfer of data.
  - Immediate notification of demand changes to the supplier, and action of those changes, becomes a major objective for both MPC systems.

- Understanding the sources and causes of variability is an ongoing challenge to both parties.

  - 'Special' causes of variability, such as those due to complex dual-sourcing arrangements, can and should be eliminated.
  - 'Common' causes of variability, such as those due to the market at large, should be addressed by buyer and supplier working jointly. Possible actions include buffer stocks of parts (which will be reduced over time) and agreed 'fixed' and 'adjustable' schedule periods (see Figure 10.4).

- Total conformance quality, part count accuracy, and delivery reliability become increasingly critical to success.

There are many issues to be addressed in the development of responsiveness by suppliers. Such responsiveness cannot simply be delegated to suppliers, who are expected to perform 'just-in-time'. It is the reward of mutual problem solving by all members of a supply chain. In this, the OEM has a key role to play in orchestrating logistics.

Appendix C
Problems with Total
Quality Implementation
at Company A

Many companies in recent years have been enthusiastically setting about total quality implementation. Sometimes there are fatal flaws in what is being planned, or in how implementation is being carried out in practice. This was the case in a traditional company in the UK engineering industry, which we will refer to as 'Company A'. Just 2 years into total quality implementation, an investigative group from Company A's parent concluded the following.

- A major effort was needed to improve the fundamentals of the business. The first priority was to establish effective disciplines and controls within each function.
- TQ consumes a great deal of management time and resource. Additional time and effort in further development should be deferred until the priority issues have been addressed.

This marked the end of TQ development at Company A. But the background to the investigative group's conclusions are highly instructive. A brief description of some of the major issues follows.

Early initiatives directed at improving product quality at Company A had been very successful, but the Board realized that progress had reached a plateau, and that new ideas were needed to propel the company into the 'world-class' league. It was decided that a study team of senior managers would be set up to examine the company's approach to 'putting quality first', and to report in 3 months' time. The study group concluded that there was no magic solution to improving quality. Although previous one-off initiatives had yielded some benefits, several examples were quoted where an inconsistent and uncertain management approach prevailed:

- While management preached quality, production quotas were always the real priority.
- New product introduction always led to many late modifications and high costs of returns.

- While management preached 'right the first time', mass inspection and large areas for rectification were still features of the business.
- New tools and techniques like SPC had been introduced in a disjointed way. Some areas used SPC but did not know why.

The study group identified over 30 specific quality-related issues which needed to be addressed as a matter of urgency. These included the need to:

- review the role of the supervisor and shop-floor control;
- improve discipline and control on working practices;
- reduce the number of suppliers, some of whom had a poor quality record;
- improve the control of design changes;
- introduce process failure mode and effect analysis (FMEA);
- considerably improve preventive maintenance disciplines.

The study group went on to stress the need to commit everyone in the company by means of a single management quality philosophy which encompased the elimination of waste and an integrated human resource plan. In order to progress this point, it was recommended that the Board should seek the advice of Dr Deming, and a series of seminars took place. This phase of development culminated in the appointment of consultants to help facilitate the initial stages of TQ implementation.

The time from presentation of the internal study group report (which the Board had accepted in its entirety) to the decision to go ahead with TQ implementation had been less than 5 months. It is important to take stock here of some of the issues:

- The chairman was totally convinced that acceptance of TQ was the only way forward. He became very enthusiastic. When it was stressed that adoption of some of the TQ ideas and perceived benefits could take 5 years to bear fruit, he replied: 'We are Company A – we do things quicker here. We'll do it in 2.'
- While some Board members shared the chairman's enthusiasm, others were totally unconvinced about TQ and very lukewarm to some of the key issues.
- The need to address the list of over 30 quality-related issues referred to above as a matter of urgency was quickly forgotten in the rush to progress with TQ implementation.

Some of the seeds of failure had already been sown.

■ The new quality management system

Changes were to be implemented by means of a structure of committees and teams with clearly defined roles. These are illustrated in Figure C.1. The new

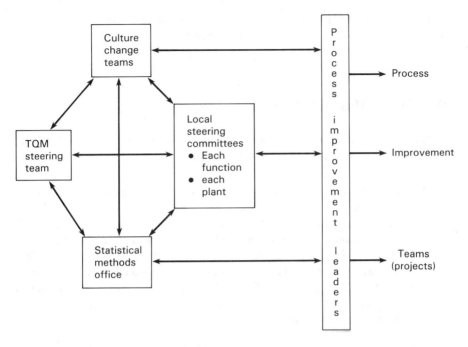

Figure C.1 Structure of committees and teams for new quality management system

system mirrored existing organizational structures, so that the transition from process improvement being a 'special' activity to becoming a normal way of life was managed by the same group of people. The following is a brief summary of the structure:

- The steering team was the Board, and its task was to lead the transition by supporting the work of other groups.
- Local steering committees were set up to manage the improvement activities in each function and each plant. They were chaired by a member of the steering team.
- The statistical methods office provided technical support in the areas of training, behavioural science, and statistics, and worked on the structure and systems of the change process.
- Process improvement leaders were statistical facilitators who helped members of project teams and local steering committees.
- Culture change teams examined Deming's 14 principles and identified areas where there was conflict with the existing management culture. The team's recommendations were championed by a Board member for implementation.

While this was the theory of the new quality management system, the reality was somewhat different. The lukewarm commitment of some Board members meant that some of the steering committees floundered and that some of the culture change teams never got off the ground.

■ The change process

Figure C.2 shows how actions were planned and implemented under four distinct but related fronts. These were as follows:

1. **Training and education:** This was carried out as a 'cascade' exercise, with consultants and the statistical methods office training the Board who in turn trained their direct reports and so on down the hierarchy. The method was a huge success. But training in philosophy was not followed up with training in tools and techniques for some months. Philosophy training emphasized attitude changes like driving out fear and treating everyone as if they want to do a good job. But no new systems were in place to support the new philosophy. Also, without tools and techniques, there was nothing that could be done with it.

2. **Quality planning and focus:** This was intended to cover the priorities and measures of quality improvement, integration of quality initiatives like SPC, and improvement of management processes like reward systems and appraisal. This whole area proved to be a particular problem. Because existing processes were in many cases not under adequate control, there was little that could be achieved in focusing on improving them. Major changes in systems were required. Appraisal systems were addressed by replacing management by objectives and target numbers by a less specific 'process improvement plan' which managers never properly understood. Issues of work measurement were also never sorted out. (Appraisal systems and management by numbers are strongly criticized by Dr Deming.)

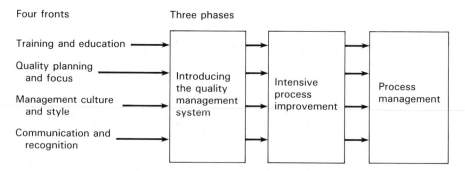

Figure C.2 Planned evolution of change process

3. **Management culture and style:** These covered corporate and functional missions, values, and goals, the interpretation of Deming's principles, and work on the recommendations of the culture change teams. While the corporate missions, values, and goals were well handled, functional efforts depended very much on the attitude of the Board member concerned. Those keen on TQ were the first to present. Interpretation of Deming's principles was never undertaken. The failure of the culture change teams referred to above led to a lack of progress in defining operating philosophy and in reviewing company policies.

4. **Communication and recognition:** This was handled by means of conferences, management briefs, company newsletters, and handouts to explain the new philosophies. A conscious effort was made not to overplay the publicity, but to ensure that people understood what was happening and why.

It was intended that these four actions would evolve through the three phases shown in Figure C.2 and would not therefore have defined start or finish dates.

■ Conclusions

A useful starting point for evaluating Company A's TQ programme is to consider good and bad aspects.

Good aspects

The 'top-down' approach to TQ implementation − reinforced by the cascade approach to training − demonstrated management's belief in the philosophy, and helped to ensure that everyone was involved in a structured way. Tools and techniques − once they had been introduced − were helpful in attacking waste. Encouraging people to think in a process/quality way was a helpful reorientation of their thinking. This was enhanced by helping people to think with a philosophy of internal and external customers. New ways of managing by facilitating what is done were accepted and used by many managers: managers work 'on the system', while their subordinates work 'in the system'. This helped to stop managers from changing processes which they did not understand. Development of mission, goals, and operating principles encouraged a teamwork approach and helped to develop consistency of purpose.

Bad aspects

A major problem was that many processes needed to be radically changed, not simply subjected to small, incremental changes. Failure to work on the fundamental issues which had been identified in the initial study team's report on 'putting quality first' contributed considerably to the lack of impact by TQ on the company's processes. TQ implementation at Company A was high on attitudes, low on systems. So there was poor measurement of the effect of the new policies on the business, or of any control mechanism to focus process improvement and quality progress. This was made worse by the dismantling of existing work standards and financial objectives with nothing to replace them. The impatience of the chairman created a sense of frustration about lack of progress, while some Board members never became committed to TQ at all.

Company A shows how TQ development depends on progress across a broad front. Excellence in certain areas does not yield success. Figure C.3 proposes four positions on a matrix of quality culture and systems/processes. Company A would be placed somewhere in the 'naïve' quadrant, depending too much on philosophy and beliefs with little application. Yet given greater systems and process expertise, and of course the will and the skill, it may be possible to make the transition to the 'total' quadrant.

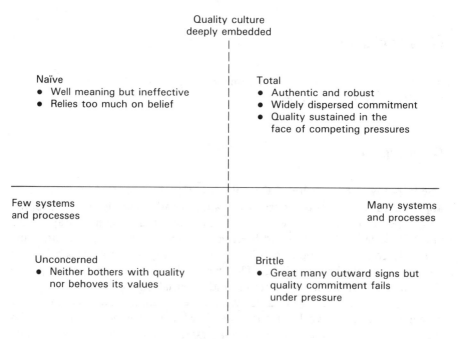

Figure C.3 TQ development matrix

Glossary

ABC inventory analysis: a system for classifying materials by annual usage value (unit cost × usage). *Pareto analysis* shows up the expensive few (top 20% by number but 80% by value), called class A items, which must be closely controlled and which are prime candidates for JIT delivery. Class C items are the trivial many – such as nuts, bolts, and washers – which must not run out.

Acceptable quality level (AQL): a proportion or number of defects which are permitted when a sample is taken from a batch of parts. The AQL is calculated statistically, and has been strongly criticized in recent years because it permits a 'fixed' number of defects to be perpetuated in inspection plans.

Activity-based costing (ABC): a system for product costing which allocates costs to activities carried out in a company by means of 'cost drivers'. Cost drivers are reckoned to be the major cause for performance of a given activity. The system aims to allocate costs more accurately to products than is the case for absorption costing.

Andon: Japanese for lantern. The visible display of condition of a line, usually by means of lights held above a production process on *andon* boards.

Backflushing: a method of reducing stock record transactions. Instead of accounting for each issue transaction separately, the daily output is used to identify what parts must have been used. These parts are then debited from the stock record.

Band width: the band width of a process is a measure of its capability to handle surges in demand across a mix of products. The aim of a system with high band width is to be capable of making any product in any order with no disruption.

Bill of materials (BOM): a structured list of parts which go into an assembly, showing how each component and subassembly relates with each other.

Bottleneck: a process at which demand exceeds capacity.

Buffer stock (safety stock): inventory which is held to buffer a process from variations in demand, or from uncertainty in the process itself.

Cellular manufacture: an aspect of *group technology* whereby a family of parts which follow similar processes is made in a product-oriented layout, or cell.

Comaker: supplier who is closely bound into an original equipment manufacturer (OEM) by cooperation across a broad front. This may include early involvement in new designs, quality improvement programmes, and plant focus on to specific OEM products.

Computer-aided design (CAD): use of computer graphics to facilitate the preparation, storage, and transmission of engineering designs.

Computer numerical control (CNC): use of computers in the preparation, storage, and execution of given designs in production processes.

Condition-based maintenance (CBM): maintenance methods based on the assumption that the condition of a given component of a machine can be predicted by monitoring a major characteristic (for example, heat, vibration).

Customer: the next process, that is, where the work goes to next.

Deming's 14 points for management: a set of points developed by Dr W. E. Deming aimed at helping Western management to close the gap with Japanese companies. Published in his book *Out of the Crisis*.

Design for manufacture (DFM): the focusing of design team effort on the cost-effective use of parts and processes to produce, on time, high-quality products that meet customer and business requirements (Lucas).

Drumbeat: the pulse, rhythm, or 'takt time' by which material movements are synchronized throughout the factory, normally derived from the *master production schedule*.

Economic batch quantity (EBQ): a variation of the EOQ concept which applies to made-in parts.

Economic order quantity (EOQ): a fixed quantity of parts which is purchased in each order cycle. The EOQ aims to optimize inventory-carrying costs with the costs of preparing an order so that total inventory costs are minimized.

Electronic data interchange (EDI): the exchange of data from computer to computer by means of agreed message standards.

Engineering change order (ECO): formal notification of a change to design which affects BOMs, production routing, or processes.

Failure mode and effects analysis (FMEA): a tool which helps to eliminate risk by a disciplined analysis of possible causes of failure of a part or assembly, ranked on grounds of seriousness, probability, and likelihood of detection. FMEA can be applied to both design and manufacturing processes.

Final assembly schedule: a short-term build schedule (typically 2–4 weeks ahead only) which sets track sequence.

Fishbone chart: a problem analysis technique whereby team members can systematically analyse the major causes of a given problem. Also known as cause and effect diagram and Ishikawa diagram.

Focused factory: a concept where a factory which does one or two tasks really well will outperform a factory which is asked to perform across many, conflicting tasks.

Forrester effect: the amplification of demand changes upstream. Suppliers who are several levels away from end customer demand often produce to schedules which are very different from that demand.

Group technology (GT): a set of manufacturing techniques which enable designers and manufacturing engineers to exploit the basic similarity of parts and processes. Families can be classified by size, shape, manufacturing routing requirements, or volume.

Hawthorne effect: a theory, based on experimental evidence, that motivation comes from recognition.

Heijunka: Japanese term for levelling and balancing production.

Jidoka: the halting of a production process, automatically or by an operator, when abnormal conditions are sensed or seen to occur.

Just-in-time (JIT): a philosophy which aims to improve competitive performance by eliminating waste from, and improving quality in, all business operations. JIT philosophy is accomplished as a result of the application of tools and techniques which require total employee involvement and teamwork.

Kanban: Japanese for card or signal. Its most widely reported use is as a means for an upstream process to instruct a downstream process to make more parts (pull scheduling). But *kanban* can be used more widely to make issues like inventory status, parts location, and production status more visible.

Lean production: manufacture of a relatively wide product range to specific customer needs to very high quality standards and with very low assembly man hours.

Life cycle: stages in the useful life of a product or process. Stages in the product life cycle are often identified as introduction, growth, maturity, and decline. In the process life cycle, they are referred to as acquisition, deployment, maintenance, and disposal.

Line balancing: a procedure for evenly distributing tasks among operators in a product (for example, flowline or cellular) layout.

Make to order (MTO): parts are only authorized for procurement and production work to be carried out if a customer order has been placed.

Make to stock (MTS): production and procurement is authorized to take place up to a predetermined level of finished product inventory.

Manufacturing planning and control (MPC) systems: the generic term for planning and controlling manufacture. Three principal phases are involved. They are planning manufacture ('front end'), disaggregating front-end plans into time-phased material requirements ('engine room'), and detailed scheduling of the factory and suppliers ('back end').

Manufacturing resource planning (MRP II): a comprehensive, computer-aided planning and control system for company operations which extends the MPC system into areas of financial planning and simulation.

Mass production: high-volume, repetitive manufacture of a relatively narrow range of products using economies of scale to keep costs low. Manufacture usually strongly decoupled from distribution.

Master production schedule (MPS): a manufacturing plan of what it is intended to produce as end items or product options offered to customers by time period.

Material requirements planning (MRP): computer-based disaggregation of the MPS into detailed material requirements by time period. The output from MRP is a time-phased plan of material requirements for both bought-out and made-in parts.

Mixed model production: production schedules that are repetitive in short cycles. The time interval between models is reduced to the shortest possible so that levelled production can be maximized internally and passed on to suppliers.

Muda, Mura, and *Muri* **(3-MU):** the Japanese words for the main inhibitors to flow in a system. Roughly translated they mean waste, inconsistency, and strained performance.

Nagare: the Japanese word for flow.

Non-value-added activities: activities which are forms of waste. Examples are storage, transport, and inspection activities.

Operations: Shingo's definition of the chain of events whereby workers and machines work on parts or products.

Optimized production technology (OPT): a philosophy of increasing throughput combined with a computerized system of shop scheduling and capacity planning. Work flow is smoothed by giving special attention to bottleneck work centres (larger process batch sizes) and to non-bottleneck work centres (smaller transfer batch sizes).

$P:D$ ratio: the ratio between the actual product lead time and the lead time expected by the customer.

Pareto chart: a means of arranging items in any population from most frequently occurring to least frequently occurring. Often, 80% of the response comes from 20% of the items; hence the alternative term for Pareto chart: the 80/20 rule.

Poka-yoke: Japanese term for error-proofing. The development of devices which make it impossible to produce goods with defects.

Preventive maintenance (PM): actions which are taken to forestall equipment failure. Actions could include overhaul, inspection, lubrication, and calibration.

Processes: Shingo's definition of the chain of events whereby raw materials are converted into products.

Process flowcharts: a methods study technique whereby a subject (such as a component or a document) is followed through processes in a systematic way. Valuable as a means of distinguishing value-added from non-value-added activities and hence for improving flow.

Program evaluation and review technique (PERT): a network-based technique for planning and controlling large-scale projects.

Pull scheduling: a system of material control whereby the user signals to the maker that more parts are needed, and where the maker only produces more parts in response to such a signal.

Push scheduling: a system of material control whereby the maker produces parts in response to a pre-set schedule regardless of whether the next process can use them.

Quality control circle (QCC) or quality circle (QC): a small group of people who volunteer to meet regularly to identify and solve problems which affect the work they do.

Reliability-centred maintenance (RCM): an umbrella philosophy to develop sensitivity to the actual maintenance requirements of each item of equipment in its operating environment.

Reorder point (ROP): the quantity of stock which acts as a trigger for a replenishment order to be placed.

Run to breakdown (RTB): an approach to maintenance for selected items which are allowed to fail. Maintenance action is then initiated to replace the part.

Runners, repeaters and strangers: notional breakdown of three categories of part:

- runners: products or key features produced every day, every week
- repeaters: products or key features produced regularly, but at longer time intervals
- strangers: products or key features produced at irregular time intervals

Seiri, seiton, seiso, **and** *seiketsu* **('4S'):** Japanese words for key aspects of housekeeping. Roughly translated, they mean sort things out, put into order, keep things clean, and keep things neat and tidy.

Setup time (changeover time): the time taken to change over a given piece of equipment from the last piece of good product from the preceding batch to the first good piece from the succeeding batch.

Small-group improvement activities (SGIAs): small cross-functional groups which are appointed to investigate and solve a given problem. Usually, they are disbanded on completion.

Statistical process control (SPC): a technique for helping the control of processes within specified limits by sampling measured process outputs and recording the results on a control chart. The purpose is to find out whether the process is under normal statistical control, or whether changes need to be made.

Time-based competition: theory that proposes that the manufacturers with lowest lead times get the highest market share.

Total productive maintenance (TPM): an evolutionary approach to excellence in maintenance which aims to eliminate breakdowns by use of the full range of maintenance and housekeeping techniques. TPM builds up the role of the operators and of the maintenance engineers.

Total quality: the complementary philosophy to JIT which emphasized that control over quality is embedded within and driven by the organization. 'Total' refers to everyone and every process.

Undercapacity scheduling: not scheduling at full capacity to allow operators regular time to work on improvement activities and TPM.

Value analysis (VA): examining designs which already exist for possible improvements and cost savings. Traditionally based on the purchasing function.

Value engineering (VE): a *DFM technique* which allows designs or design concepts to be questioned and improved, typically by a multi-functional team.

Work-in-progress (WIP): partly completed work that is either waiting between processes or is being worked on.

Recommended Further Reading

■ General books on just-in-time

1. *Japanese Manufacturing Techniques: Nine Hidden Lessons in Simplicity*, Richard Schonberger, Free Press, New York, 1982.
2. *Zero Inventories*, Robert Hall, Dow Jones Irwin, Homewood, IL, 1983.
3. *World Class Manufacturing*, Richard Schonberger, Free Press, New York, 1986.
4. *Attaining Manufacturing Excellence*, Robert Hall, Dow Jones Irwin, Homewood, IL, 1987.
5. *Just-in-Time Manufacture*, Chris Voss (ed.), IFS Publications, Beford, 1987.
6. *The Machine that Changed the World*, J. Womack, D. Jones, and D. Roos, Rawson Associates, New York, 1990.
7. *Just-in-Time: A Global Status Report*, Chris Voss and David Clutterbuck, IFS Publications, Bedford, 1989.
8. *How to Make Japanese Management Methods Work in the West*, Kazuo Murata and Alan Harrison, Gower, Aldershot, 1991.
9. *Lucas Manufacturing Engineering Systems Handbook*, J. Parnaby (ed.), Lucas Engineering & Systems, 2nd edn, Birmingham, 1991.
10. *Implementing JIT*, John Bicheno, IFS Publications, 1991.
11. *The Road to Nissan*, Peter Wickens, Macmillan, Basingstoke, 1987.

■ General books on total quality

1. *Managing for Total Quality*, N. Logethetis, Prentice Hall International, Hemel Hempstead, 1992.
2. *Total Quality Management*, John Oakland, Heinemann, Oxford, 1989.
3. *Out of the Crisis*, W. Edwards Deming, MIT Center for Advanced Engineering Study: Cambridge, MA, 1982.
4. *What is Total Quality Control: The Japanese Way*, K. Ishikawa, trans. David J. Lu, Prentice Hall, Englewood Cliffs, NJ, 1985.
5. *Managing Quality*, David Garvin, Free Press, New York, 1988.

■ Books on JIT techniques

1. *Production Flow Analysis for Planning Group Technology*, John L. Burbidge, Oxford Science Publications, 1989.
2. The excellent series of books published by Productivity Press: Cambridge, MA, including:
   TPM Development Programme: Implementing Total Productive Maintenance, Seiichi Nakajima, 1989.
   A Revolution in Manufacturing: The SMED System, Shigeo Shingo, 1985.
   Zero Quality Control: Source Inspection and the Poka-yoke System, Shigeo Shingo, trans. A. P. Dolan, 1986.
   A Study of the Toyota Production System from an Industrial Engineering Viewpoint, Shigeo Shingo, 1989.
3. *Manufacturing Planning and Control Systems*, T. Vollman, W. Berry, and C. Whybark, Irwin, 1989 (3rd edn due 1992).
4. *Just-in-Time Purchasing*, A. Ansari and B. Moderress, Free Press, New York, 1990.
5. *Improving the Supply Chain*, D. McBeth, L. Baxter, N. Ferguson, and G. Neil, IFS Publications, Beford, 1991.

■ Books on improving design methodology

1. *Total Design*, Stuart Pugh, Addison-Wesley, Wokingham, 1990.
2. *Managing Integration in CAD/CAM and Simultaneous Engineering*, D. Twigg and C. A. Voss, Chapman and Hall, London, 1992.
3. *Time-based Competition: The Next Battleground in American Manufacturing*, J. D. Blackburn, Business One Irwin, Homewood, IL, 1991.

■ Books on manufacturing strategy

1. *Manufacturing: The Formidable Competitive Weapon*, Whickam Skinner, Wiley, New York, 1985.
2. *Restoring our Competitive Edge: Competing through Manufacturing*, R. Hayes and S. C. Wheelwright, Wiley, New York, 1984.
3. *Competitive Manufacturing*, M. Gregory, IFS Publications, Bedford, 1990.
4. *Manufacturing Strategy*, Terry Hill, Irwin, 1989.
5. *The Manufacturing Advantage*, N. Slack, Mercury, London, 1991.

Index